A Practitioner's Guide to Enhancing Parenting Skills

A Practitioner's Guide to Enhancing Parenting Skills: Assessment, Analysis and Intervention offers a detailed and stepwise approach to problem behaviour analysis and management, based on the successful and evidence-based Enhancing Parenting Skills Programme (EPaS). This unique programme, based on 40 years of Professor Hutchings' clinical work, draws on social learning theory (SLT) principles designed to support families of young children with behavioural challenges.

In this book, Hutchings and Williams combine clear practical guidance with case examples and useful checklists to deliver SLT-based interventions tailored to the unique needs of individual families. The case analysis identifies the assets and skills in the home situation and the functions of problem behaviours before creating a set of achievable goals. The latter part of the manual includes examples of intervention strategies to address several common problems, including toileting, eating and night-time problems.

This book is an invaluable tool for all practitioners working in Early Years including CAMHS primary care staff, social workers, clinical psychologists, health visitors and school nurses.

Professor Judy Hutchings was an NHS Clinical Child Psychologist for 37 years, and since 1988 has also worked as a researcher in Bangor University, where she set up the Centre for Evidence Based Early Intervention. She introduced parenting programmes into treatment and preventive services and undertook research trials on services for children with behavioural problems, including developing the EPaS programme. In 2011, she was awarded an OBE for her work with children and families.

Dr Margiad Williams' PhD evaluated the Enhancing Parenting Skills (EPaS) programme in health visiting services across north Wales and Shropshire. She has studied/worked at the Centre for Evidence Based Early Intervention since 2009 evaluating programmes for parents, teachers and children.

D1600217

A Practitioner's Guide to Enhancing Parenting Skills

Assessment, Analysis and
Intervention

Judy Hutchings and Margiad Williams

Routledge
Taylor & Francis Group

LONDON AND NEW YORK

First published 2019
by Routledge
2 Park Square, Milton Park, Abingdon, Oxon OX14 4RN

and by Routledge
52 Vanderbilt Avenue, New York, NY 10017

Routledge is an imprint of the Taylor & Francis Group, an informa business

British Library Cataloguing-in-Publication Data
A catalogue record for this book is available from the British Library

Library of Congress Cataloging-in-Publication Data
Names: Hutchings, Judy, author. | Williams, Margiad, author.
Title: A practitioner's guide to enhancing parenting skills : assessment,
    analysis and intervention / Judy Hutchings and Margiad Williams.
Description: First Edition. | New York : Routledge, 2019. | Includes
    bibliographical references and index.
Identifiers: LCCN 2018056473 (print) | LCCN 2018057495 (ebook) | ISBN
    9780203711538 (Ebook) | ISBN 9781138560529 (hardback) | ISBN
    9781138560536 (pbk.) | ISBN 9780203711538 (ebk)
Subjects: LCSH: Parenting. | Parent and child.
Classification: LCC HQ755.8 (ebook) | LCC HQ755.8 .H8877 2019 (print)
    | DDC 649.1—dc23
LC record available at https://lccn.loc.gov/2018056473

ISBN: 978-1-138-56052-9 (hbk)
ISBN: 978-1-138-56053-6 (pbk)
ISBN: 978-0-203-71153-8 (ebk)

Typeset in Sabon
by Swales & Willis Ltd, Exeter, Devon, UK

Contents

PART III
Typical problems 169

Part I
Background

1 Conduct problems and the risk factors for poor outcomes

Introduction

Between the ages of 3 and 10 years, children's behavioural problems are easy to identify, remain relatively stable and, if not resolved, put them at risk of later conduct problems, significant antisocial behaviour problems in adolescence and subsequent lifelong problems (Hutchings and Gardner, 2012). Conduct problems comprise the single biggest source of referral to child mental health services and are extremely costly to educational, health, social care and justice systems (Bonin, Stevens, Beecham, Byford and Parsonage, 2011; National Collaborating Centre for Mental Health (NCCMH), 2013). Young children's conduct problems typically involve simple aggressive, disruptive and non-compliant behaviours that produce immediate consequences, whereas the replacement behaviours, cooperation, compliance and self-regulation, are complex and harder to learn (Allen and Duncan-Smith, 2009).

Early childhood behavioural difficulties, that have the potential to develop into conduct disorders, are a large and growing problem. A recent meta-analysis estimated that worldwide prevalence of disruptive behaviour disorders was 5.7 per cent (Polanczyk, Salum, Sugaya, Caye and Rohde, 2015). The 1999 and 2004 British surveys concluded that 8 per cent of boys aged 5 to 16, and 4 per cent of girls, were conduct disordered (Green, McGinnity, Meltzer, Ford and Goodman, 2005) and for children living in disadvantaged neighbourhoods the proportion is nearer to 15 per cent (Green et al., 2005; Meltzer, Gatward, Goodman and Ford, 2000).

Children are diagnosed as having a behaviour disorder when they are exhibiting severely disruptive, aggressive and/or destructive behaviour that is causing problems for their parents or carers. There are currently two major diagnostic systems. The *Diagnostic and Statistical Manual of Mental Disorders, Fifth Edition* (DSM-5; American Psychiatric Association, 2013) uses the global term *Disruptive, Impulse-Control and Conduct Disorders* for children exhibiting these behaviour patterns, but this can be broken down into Oppositional Defiant Disorder (ODD) for children with symptoms of anger/irritable mood, argumentative/defiant behaviour and vindictiveness and Conduct Disorder (CD) for children who show persistent and repetitive aggression towards others, destruction of property, deceitfulness or theft, and serious violation of rules. The *International Classification of Diseases, 10th Revision* (ICD-10; World Health Organization, 1992) uses the term *CD* for children up to the age of 18 years, but includes ODD as a subtype for children under 10 years.

The problems associated with behaviour disorders are often associated with deficits in essential life and school readiness skills, since many of the problematic behaviours are very easy to learn (hitting, kicking, running away, etc.) and the replacement alternative behaviours, i.e. waiting, asking, recognising feelings and managing frustration, are much more complex skills. Without intervention, child behaviour problems, especially those that have their origins in the preschool years, are relatively stable over time (Côté, Vaillancourt, Barker, Nagin and Tremblay, 2007; Dishion and Patterson, 2006; Piquero, Carriaga, Diamond, Kazemian and Farrington, 2012). When young children with behaviour problems start school, they experience secondary effects of their behaviour that can hamper their education and development. Their lack of social skills and aggressive behaviour can make them difficult to teach (Webster-Stratton, Reid and Stoolmiller, 2008) and can lead to them being rejected by their peers (Ladd and Troop-Gordon, 2003) and more likely to associate with other antisocial children and turn to more antisocial ways of obtaining attention. Approximately half of young children diagnosed with CD go on to develop serious psychosocial problems in adulthood, including criminal convictions, drug misuse and violent behaviour (NCCMH, 2013).

There are now several longitudinal studies that indicate that, although many of those young children assessed as "antisocial" do not go on to become antisocial adults, antisocial adults have almost always been antisocial children (Farrington and Welsh, 2007). The Cambridge Study in Delinquent Development has followed the development of 411 South London males from the age of eight to 32 years (Farrington, 2000). Measures of the sample's antisocial behaviour taken at ages 10, 18 and 32 were significantly correlated, supporting the view that antisocial behaviour is stable over time. They found that overall frequency of offending peaked at around the age of 18 and then decreased. Participants were less antisocial at 32 than at age 18, but those who were most deviant at 18 tended to be the most deviant at 32 years old. The Christchurch Health and Development Study found that children with high levels of conduct problems at ages 7 to 9 years had significantly higher rates of adverse outcomes in adulthood, including crime, substance misuse, mental health problems and sexual/partner relationships (Fergusson, Horwood and Ridder, 2005). Other longitudinal studies have found similar results (e.g. Dunedin Health and Development Study: Caspi, Moffitt, Newman and Silva, 1996; Oregon Youth Study: Patterson, Capaldi and Bank, 1991; Pittsburgh Youth Study: Loeber and Hay, 1997).

Early childhood difficulties that remain untreated can result in long-term problems that are costly to society (Sainsbury Centre for Mental Health, 2009; Welsh et al., 2008). As time passes, behaviour difficulties can become more resistant to preventive services and treatment (Allen, 2011) and incur the need for increasingly costly services. Using data from a longitudinal study of Inner London children, Scott and colleagues (2001) have demonstrated how childhood antisocial behaviour leads to quantifiable costs to society. By the time they were 27 years old, children who at age 10 had displayed no signs of antisocial behaviour were estimated to have cost the state £7,400 in relation to crime, special education, social security, health, foster/residential care and relationship breakdown. The equivalent figure for those with conduct problems at the age of 10 was £24,300, increasing to £70,000 for those with diagnosed, chronic CD. A UK study, Romeo, Knapp and Scott (2006) estimated an annual cost of £5,960 per child with conduct problems without criminal justice costs with 78 per cent of the total cost falling on families. Health, education and voluntary services accounted for 8 per cent, 1 per cent and 3 per cent of the total cost, respectively. However, early interventions to reduce problem behaviour have been shown to be cost-effective in the long-term (Bonin et al., 2011; Edwards et al., 2007; Muntz, Hutchings, Edwards, Hounsome and O'Ceilleachair, 2004; Sainsbury Centre for Mental Health, 2009).

Between 3 and 8 years, most children experience nursery and then commence compulsory school attendance. Children who start school without the necessary social and self-regulation skills needed in a school environment are likely to have negative academic and social experiences in school that contribute further to the development and/or maintenance of conduct problems (Duncan et al., 2007). Antisocial children tend to be isolated, with few friends (Gross, 2008), and are more likely to respond aggressively to benign situations. Rejection by peers can draw them towards similarly antisocial peers during later childhood years, further increasing the risk of long-term involvement in drug misuse, offending and/or mental health problems (Allen, 2011; Farrington and Welsh, 2007).

Risk and protective factors

Several environmental variables are associated with early childhood behaviour problems and it is possible to recognise factors that place young children at increased risk of developing conduct problems. There is evidence that the greater the number of associated risk factors present in the child's living environment, the higher the risk for the child (Barker, Copeland, Maughan, Jaffee and Uher, 2012; Sabates and Dex, 2015; Trentacosta et al., 2008). Risk factors can be considered under a number of headings: family and social circumstances, individual factors, parental factors, and school and community.

Individual factors

Boys are more likely than girls to develop behaviour problems (Hutchings, Williams, Martin and Pritchard, 2011; Zahn-Waxler, Shirtcliff and Marceau, 2008) with the risk three to four times higher than for girls (Martel, 2013; Merikangas, Nakamura and Kessler, 2009). Boys are rated as having more behaviour problems by both parents and teachers (Miner and Clarke-Stewart, 2008). Differences have also been shown in the type of behaviour problems with young boys showing more physical aggression than girls (Alink et al., 2006).

A significant proportion of children with behavioural problems also show increased levels of attentional/impulsivity problems (Biederman, 2005; Hartman, Stage and Webster-Stratton, 2003; Jones, Daley, Hutchings, Bywater and Eames, 2008). Impulsivity is positively associated with externalising behaviour in three-year-olds (Karreman, de Haas, van Tuijl, van Aken and Dekovic, 2010) and higher levels of impulsivity in childhood has been linked to externalising behaviour problems in adolescence (Leve, Kim and Pears, 2005). Both attentional/impulsivity and behaviour problems are associated with language and cognitive delays (Daley, Jones and Hutchings, 2009), leading to further difficulties, including poor literacy skills (Gross, 2008).

Genetics also have a role to play in the development of childhood behaviour problems. A review by Moffitt (2005) exploring the behavioural-genetic literature found that the estimated genetic influence on behaviour problems was approximately 50 per cent, with an estimated 20 per cent of the variance due to shared environment (e.g. living in poverty) and the remaining 30 per cent due to environmental factors experienced uniquely by individuals (e.g. victims of abuse). Patterns within families have also been found, with higher rates of behaviour problems in the first-degree relatives of boys with diagnosed CD (Blazei, Iacono and Krueger, 2006). Herndon and Iacono (2005) found that children born to parents exhibiting behaviour problems were at increased risk of developing CD by adolescence.

Parental factors

Poor parenting affects every aspect of children's development (Allen and Duncan-Smith, 2008; Belsky and de Haan, 2011). Harsh parenting, physical punishment, lax supervision and inconsistent discipline play a significant role in the development and maintenance of child behaviour problems (Hoeve et al., 2009). By contrast, positive parenting practices, including frequent joint activities, monitoring, structuring the child's time and constructive discipline strategies, are protective (Gardner, Burton and Klimes, 2006). Interventions that develop these skills are associated with improvements in serious behaviour problems over time that are independent of other risk factors, including single and/or young parenthood, maternal depression and poverty (Gardner, Hutchings, Bywater and Whitaker, 2010;

Hartman et al., 2003; Hoeve et al., 2009). These studies further demonstrate that it is parenting, rather than these disadvantaging factors per se, that both predicts behavioural problems in children (Patterson, Forgatch, Yoerger and Stoolmiller, 1998) and can be successfully supported in interventions (Hutchings et al., 2007).

Parenting behaviours

Poor parenting has been shown to be the major factor associated with early antisocial behaviour and later delinquency (Farrington and Welsh, 2007). Patterson's detailed observation of parent–child interactions first demonstrated the way in which antisocial child behaviour patterns were reinforced by parental responses (Patterson, 1982). The evidence is now clear that many children learn and establish problem behaviours because parents lack key parenting skills, use them inconsistently (Lunkenheimer et al., 2016) and/or fail to use them at appropriate times (Hoeve et al., 2009). Studies, including longitudinal studies, have consistently identified children's experience of harsh parenting and inconsistent discipline, with little supervision and positive parental involvement with the child, as significant factors in the development of child behaviour problems and later adult offending (Farrington and Welsh, 2007; Hoeve et al., 2009). By contrast, the use of positive parenting skills, such as frequent joint activities, monitoring, structuring the child's time and constructive discipline strategies, appears to be protective and has been associated with improvements in child behaviour over time that are independent of other risk factors (Forgatch and DeGarmo, 2002). The identification of parenting style as a major influence on child behaviour has been borne out by the fact that many well-designed parent training programmes have led to improvements in children's behaviour (Furlong et al., 2012).

Parents do not set out to be harsh parents. Rearing children is one of the hardest jobs and many parents are not well prepared for it. A limited experience of young children, together with other factors, described here, make parenting more challenging. Having a child with a "difficult" temperament from the start is likely to be a factor which influences how parents behave towards their child. Patterson has suggested that the most severe behaviour problems start with a combination of temperamentally difficult toddlers and inexperienced parents. He describes a downward spiral where parents' ineffective monitoring and discipline inadvertently reinforce their child's discovery that whining, temper tantrums and other aggressive behaviours are successful strategies for gaining attention (Patterson and Yoerger, 2002). Several studies have shown that young children displaying behaviour problems with parents who were unable to manage their behaviour were statistically more likely than other children to grow into adult violent offenders (Leschied, Chiodo, Nowicki and Rodger, 2008).

Maternal observation and attending skills

Parents of conduct problem children tend to focus on their children's deviant behaviour and are poor at accurately describing the details of that behaviour (McMahon and Frick, 2005; Wahler and Dumas, 1989; Wahler and Sansbury, 1990). They will describe their child's behaviour in a global blame-oriented way rather than report specific incidents, saying things like "He never does what I ask" or "He always tries to annoy me when we go out" (Wahler and Hann, 1984). Such mothers are quick to classify their child's behaviour as deviant and respond aversely to it and are relatively inflexible in their parenting style. Parents of children with behaviour problems also show insensitivity to the cues of others, have poor observation skills (Meunier, 2007; van Vreeswijk and Wilde, 2004) and poor problem-solving (DeGarmo and Forgatch, 1997; Evans, Williams, O'Loughlin and Howells, 1992). Hutchings, Smith and Gilbert (2000) showed that their measures of maternal observational style, autobiographical memory and parental problem-solving were highly correlated and differentiated well between the parents of children referred for treatment of CD and parents of non-referred children.

The inability of parents of conduct problem children to accurately describe their child's behaviour has been demonstrated in studies which examined the way parents responded when asked to observe and rate their child's videotaped behaviour (Sansbury and Wahler, 1992; Wahler and Sansbury, 1990). Parenting young children involves the continual monitoring of their behaviour (Wahler and Dumas, 1984). Mothers who attend to the complex range of specific child behaviours and their context are more likely to make flexible responses that are appropriate for the situation. Wahler and Dumas (1989) suggest that this deficiency in maternal attending is induced by the presence of other distracting stresses and difficulties in the parent's life. The poor observation skills demonstrated by the parents of conduct problem children and their focus on negative behaviours means that they are more likely to be giving attention to, and therefore reinforcing, their child's deviant behaviour.

Maternal mental health problems

There is a substantial literature showing the co-occurrence of maternal depression and child behaviour problems (see review by Goodman et al., 2011). Alpern and Lyons-Ruth (1993) report that 50 per cent of mothers of children referred for treatment of behavioural difficulties show clinical levels of depression. Mothers' depressive symptoms are positively correlated with child behaviour problems, in that higher levels of depression are associated with higher levels of behaviour problems (Goodman et al., 2011; Gross, Shaw, Moilanen, Dishion and Wilson, 2008).

The skill deficits associated with parents of children with behaviour problems (poor observation, poor problem-solving, insensitivity to social cues) are also associated with depression. Forehand and colleagues (1982, 1984) found that maternal depression was a predictor of maternal perceptions of child behaviour, with mothers who perceived their children as more non-compliant reporting higher levels of depression. They conclude that mothers of clinic-referred children were less objective in their perceptions of child behaviour when levels of depression were high. Parenting intervention programmes that have been most effective with parents of children with behaviour problems have also been effective in improving parental depression (Furlong et al., 2012). Behavioural parenting interventions include components that address these skill deficits (Hutchings, Gardner and Lane, 2004). Specifically, parents are taught accurate problem-solving and observation skills and have opportunities to practise and reinforce those skills, initially with the support from facilitators and subsequently at home with their children (Hutchings, Lane and Kelly, 2004). Gaining experience of successfully using new skills is important for depressed parents. Depression is characterised by an inability to deal with problems, leading to an avoidance of stressful situations, which is highlighted in the learned helplessness theory of depression (Seligman, 1975). Forced exposure to success is the best way of overcoming learned helplessness, which is essentially what parenting programmes do. Teaching parents observation and problem-solving skills, as well as realistic goal setting, accompanied by rehearsal of the new skills, increases the chance that these skills will be reinforced in the home environment by their success. This gives depressed parents more confidence in their parenting abilities and their ability to manage other aspects of their life, leading to reductions in depressive symptoms (Hutchings, Bywater, Williams, Lane and Whitaker, 2012).

Maternal depression co-exists with childhood behavioural problems and some research argues that it can be a causal factor in the emergence of conduct problems (Goodman et al., 2011; Rutter, 1996). There are differences in the behaviour of depressed mothers towards their children from early in their children's lives, which can result in impaired bonding and early mother–baby interaction difficulties (Moehler, Brunner, Wiebel, Reck and Resch, 2006). Depressed mothers exhibit many of the features known to be associated with the development of conduct problems such as lower rates of praise, failure to monitor their child's behaviour, and spending less time playing with them (Lovejoy, Graczyk, O'Hare and Neuman, 2000; Paulson, Dauber and Leiferman, 2006; Webster-Stratton and Herbert, 1994).

Parental mental health problems can also be precipitated by problematic child behaviour, particularly where the child has characteristics, either health problems or temperament, that make the parenting task more difficult (Webster-Stratton and Spitzer, 1996). Repeated failures in disciplining their child may lead to mothers' decreased self-esteem, lack of perceived control over situations and lack of confidence (Dix and Meunier, 2009; Lyons-Ruth et al., 2002; Teti, Gelfand and Pompa, 1990). Improvements in child behaviour problems following treatment have been associated with improvements in parental depressive symptoms (Furlong et al., 2012; Hutchings et al., 2007), and mediation studies show that changes in maternal depression mediate the relationship between intervention effects and changes in child behaviour (Hutchings et al., 2012; Shaw, Connell, Dishion, Wilson and Gardner, 2009). Recent developments suggest that the relationship between parental depression and child behaviour problems is reciprocal (Bagner, Pettit, Lewinsohn, Seeley and Jaccard, 2013).

Family/social factors

Family/social risk factors for poor outcomes include socio-economic disadvantage, disrupted families, e.g. divorce, and large families (Farrington and Welsh, 2007).

Socio-economic disadvantage has long been associated with greater risk of childhood behaviour problems as well as subsequent adult mental health problems (Farrington, 2000; Kiernan and Mensah, 2009; Najman et al., 2010). Research indicates that major life stressors such as poverty, unemployment, cramped living conditions and illness are related to many childhood problems, including conduct disorders (Flouri, Mavroveli and Tzavidis, 2010; Rydell, 2010; Tiet et al., 2001). Farrington and colleagues found that low income, low socio-economic status and large family size (more than four children) were all risk factors for chronic offending and antisocial personality at age 32 (Farrington, 2000).

Disruption in families occurs for a number of reasons, including parental separation or divorce. Children who have experienced parental divorce/separation are at increased risk for developing behaviour problems (Farrington, 2000; McLanahan, Tach and Schneider, 2013; Mitchell et al., 2015). This is especially true for young children (Sigle-Rushton and McLanahan, 2004), and boys more than girls (Mitchell et al., 2015). However, the relationship between parental divorce/separation and child behaviour problems is not straightforward. Some have argued that the child's pre-existing behaviour problems may put a strain on the marital relationship leading to separation (Blazei et al., 2006), whilst others highlight the role of marital conflict in the development of behaviour problems (Amato, 2001). Recently, research has suggested that parental divorce/separation may have a causal role in the development of child behaviour problems (see McLanahan et al., 2013).

Family size can also affect children's later outcomes. Children from large families (more than four children) have worse outcomes, including increased behaviour problems (Farrington, 2000; Kolthof, Kikkert and Dekker, 2014), even in very young children (Murray, Irving, Farrington, Colman and Bloxsom, 2010). A recent meta-analysis, Derzon (2010) found that family size was a strong predictor of aggressive and violent behaviour in children and adolescents. Researchers have suggested that the effect of family size on child behaviour problems could be due to its link with poverty or because of the lack of sufficient attention given to children within this environment (Farrington, 2000).

School and community

Once children with behaviour problems enter school, negative academic and social experiences contribute further to the development of conduct problems. Antisocial children lack the social skills to maintain friendships and risk being isolated from peer groups (Asher and McDonald, 2009; Bierman, 2004). They are more likely to interpret social cues as provocative and to respond aggressively to benign situations. Rejection by peers is often the prelude to being drawn towards a group of similarly antisocial peers, further increasing the risks of later involvement in drug misuse and offending (Dishion et al., 1991; Laird, Jordan, Dodge, Pettit and Bates, 2001; Vitaro, Pedersen and Brendgen, 2007). Poor classroom management strategies where a large amount of negative attention is afforded to "misbehaviour", and children are rarely or inadequately praised for positive work and behaviour, are associated with classroom aggression, delinquency and poor academic performance (Gable, Hester, Rock and Hughes, 2009; Reinke and Herman, 2002). Behaviour problems also lead to poor relations with teachers as the child becomes labelled as "a troublemaker" and receives less encouragement and more criticism and disciplinary action (Gable et al., 2009). The lack of encouragement in the classroom often results in children becoming disenchanted with basic school activities such as learning to read, write and count. Once children begin to fail, or to believe that they are failing in achievements, which they discover are highly rated at school, it is not easy to re-establish their confidence. The children may all too readily find that there are greater satisfactions to be won by gaining attention through difficult behaviour or, indeed, as they grow older, by joining other children reacting to similar difficulties by truanting. This may result in exclusion from school and referral to pupil support, where they can be drawn even deeper into antisocial behaviour as a result of their enforced association with children who have similar problems (Dishion, McCord and Poulin, 1999; Dodge, Dishion and Lansford, 2007).

Protective factors

As well as the risk factors, there are also other factors operating in the child's life that can help to counter the adverse influence of multiple risk factors (Farrington and Welsh, 2007). These have been called protective factors, and among those identified are effective child self- and emotion regulation skills; positive parenting, including high warmth and acceptance; and stimulating environments (Andershed and Andershed, 2015). One of the most important, and modifiable, protective factors is positive parenting (Farrington and Welsh, 2007). Positive parenting is important for child health and well-being; behavioural and educational development (Farrington and Welsh, 2007); reducing violence against children in and outside the home (Farrington and

Welsh, 2007); reducing risk of problem behaviours and lifestyles, especially in teenagers (DeVore and Ginsburg, 2005); and increasing children's resilience in the face of stress (Benzies and Mychasiuk, 2009).

Conclusion

Different risk factors become salient at different stages in children's development. While the school and community environments provide important influencing factors, problem behaviours are frequently established in the preschool years, when influences on the child's behaviour come primarily from the family environment. Although families may be experiencing a range of problems associated with the development of conduct problems, the evidence suggests that these problems may be viewed as risk factors because of their adverse effect on the quality of parenting (Patterson et al., 1998). Parenting practices and parent–child relationships during early childhood are key factors in the development of antisocial behaviour in children and early family interventions are needed to enhance more effective parenting skills.

References

Alink, L. R., Mesman, J., Van Zeijl, J., Stolk, M. N., Juffer, F., Koot, H. M., . . . Van IJzendoorn, M. H. (2006). The early childhood aggression curve: Development of physical aggression in 10- to 50-month-old children. *Child Development, 77,* 954–966. doi:10.1111/j.1467-8624.2006.00912.x

Allen, G. (2011). *Early intervention: The next steps. An independent report to Her Majesty's Government.* London, UK: The Smith Institute and the Centre for Social Justice. Retrieved from: http://dera.ioe.ac.uk/14161/1/graham%20 allen%20review%20of%20early%20intervention.pdf

Allen, G. & Duncan-Smith, I. (2009). *Early intervention: Good parents, great kids, better citizens.* London, UK: Centre for Social Justice and the Smith Institute.

Alpern, L. & Lyons-Ruth, K. (1993). Pre-school children at social risk: Chronicity and timing of maternal depressive symptoms and child behavior problems at school and at home. *Development and Psychopathology, 5*(3), 371–387.

Amato, P. R. (2001). Children of divorce in the 1990s: An update of the Amato and Keith (1991) meta-analysis. *Journal of Family Psychology, 15,* 355–370. doi:10.1037//0893-3200.15.3.355

American Psychiatric Association (2013). *Diagnostic and Statistical Manual of Mental Disorders (DSM-5®).* Washington, DC: American Psychiatric Association.

Andershed, A. & Andershed, H. (2015). Risk and protective factors among preschool children: Integrating research and practice. *Journal of Evidence-Informed Social Work, 12,* 412–424. doi:10.1080/15433714.2013.866062

Asher, S. R. & McDonald, K. L. (2009). The behavioral basis of acceptance, rejection, and perceived popularity. In: K. H. Rubin, W. M. Bukowski, & B. Laursen (Eds.), *Handbook of peer interactions, relationships, and groups* (pp. 232–248). New York: Guilford Press.

Bagner, D. M., Pettit, J. W., Lewinsohn, P. M., Seeley, J. R., & Jaccard, J. (2013). Disentangling the temporal relationship between parental depressive symptoms and early child behavior problems: A transactional framework. *Journal of Clinical Child and Adolescent Psychology*, 42, 78–90. doi:10.108 0/15374416.2012.715368

Barker, E. D., Copeland, W., Maughan, B., Jaffee, S. R., & Uher, R. (2012). Relative impact of maternal depression and associated risk factors on offspring psychopathology. *British Journal of Psychiatry*, 200, 124–129. doi:10.1192/bjp. bp.111.092346

Belsky, J. & de Haan, M. (2011). Annual research review: Parenting and children's brain development: The end of the beginning. *Journal of Child Psychology and Psychiatry*, 52(4), 409–428. doi:10.1111/j.1469-7610.2010.02281.x

Benzies, K. & Mychasiuk, R. (2009). Fostering family resiliency: A review of the key protective factors. *Child and Family Social Work*, 14, 103–114. doi:10.1111/ j.1365-2206.2008.00586.x

Biederman, J. (2005). Attention-deficit/hyperactivity disorder: A selective overview. *Biological Psychiatry*, 57, 1215–1220. doi:10.1016/j.biopsych.2004.10.020

Bierman, K. L. (2004). *Peer rejection: Developmental processes and intervention strategies*. New York, NY: Guilford Press.

Blazei, R. W., Iacono, W. G., & Krueger, R. F. (2006). Intergenerational transmission of antisocial behavior: How do kids become antisocial adults? *Applied and Preventive Psychology*, 11, 230–253. doi:10.1016/j.appsy.2006.07.001

Bonin, E. M., Stevens, M., Beecham, J., Byford, S., & Parsonage, M. (2011). Costs and longer-term savings of parenting programmes for the prevention of persistent conduct disorder: a modelling study. *BMC Public Health*, 11, 803. doi. org/10.1186/1471-2458-11-803

Caspi, A., Moffitt, T. E., Newman, D. L., & Silva, P. A. (1996). Behavioral observations at age 3 years predict adult psychiatric disorders: Longitudinal evidence from a birth cohort. *Archives of General Psychiatry*, 53, 1033–1039. doi:10.1001/ archpsyc.1996.01830110071009

Côté, S. M., Vaillancourt, T., Barker, E. D., Nagin, D., & Tremblay, R. E. (2007). The joint development of physical and indirect aggression: Predictors of continuity and change during childhood. *Development and Psychopathology*, 19, 37–55. doi:10.1017/S0954579407070034

Daley, D., Jones, K., & Hutchings, J. (2009). Attention deficit hyperactivity disorder (ADHD) in preschool children: Current findings, recommended interventions and future directions. *Child: Care, Health and Development*, 35, 754–766. doi:10.1111/j.1365-2214.2009.00938.x

DeGarmo, D. S. & Forgatch, M. S. (1997). Confidant support and maternal distress: Predictors of parenting practices for divorced mothers. *Personal Relationships*, 4(4), 305–317.

Derzon, J. H. (2010). The correspondence of family features with problem, aggressive, criminal, and violent behavior: A meta-analysis. *Journal of Experimental Criminology*, 6, 263–292. doi:10.1007/s11292-010-9098-0

DeVore, E. R. & Ginsburg, K. R. (2005). The protective effects of good parenting on adolescents. *Current Opinion in Pediatrics*, 17, 460–465. doi:10.1097/01. mop.0000170514.27649.c9

Dishion, T. J. & Patterson, G. R. (2006). The development and ecology of antisocial behavior in children and adolescents. In: D. Cicchetti & D. J. Cohen (Eds.), *Developmental Psychopathology*, Vol. 3, *Risk, Disorder, and Adaptation* (pp. 503–541). New York: Wiley.

Dishion, T. J., McCord, J., & Poulin, F. (1999). When interventions harm: Peer groups and problem behavior. *American Psychologist, 54*, 755–764. doi:10.1037/0003-066X.54.9.755

Dishion, T. J., Patterson, G. R., Stoolmiller, M., & Skinner, M. L. (1991). Family, school, and behavioral antecedents to early adolescent involvement with antisocial peers. *Developmental Psychology, 27*, 172–180. doi:10.1037/0012-1649.27.1.172

Dix, T. & Meunier, L. N. (2009). Depressive symptoms and parenting competence: An analysis of 13 regulatory processes. *Developmental Review, 29*, 45–68. doi:10.1016/j.dr.2008.11.002

Dodge, K. A., Dishion, T. J., & Lansford, J. E. (Eds.). (2007). *Deviant peer influences in programs for youth: Problems and solutions*. New York: Guilford Press.

Duncan, G. J., Dowsett, C. J., Claessens, A., Magnuson, K., Huston, A. C., Klebanov, P., . . . Duckworth, K. (2007). School readiness and later achievement. *Developmental Psychology, 43*, 1428–1446. doi:10.1037/0012-1649.43.6.1428

Evans, J., Williams, J. M. G., O'Loughlin, S., & Howells, K. (1992). Autobiographical memory and problem solving strategies of parasuicide patients. *Psychological Medicine, 22*, 399–405. doi:10.1017/S0033291700030348

Farrington, D. P. (2000). Psychosocial predictors of adult antisocial personality and adult convictions. *Behavioral Sciences and the Law, 18*, 605–622. doi:10.1002/1099-0798(200010)18:5%3C605::AID-BSL406%3E3.0.CO;2-0

Farrington, D. & Welsh, B. C. (2007). *Saving children from a life of crime: Early risk factors and effective interventions*. New York: Oxford University Press.

Fergusson, D. M., Horwood, L. J., & Ridder, E. (2005). Show me the child at seven: The consequences of conduct problems in childhood for psychosocial functioning in adulthood. *Journal of Child Psychology and Psychiatry, 46*, 837–849. doi:10.1111/j.1469-7610.2004.00387.x

Flouri, E., Mavroveli, S., & Tzavidis, N. (2010). Modeling risks: Effects of area deprivation, family socio-economic disadvantage and adverse life events on young children's psychopathology. *Social Psychiatry and Psychiatric Epidemiology, 45*, 611–619. doi:10.1007/s00127-009-0101-x

Forehand, R. L. & McMahon, R. J. (1984). *Helping the Non-Compliant Child: A Clinician's Guide to Parent Training*. London, UK: Guilford Press.

Forehand, R., Wells, K. C., McMahon, R. J., Griest, D., & Rogers, T. (1982). Maternal perceptions of maladjustment in clinic-referred children: An extension of earlier research. *Journal of Behavioral Assessment, 4*, 145–151. doi:10.1007/BF01321388

Forgatch, M. S. & DeGarmo, D. (2002). Extending and testing the social interaction learning model with divorce samples. In: J. B. Reid, G. R. Patterson, & J. Snyder (Eds.), *Antisocial behavior in children and adolescents: A developmental analysis and model for intervention* (pp. 235–256). doi:10.1037/10468-012

Furlong, M., McGilloway, S., Bywater, T., Hutchings, J., Smith, S. M., & Donnelly, M. (2012). Behavioural and cognitive-behavioural group-based parenting programmes for early-onset conduct problems in children aged 3 to 12 years (Cochrane review). *Cochrane Database for Systematic Reviews, 2*, 1–362. doi:10.1002/14651858.CD008225.pub2

Gable, R. A., Hester, P. H., Rock, M. L., & Hughes, K. G. (2009). Back to basics: Rules, praise, ignoring, and reprimands revisited. *Intervention in School and Clinic, 44*, 195–205. doi:10.1177/1053451208328831

Gardner, F., Burton, J., & Klimes, I. (2006). Randomised controlled trial of a parenting intervention in the voluntary sector for reducing child conduct problems: outcomes and mechanisms of change. *Journal of Child Psychology and Psychiatry, 47*, 1123–1132. doi:10.1111/j.1469-7610.2006.01668.x

Gardner, F., Hutchings, J., Bywater, T., & Whitaker, C. J. (2010). Who benefits and how does it work? Moderators and mediators of outcome in an effectiveness trial of a parenting intervention. *Journal of Clinical Child and Adolescent Psychology, 39*, 568–580. doi:10.1080/15374416.2010.486315

Goodman, S. H., Rouse, M. H., Connell, A. M., Broth, M. R., Hall, C. M., & Heyward, D. (2011). Maternal depression and child psychopathology: A meta-analytic review. *Clinical Child and Family Psychology Review, 14*, 1–27. doi:10.1007/s10567-010-0080-1

Green, H., McGinnity, A., Meltzer, H., Ford, T., & Goodman, R. (2005). *Mental health of children and young people in Great Britain, 2004: Summary report.* Newport, UK: Office for National Statistics.

Gross, H. E., Shaw, D. S., Moilanen, K. L., Dishion, T. J., & Wilson, M. N. (2008). Reciprocal models of child behavior and depressive symptoms in mothers and fathers in a sample of children at risk for early conduct problems. *Journal of Family Psychology, 22*, 742–751. doi:10.1037/a0013514

Gross, J. (2008). *Getting in early: Primary schools and early intervention.* London, UK: The Smith Institute/Centre for Social Justice.

Hartman, R. R., Stage, S. A., & Webster-Stratton, C. (2003). A growth curve analysis of parent training outcomes: Examining the influence of child risk factors (inattention, impulsivity, and hyperactivity problems), parental and family risk factors. *Journal of Child Psychology and Psychiatry, 44*, 388–398. doi:10.1111/1469-7610.00129

Herndon, R. W. & Iacono, W. G. (2005). Psychiatric disorder in the children of antisocial parents. *Psychological Medicine, 35*, 1815–1824. doi:10.1017/S0033291705005635

Hoeve, M., Dubas, J. S., Eichelsheim, V. I., van der Laan, P. H., Smeenk, W., & Gerris, J. R. M. (2009). The relationship between parenting and delinquency: A meta-analysis. *Journal of Abnormal Child Psychology, 37*, 749–775. doi:10.1007/s10802-009-9310-8

Hutchings, J. & Gardner, F. (2012). Support from the Start: Effective programmes for three to eight year-olds. *Journal of Children's Services, 7*, 29–40. doi:10.1108/17466661211213652

Hutchings, J., Gardner, F., & Lane, E. (2004). Chapter 5: Making evidence-based interventions work. In: C. Sutton, D. Utting, & D. Farrington (Eds.), *Support from the start: Working with young children and their families to reduce the risks of crime and anti-social behaviour*, Nottingham, UK: Department for Education and Skills.

Hutchings, J., Lane, E., & Kelly, J. (2004). Comparison of two treatments for children with severely disruptive behaviours: A four-year follow-up. *Behavioural and Cognitive Psychotherapy, 32*, 15–30. doi:10.1017/S1352465804001018

Hutchings, J., Smith, M., & Gilbert, H. (2000). *The Parent–Child Autobiographical Memory Test (PCAMT). Identifying potential deficits in maternal observation style.* Spotlight No. 43, Cardiff: Wales Office for Research and Development (WORD).

Hutchings, J., Williams, M. E., Martin, P., & Pritchard, R. O. (2011). Levels of behavioural difficulties in young Welsh school children. *Welsh Journal of Education, 15*(1), 103–115.

Hutchings, J., Bywater, T., Williams, M. E., Lane, E., & Whitaker, C. J. (2012). Improvements in maternal depression as a mediator of child behaviour change. *Psychology*, 3, 795–801. doi:10.4236/psych.2012.329120

Hutchings, J., Bywater, T., Daley, D., Gardner, F., Whitaker, C. J., Jones, K., . . . Edwards, R. T. (2007). Parenting intervention in Sure Start services for children at risk of developing Conduct Disorder: Pragmatic randomised controlled trial. *British Medical Journal*, 334, 678–684. doi:10.1136/bmj.39126.620799.55

Jones, K., Daley, D., Hutchings, J., Bywater, T., & Eames, C. (2008). Efficacy of the Incredible Years programme as an early intervention for children with conduct problems and ADHD: Long-term follow-up. *Child Care, Health, and Development*, 34, 380–390. doi:10.1111/j.1365-2214.2008.00817.x

Karreman, A., de Haas, S., van Tuijl, C., van Aken, M. A. G., & Dekovic, M. (2010). Relations among temperament, parenting, and problem behavior in young children. *Infant Behavior and Development*, 33, 39–49. doi:10.1016/j.infbeh.2009.10.008

Kiernan, K. E. & Mensah, F. K. (2009). Poverty, maternal depression, family status and children's cognitive and behavioural development in early childhood: A longitudinal study. *Journal of Social Policy*, 38, 569–588. doi:10.1017/s0047279409003250

Kolthof, H. J., Kikkert, M. J., & Dekker, J. (2014). Multiproblem or multirisk families? A broad review of the literature. *Journal of Child and Adolescent Behavior*, 2, 4148–4153. doi:10.4172/2375-4494.1000148

Ladd, G. W. & Troop-Gordon, W. (2003). The role of chronic peer difficulties in the development of children's psychological adjustment problems. *Child Development*, 74, 1344–1367. doi:10.1111/1467-8624.00611

Laird, R. D., Jordan, K. Y., Dodge, K. A., Pettit, G. S., & Bates, J. E. (2001). Peer rejection in childhood, involvement with antisocial peers in early adolescence, and the development of externalizing behavior problems. *Development and Psychopathology*, 13(2), 337–354.

Leschied, A., Chiodo, D., Nowicki, E., & Rodger, S. (2008). Childhood predictors of adult criminality: A meta-analysis drawn from the prospective longitudinal literature. *Canadian Journal of Criminology and Criminal Justice*, 50(4), 435–467. doi:10.3138/cjccj.50.4.435

Leve, L. D., Kim, H. K., & Pears, K. C. (2005). Childhood temperament and family environment as predictors of internalizing and externalizing trajectories from ages 5 to 17. *Journal of Abnormal Child Psychology*, 33, 505–520. doi:10.1007/s10802-005-6734-7

Loeber, R. & Hay, D. (1997). Key issues in the development of aggression and violence from childhood to early adulthood. *Annual Review of Psychology*, 48, 371–410. doi:10.1146/annurev.psych.48.1.371

Lovejoy, M. C., Graczyk, P. A., O'Hare, E., & Neuman, G. (2000). Maternal depression and parenting behavior: A meta-analytic review. *Clinical Psychology Review*, 20(5), 561–592.

Lunkenheimer, E., Lichtwarck-Aschoff, A., Hollenstein, T., Kemp, C. J., & Granic, I. (2016). Breaking down the coercive cycle: How parent and child risk factors influence real-time variability in parental responses to child misbehavior. *Parenting*, 16, 237–256. doi:10.1080/15295192.2016.1184925

Lyons-Ruth, K., Wolfe, R., Lyubchik, A., & Steingard, R. (2002). Depressive symptoms in parents of children under age 3: Sociodemographic predictors, current correlates, and associated parenting behaviors. In: N. Halfon, K. T. McLearn, & M. A. Schuster (Eds.), *Child rearing in America: Challenges facing parents with young children* (pp. 217–259). Cambridge UK: Cambridge University Press.

Martel, M. M. (2013). Sexual selection and sex differences in the prevalence of childhood externalizing and adolescent internalizing disorders. *Psychological Bulletin, 130*, 1221–1259. doi:10.1037/a0032247

McLanahan, S., Tach, L., & Schneider, D. (2013). The causal effects of father absence. *Annual Review of Sociology, 399*, 399–427. doi:10.1146/annurev-soc-071312-145704

McMahon, R. J. & Frick, P. J. (2005). Evidence-based assessment of conduct problems in children and adolescents. *Journal of Clinical Child and Adolescent Psychology, 34*, 477–505. doi:10.1207/s15374424jccp3403_6

Meltzer, H., Gatward, R., Goodman, R., & Ford, T. (2000). *The mental health of children and adolescents in Great Britain: Summary report.* London, UK: Office for National Statistics.

Merikangas, K. R., Nakamura, E. F., & Kessler, R. C. (2009). Epidemiology of mental disorders in children and adolescents. *Dialogues in Clinical Neuroscience, 11*(1), 7–20.

Meunier, L. J. (2007). *Maternal depressive symptoms and parenting behavior: Child behavior as an activator of maternal responsiveness.* PhD thesis, Austin, University of Texas.

Miner, J. L. & Clarke-Stewart, A. (2008). Trajectories of externalizing behaviour from age 2 to age 9: Relations with gender, temperament, ethnicity, parenting, and rater. *Developmental Psychology, 44*, 771–786. doi:10.1037/0012-1649.44.3.771

Mitchell, C., McLanahan, S., Notterman, D., Hobcraft, J., Brooks-Gunn, J., & Garfinkel, I. (2015). Family structure instability, genetic sensitivity, and child well-being. *American Journal of Sociology, 120*, 1195–1225. doi:10.1086/680681

Moehler, E., Brunner, R., Wiebel, A., Reck, C., & Resch, F. (2006). Maternal depressive symptoms in the postnatal period are associated with long-term impairment of mother–child bonding. *Archives of Women's Mental Health, 9*, 273–278. doi:10.1007/s00737-006-0149-5

Moffitt, T. E. (2005). Genetics and environmental influences on antisocial behaviors: Evidence from behavioural-genetic research. *Advances in Genetics, 55*, 41–104. doi:10.1016/s0065-2660(05)55003-x

Muntz, R., Hutchings, J., Edwards, R. T., Hounsome, B., & O'Ceilleachair, A. (2004). Economic evaluation of treatments for children with severe behavioural problems. *Journal of Mental Health Policy, 7*(4), 177–189.

Murray, J., Irving, B., Farrington, D. P., Colman, I., & Bloxsom, C. A. J. (2010). Very early predictors of conduct problems and crime: Results from a national cohort study. *Journal of Child Psychology and Psychiatry, 51*, 1198–1207. doi:10.1111/j.1469-7610.2010.02287.x

Najman, J. M., Clavarino, A., McGee, T. R., Bor, W., Williams, G. M., & Hayatbakhsh, M. R. (2010). Timing and chronicity of family poverty and development of unhealthy behaviors in children: A longitudinal study. *Journal of Adolescent Health, 46*, 538–544. doi:10.1016/j.jadohealth.2009.12.001

National Collaborating Centre for Mental Health [NCCMH] (2013). *Antisocial behaviour and conduct disorders in children and young people: The NICE guideline on recognition, intervention, and management* (No. 158). Leicester, UK: RCPsych Publications.

Patterson, G. R. (1982). *Coercive family process.* Eugene, OR: Castalia.

Patterson, G. R. & Yoerger, K. A. (2002). A developmental model for early- and late-onset delinquency. In: J. B. Reid, G. R. Patterson, & J. J. Snyder (Eds.), *Antisocial behaviour in children and adolescents: A developmental analysis and model for intervention* (pp. 147–172). Washington DC: American Psychological Association.

Patterson, G. R., Capaldi, D., & Bank, L. (1991). An early starter model for predicting delinquency. In: D. J. Pepler & K. H. Rubin (Eds.), *The development and treatment of childhood aggression* (pp. 139–168). Hillsdale, NJ: Lawrence Erlbaum.

Patterson, G. R., Forgatch, M. S., Yoerger, K. L., & Stoolmiller, M. (1998). Variables that initiate and maintain an early-onset trajectory for juvenile offending. *Development and Psychopathology, 10,* 531–547.

Paulson, J. F., Dauber, S., & Leiferman, J. A. (2006). Individual and combined effects of postpartum depression in mothers and fathers on parenting behavior. *Pediatrics, 118,* 659–668. doi:10.1016/j.infbeh.2009.10.005

Piquero, A. R., Carriaga, M. L., Diamond, B., Kazemian, L., & Farrington, D. P. (2012). Stability in aggression revisited. *Aggression and Violent Behavior, 17,* 365–372. doi:10.1016/j.avb.2012.04.001

Polanczyk, G. V., Salum, G. A., Sugaya, L. S., Caye, A., & Rohde, L. A. (2015). Annual research review: A meta-analysis of the worldwide prevalence of mental disorders in children and adolescents. *Journal of Child Psychology and Psychiatry, 56,* 345–365. doi:10.1111/jcpp.12381

Reinke, W. M. & Herman, K. C. (2002). Creating school environments that deter antisocial behaviors in youth. *Psychology in the Schools, 39,* 549–560. doi:10.1002/pits.10048

Romeo, R., Knapp, M., & Scott, S. (2006). Economic cost of severe antisocial behaviour in children–and who pays it. *British Journal of Psychiatry, 188,* 547–553. doi:10.1192/bjp.bp.104.007625

Rutter, M. (1996). Connections between child and adult psychopathology. *European Child and Adolescent Psychiatry, 5*(1), 4–7.

Rydell, A. M. (2010). Family factors and children's disruptive behaviour: An investigation of links between demographic characteristics, negative life events and symptoms of ODD and ADHD. *Social Psychiatry and Psychiatric Epidemiology, 45,* 233–244. doi:10.1007/s00127-009-0060-2

Sabates, R. & Dex, S. (2015). The impact of multiple risk factors on young children's cognitive and behavioural development. *Children and Society, 29,* 95–108. doi:10.1111/chso.12024

Sainsbury Centre for Mental Health (2009). *The chance of a lifetime: Preventing early conduct problems and reducing crime.* London, UK: Sainsbury Centre for Mental Health.

Sansbury, L. S. & Wahler, R. G. (1992). Pathways to maladaptive parenting with mothers and their conduct disordered children. *Behavior Modification, 16*(4), 574–592.

Scott, S., Knapp, M., Henderson, J., & Maughan, B. (2001). Financial cost of social exclusion: Follow up study of antisocial children into adulthood. *British Medical Journal, 323,* 191. doi:10.1136/bmj.323.7306.191

Seligman, M. E. P. (1975). *Helplessness: On depression, development and death.* San Francisco, CA: W. H. Freeman.

Shaw, D. S., Connell, A., Dishion, T. J., Wilson, M. N., & Gardner, F. (2009). Improvements in maternal depression as a mediator of intervention effects on early childhood problem behaviour. *Development and Psychopathology*, *21*, 417–439. doi:10.1017/s0954579409000236

Sigle-Rushton, W. & McLanahan, S. S. (2004). Father absence and child wellbeing: A critical review. In: D. P. Moynihan, T. Smeeding, & L. Rainwater (Eds.), *The future of the family* (pp. 116–158). New York: Russell Sage Foundation.

Teti, D. M., Gelfand, D. M., & Pompa, J. (1990). Depressed mothers' behavioural competence with their infants: demographic and psychosocial correlates. *Development and Psychopathology*, *2*, 259–270.

Tiet, Q. Q., Bird, H. R., Hoven, C. W., Moore, R., Wu, P., Wicks, J., . . . & Cohen, P. (2001). Relationship between specific adverse life events and psychiatric disorders. *Journal of Abnormal Child Psychology*, *29*, 153–164. doi:10.1023/A:1005288130494

Trentacosta, C. J., Hyde, L. W., Shaw, D. S., Dishion, T. J., Gardner, F., & Wilson, M. (2008). The relations among cumulative risk, parenting, and behavior problems during early childhood. *Journal of Child Psychology and Psychiatry*, *49*, 1211–1219. doi:10.1111/j.1469-7610.2008.01941.x

van Vreeswijk, D. F. & de Wilde, E. J. (2004). Autobiographical memory specificity, psychopathology, depressed mood and the use of the Autobiographical Memory Test: A meta-analysis. *Behaviour Research and Therapy*, *42*, 731–743. doi:10.1016/S0005-7967(03)00194-3

Vitaro, F., Pedersen, S., & Brendgen, M. (2007). Children's disruptiveness, peer rejection, friends' deviancy, and delinquent behaviors: A process-oriented approach. *Development and Psychopathology*, *19*, 433–453. doi:10.1017/S0954579407070216

Wahler, R. G. & Dumas, J. E. (1984). Changing the observational coding styles of insular and non-insular mothers: A step towards maintenance of parent training effects. In: R. F. Dangel & R. A. Polster (Eds.), *Parent training: Foundations of research and practice* (pp. 379–416). New York: Guilford Press.

Wahler, R. G. & Dumas, J. E. (1989). Attentional problems in dysfunctional mother–child interactions: An interbehavioral model. *Psychological Bulletin*, *105*, 116–130. doi:10.1037/0033-2909.105.1.116

Wahler, R. G. & Hann, D. M. (1984). The communication patterns of troubled mothers: In search of a keystone in the generalisation of parenting skills. *Education and Treatment of Children*, *7*(4), 335–350.

Wahler, R. G. & Sansbury, L. E. (1990). The monitoring skills of troubled mothers: Their problems in defining child deviance. *Journal of Abnormal Child Psychology*, *18*, 577–589. doi:10.1007/BF00911109

Webster-Stratton, C. & Herbert, M. (1994). *Troubled families – problem children: Working with parents: A collaborative process*. West Sussex, UK: John Wiley & Sons.

Webster-Stratton, C. & Spitzer, A. (1996). Parenting a young child with conduct problems: New insights using qualitative methods. *Advances in Clinical Child Psychology*, *18*, 1–62.

Webster-Stratton, C., Reid, M. J., & Stoolmiller, M. (2008). Preventing conduct problems and improving school readiness: Evaluation of the incredible years teacher and child training programs in high-risk schools. *Journal of Child Psychology and Psychiatry*, *49*, 471–488. doi:10.1111/j.1469-7610.2007.01861.x

Welsh, B. C., Loeber, R., Stevens, B. R., Stouthamer-Loeber, M., Cohen, M. A., & Farrington, D. P. (2008). Costs of juvenile crime in urban areas: A longitudinal perspective. *Youth Violence and Juvenile Justice, 6*, 3–27. doi:10.1177/1541204007308427

World Health Organization (1992). *The ICD-10 classification of mental and behavioural disorders: Clinical description and diagnostic guidelines.* Geneva: WHO.

Zahn-Waxler, C., Shirtcliff, E. A., & Marceau, K. (2008). Disorders of childhood and adolescence: Gender and psychopathology. *Annual Review of Clinical Psychology, 4*, 275–303. doi:10.1146/annurev.clinpsy.3.022806.091358

2 Interventions

Behavioural family interventions

Helping parents to develop effective child management strategies by way of behaviourally based family interventions is a proven effective treatment approach that is recommended with parents (National Collaborating Centre for Mental Health (NCCMH), 2013; Furlong et al., 2012). More than 50 years of research into behavioural family interventions have provided strong evidence that they are effective for children with high levels of disruptive behaviour (Farrington and Welsh, 2007). There is also evidence of positive long-term outcomes (Sandler et al., 2011) and their effectiveness as crime prevention measures (Farrington and Welsh, 2007).

Early intervention, before children become more independent of their parents, has a greater likelihood of success (Allen, 2011; Farrington and Welsh, 2007). A substantial weight of evidence, accumulated over the past 40 plus years, has come from randomised controlled trials (RCTs) and systematic reviews of these evidence-based programmes. Most effective interventions are based on social learning theory, are "cognitive-behavioural" in orientation, and such programmes are increasingly being used in the UK.

Behavioural parent training is based on social learning theory, which provides a way of understanding the nature of the problem and the principles that underpin strategies, such as modelling and behavioural rehearsal, that help both the parent and the child to establish more appropriate behaviours (see Chapter 11). Parents are taught to observe and record specific problem behaviours at home, to give clear and specific instructions, to establish clear rules and consistent limits for their child to follow, to praise and reward pro-social behaviours and to apply non-violent discipline approaches, such as time out, in response to inappropriate behaviour.

One of the first and the most influential parenting programmes was developed by Patterson and colleagues at the Oregon Social Learning Center. Patterson's (1982) early work first described the development of problem behaviour as a *coercive family process*, a downward spiral in which both parents and children learn that they can stop, or escape, the aversive behaviour of the other by behaving in an aversive way themselves and so develop increasingly negative and aggressive patterns of behaviour. Patterson's parenting programme was designed to alter the pattern of exchanges between parent and child, so that pro-social rather than coercive child behaviour is directly reinforced and supported within the family (Patterson, 1982; Patterson, Reid, Jones and Conger, 1975).

Family behavioural programmes are considered to be the most effective method of intervention, but this does not work for everyone. Some studies report a parent dropout of up to 40 per cent (NCCMH, 2013; Reyno and McGrath, 2006), and it is reported that 30–40 per cent of parents who received parent training continue to have children with levels of behaviour problems in the clinical range (Patterson, 1982).

Factors reported to influence treatment outcome

A major factor is the age of the child at the time of treatment. Many families will have been trying to cope with their child's behaviour for some time before seeking help, and the older the child is at the start of treatment, the poorer the outcome (Ogden and Hagen, 2008). In addition, many of the problems associated with the development of conduct disorder have also been identified as factors which influence a family's ability to benefit from parent training. A number of associated factors have been identified, including demographic characteristics such as low socio-economic status, unemployment, low education, single parent status, younger maternal age, and ethnic minority status (e.g. Fernandez and Eyberg, 2009; Nock and Ferriter, 2005; Reyno and McGrath, 2006; Werba, Eyberg, Boggs and Algina, 2006). Dumas and Wahler (1983) reported that socially isolated mothers were more likely to relapse following intervention because of the lack of an effective support system. They found that mothers who were either socially disadvantaged or insular had only a 50 per cent probability of treatment success, and mothers who were both socially disadvantaged and insular were almost certain to fail.

However, this is not always the case with evidence-based parenting programmes. For example, evidence from the United States suggests that parenting and child behaviour can improve in families experiencing severe socio-economic disadvantage. Many of the children who qualify for the US Head Start programme are exposed to multiple risk factors for conduct problems and later offending. Yet the *Incredible Years* parenting programmes, which address the issues of engaging very disadvantaged families, have been successfully implemented with these Head Start families and studies examining their efficacy have found no adverse connection between parents' socio-economic status or ethnicity and programme uptake, satisfaction or outcomes (Hartman, Stage and Webster-Stratton, 2003; Webster-Stratton, Reid and Hammond, 2001). According to Hartman and colleagues (2003), "as mothers are given opportunities to acquire further positive parenting skills, levels of economic disadvantage become less important in predicting treatment success or failure" (p. 396). In a UK-based study of a parenting programme in Sure Start centres, Gardner and colleagues (2010) found that depressed mothers reported greater improvements in their child's behaviour problems than non-depressed mothers, and that teen parents, single parents, low-income families and children with the most severe levels of behaviour problems benefited as much as other parents. This suggests that parenting programmes can be beneficial for all families regardless of risk factors that influence treatment outcome.

Key components of effective behavioural family interventions

In terms of necessary components, it has been established that:

- New parenting skills must be actively rehearsed (Bandura, 1977; Knapp and Deluty, 1989). Approaches such as videotape feedback, role play and rehearsal are very effective in improving parent behaviours and confidence (Barth and Liggett-Creel, 2014; Kaminski, Valle, Filene and Boyle, 2008).
- Parenting programmes must teach principles rather than prescribed techniques. When parents learn behavioural principles, they acquire the tools to decide what works best for them and to respond positively and appropriately when new situations arise (Hutchings, Gardner and Lane, 2004; McMahon, Forehand and Griest, 1981). This also enables them to set and achieve their own goals (Webster-Stratton and Hancock, 1998).
- Since parenting practices are involved in both the establishment and maintenance of problematic child behaviour, it is essential that parents practise new parenting behaviours at home (Kaminski et al., 2008; Patterson, 1982).
- Programmes need to include (non-violent) sanctions for negative behaviour as well as strategies to build positive relationships through play and praise (Barth and Liggett-Creel, 2014; Chorpita, Daleiden and Weisz, 2005; Kaminski et al., 2008). Work that helps parents to encourage positive behaviour through play and praise, but does not help them to deal with problem behaviour, can show early improvements, but these positive changes may not be maintained (Hobbs, Walle and Hammersly, 1991; Wiltz and Patterson, 1974).

Difficulties in the relationships between adults in the family should not be ignored, since they can have significant effects on children (Cummings and Davies, 2010). For example, Cowan and colleagues (2011) found a value-added impact of participating in groups focusing on couple relationship issues with reduced conflict and greater effectiveness of both mothers' and fathers' parenting style, compared to those attending parenting-focused groups.

Common factors of effective treatment programmes

As well as the specific components essential in family interventions, there are other factors that influence the outcome of treatment. These factors are common to many different fields, including medicine, psychiatry and education, and can help to explain the positive and similar results obtained from theoretically different interventions. According to Lambert (1992), common factors include:

- *The client(s)*: including their unique strengths, beliefs, values, skills, experiences, ability to enlist the support and help of others, circumstances, potential for change and desired changes that are already happening in their lives. Effective treatment mobilises the client's resources and works in a way that is compatible with the client's beliefs and values.
- *The client–practitioner relationship*: including the client's perception of the empathy, acceptance and warmth of the therapist, the classic counselling skills (Patterson, 1984). This "therapeutic alliance" is enhanced by:
  - accepting the client's goals at face value instead of challenging them or altering them to fit a specific theoretical model
  - tailoring therapeutic tasks and suggestions to the client instead of requiring the client to conform to the therapist's chosen model and beliefs
  - collaborating with clients instead of dictating to them
  - exploring material that is relevant to the client.

- *Client expectations of a positive outcome*: This is the client's hope and expectancy of change as a result of taking part in a programme. This is harnessed when practitioners:
  - convey an attitude of hope and possibility without minimising the problem or the pain that accompanies it
  - encourage clients to focus on present and future possibilities instead of past problems.

The helping process: combining common and specific factors

The process of helping parents towards a successful outcome needs to consider these common factors as well as the specific techniques of therapy. The *Family Partnership Model* developed by Davis and Day (2010) provides a good example of the way that common factors can be incorporated into a parenting intervention. The model focuses on the parent–practitioner relationship as fundamental in determining the eventual outcomes. It stresses that this relationship is one of partnership and mutual respect and teaches practitioners how this can be achieved through skills such as attending and listening. The aim is to involve parents from the start and to value and use their expertise so that they take credit for positive changes and feel confident that they can tackle future problems (Davis and Day, 2010).

Collaborative skills are the core of client-centred therapy, which recognises the importance of strategies that enable clients to be empowered through their ownership of ideas and solutions. Webster-Stratton has given much attention to the essential collaborative process skills needed for group leaders in her Incredible Years parenting programmes (Webster-Stratton and Herbert, 1994). These have been incorporated into her training programmes and may contribute to her success in engaging much larger numbers of high-risk socially disadvantaged families than most other workers in this field. These skills are essential to engage families whose children are already at high risk of long-term delinquency.

It is clear that the effectiveness of a programme depends on the degree to which it takes account of common factors. Webster-Stratton's series of Incredible Years group-based programmes ensure that "client" risk factors are addressed in a way that minimises their impact on outcomes. They are also delivered in a way designed to ensure an effective, collaborative, client–practitioner relationship (Webster-Stratton and Herbert, 1994). By collaborating with clients and tailoring the programme delivery to their needs and circumstances, Webster-Stratton has achieved good outcomes with clients who, in other programmes, are at greatest risk of dropout or failure. Her starting point for engaging these "hard to reach" families is that non-attendance in parenting skills programmes and other interventions is a problem in the programme, not in the participants. As she puts it:

> Such families have been described as unmotivated, resistant, unreliable, disengaged, chaotic, in denial, disorganized, uncaring, dysfunctional and unlikely candidates for this kind of treatment – in short, unreachable. However, these families might well describe traditional clinic-based programs as "unreachable". Clinical programs may be too far away from home, too expensive, insensitive, distant, inflexible in terms of scheduling and content, foreign in terms of language (literally or figuratively), blaming or critical of their lifestyle. A cost–benefit analysis would, in all likelihood, reveal that the costs to these clients of receiving treatment far outweigh the potential benefits even though they do genuinely want to do what is best for their children. Perhaps this population has been "unreachable" not because of their own characteristics, but because of the characteristics of the interventions they have been offered.
>
> (Webster-Stratton, 1998, p. 184)

When this approach is taken, factors such as social and economic disadvantage and maternal mental health are not strongly related to levels of engagement or positive outcomes with the programme (Baydar, Reid and

Webster-Stratton, 2003; Hartman et al., 2003). Although working with a very disadvantaged community in Seattle, Webster-Stratton was able to demonstrate higher levels of take-up, retention and better long-term outcomes than most other programmes in this field, with 88 per cent of high-risk Head Start families being retained in the programme and completing more than two-thirds of the sessions (Webster-Stratton, 1998).

Given the importance of specific as well as common factors it is not surprising that the delivery of effective behavioural family interventions is demanding. Highly skilled therapists, experienced in both social learning theory and collaborative leader skills, are often needed to deliver evidence-based programmes. Programmes led by trainees, who are learning the intervention, have been shown to be less successful (Taylor and Biglan, 1998).

When both common and specific factors are addressed and used to best effect, they can help to bring about a successful outcome. When they are ignored, they can become barriers. The collaborative process of working with families is also summarised by Hutchings et al. (2004).

What works?

The demand for effective programmes to curb and prevent children's disruptive and antisocial behaviour has never been greater, and the recent government focus on antisocial behaviour has led to a surge in parent training programmes. These have been delivered in a variety of formats: in groups, in individual consultations, DIY programmes using videos, and television programmes. Most programmes have the core principles of helping parents to increase positive child behaviour and at the same time to set clear consistent and non-violent limits for children. But agencies setting out to deliver support for parents need to know what does and doesn't work.

The effectiveness of parenting programmes can only be determined by rigorous evaluations. The most dependable evidence is derived from studies where outcomes for a group of participants for a programme have been compared with outcomes for a similar control group. In fact, evaluation in RCTs in which participants are randomly assigned to a treatment or control (usually waiting list) are considered to provide the most reliable and meaningful evidence of effectiveness, especially if these findings are replicated and include long-term follow-up (Flay et al., 2005). The parenting programmes described below have been thoroughly evaluated in RCTs and shown to be effective in reducing problem behaviour.

Evidence based parenting programmes

The parenting programme developed by Patterson (1974, 1982) is a long-established and well-researched programme, which has influenced the development of most other behavioural parenting programmes. Parents are taught to use incentive charts and social reinforcers to encourage children's pro-social behaviour and to use discipline strategies to discourage problem behaviour. Patterson's programmes have been shown to be effective with children referred for serious conduct problems between the ages of three and 12 (Patterson, 1974; Patterson, Chamberlain and Reid, 1982) and the earlier work on their initial programmes over the last 25 years has expanded to include treatment foster care programmes (Chamberlain, 2003), step-parenting programmes (DeGarmo and Forgatch, 2007; Forgatch, DeGarmo and Beldavs, 2005) and universal school-based programmes (Eddy, Reid and Fetrow, 2000; Reid, Eddy, Fetrow and Stoolmiller, 1999).

Forehand and Long developed a five-week programme, *Addressing Strong-Willed Behaviour* (Forehand and Long, 1996, 2002), for parents to do at home. Five chapters teach five new parenting skills: attending, rewarding, ignoring, giving your child effective direction, and using time out correctly. Each new skill builds on the previously learned skill and included assignments for the parents to ensure that they practiced as well as understood these new skills. An earlier clinic-based version of this programme: *Helping the Noncompliant Child* (Forehand and McMahon, 1981) teaches parents these same five parenting skills through modelling and role play. Treatment is carried out with individual families in a treatment room set up as a playroom with a one-way mirror to an observation room and bug-in-the ear equipment to enable the therapist to talk to the parent as they interact with the child and practise skills. Parents are also given homework assignments to practise the new skills at home with their child. This treatment approach has been used in much of the research leading up to the development of the EPaS programme (see Chapter 3) and the skills taught in this programme are a core part of the parenting framework for the EPaS course. They are discussed fully in Chapters 10–12.

Webster-Stratton, another major contributor to the treatment of child behaviour problems, has built on the work of Patterson and others and developed a series of programmes for children, parents and teachers. The Incredible Years series (Webster-Stratton, Mihalic et al., 2001), referred to previously in this chapter, is based on "videotape modelling" and has been identified as a "blueprint" model programme, having been shown, using rigorous evaluation techniques, to be effective in reducing problem behaviours. In the parenting programme, parents watch video clips of parent and child models in natural situations "doing it wrong" and "doing it right". Parents are encouraged to discuss and role-play ways that they might have handled the interaction more effectively. The "Basic" programme uses a "parenting pyramid" to illustrate how parenting behaviours and strategies can be used to promote their child's social competence and confidence, to encourage their child to behave appropriately and deal with unacceptable behaviour. As well as the five parenting skills described earlier, it emphasises the importance of parents playing with their child and using this time to watch and praise the child, to build up a bank of positive experiences and the child's self-esteem. Trained facilitators work with parents within a collaborative model (Webster-Stratton and Herbert, 1994) that is a central feature of the programme. The programmes also include the provision of transport, child care, meals and flexible course times to enable and encourage all parents to participate.

The "Basic" parenting programme can also be delivered at home with the help of a self-administration manual. This mode of delivery has been found to be effective for those parents who complete the programme and that improvement is enhanced with the addition of therapist consultation (Webster-Stratton, 1990). An online interactive version of the "Basic" parenting programme has been researched by Ted Taylor in collaboration with Webster-Stratton to enable parents to work through the programme at their own pace with added professional coaching through telephone calls and home visits (Taylor et al., 2008). Parents who undertook the online programme reported high levels of satisfaction as well as achievement of their self-determined goals.

In Australia, Matt Sanders has developed and researched the *Triple P – Positive Parenting Programme*, which includes five levels of intervention (Sanders, Turner and Markie-Dadds, 2002). The five levels acknowledge that parents have differing needs and desires concerning the type, intensity and mode of intervention they are likely to find most helpful. *Level 1* includes universal services such as media strategies to provide information, raise community awareness of parenting issues, and to turn the process of learning about child behaviour into a normal, straightforward activity for parents. At higher levels, interventions become more intensive as difficulties become more severe. Thus, *Level 4* is for children with identified behaviour problems, combining information with active parenting skills training, and applying these to a broad range of behaviours and settings. Delivery formats include a 10-session programme in the clinic or home, an eight-session group programme or a self-help parenting workbook. *Level 5* is for families experiencing behaviour problems complicated by additional family problems. It extends the intervention to include marital communication, mood and stress management. There is good evidence of effectiveness from RCTs in Australia that have evaluated Triple-P preventive and clinical interventions in various delivery formats (Sanders, Markie-Dadds, Tully and Bor, 2000; Thomas and Zimmer-Gembeck, 2007).

Parenting programmes can be delivered using different formats, the most prevalent being group-based or individually delivered. Both formats have advantages and disadvantages. Group-based programmes are highly effective and cost-effective (Furlong et al., 2012) and are recommended by the National Institute for Health and Care Excellence (see NCCMH, 2013). However, they are not always appropriate or accessible to all families. For example, some families are more likely to be affected by barriers to treatment such as access, health, and lack of self-confidence (Lavigne et al., 2010; Reyno and McGrath, 2006). Offering an individually delivered programme to these families may be more appropriate, since delivering a programme on an individual basis in the families' homes can eliminate many of the associated barriers. Individually delivered parenting programmes can be tailored to meet the needs of a particular family. Parents can be actively involved in the development of appropriate strategies for dealing with their child's behaviour problems (Fettig and Ostrosky, 2011). Parents are experts on their children and the day-to-day activities and routines of the family. Their in-depth knowledge of family routines, goals, values and resources are invaluable when developing tailored intervention strategies. Parenting programmes delivered on an individual basis also allow parents to practise new skills they have learned with their own child, which is an important component of effective programmes (Kaminski et al., 2008).

Who can deliver evidence-based programmes?

Traditionally, training parents of children with behaviour problems to manage their child's behaviour was firmly in the domain of specialist services such as Child and Adolescent Mental Health services. More recently however, with government recognition that early interventions using a more preventive approach is a more effective way to tackle this problem, parenting programmes are being provided within community projects involving primary care, education and social services as well as volunteer agencies. For example, the Sure Start programme, launched by the government in 1999, provides community support for all families with children under the age of four in designated areas of high social exclusion. Also, voluntary organisations such as Parent Network and the Family Caring Trust have been important in promoting parenting education in the UK and reach at least 20,000 parents a year with a range of programmes.

Despite the growing interest in tackling this serious problem, only a small proportion of those identified as having behavioural difficulties get specialist help (British Medical Association, 2013). Many specialist services do not accept referrals of younger children, despite evidence that these early starter children are at the greatest risk of long-term problems. There is also evidence to suggest that referred children are not necessarily those most in need of help. Many families do not seek or accept help because they perceive these services as stigmatising and/or inaccessible (Corrigan, 2004; Hutchings, Bywater and Daley, 2007).

The way forward must surely be to get help to as many families as possible, as early as possible, using interventions that have been researched and shown to be effective. We have a wealth of professionals working at the "Tier one" level, the first and universal level of professional care for families. These include general practitioners, health visitors, school nurses, social workers and teachers who are in a position to support and advise parents of young children who are showing behavioural difficulties. The important role of these practitioners is highlighted by the fact that these children can be identified in the preschool and early school years before their problems have achieved clinical levels and the development of secondary difficulties such as academic failure and low self-esteem. Health visitors, in particular, are highly skilled in the recognition of such problems and are in a unique position to help the families of preschool children to address any emerging difficulties (Kendrick et al., 2000). For parents seeking ways to cope with their children's difficult behaviour, the health visitor is often the only person to whom they can/will turn to for advice. Health visitors can be reasonably impartial, but very supportive, and are usually accepted in the home by parents because they provide a universal service and are not seen as stigmatising.

Health visitors have become increasingly interested in the use of behavioural management principles (Hutchings and Nash, 1998) and, although dealing with behaviour problems constitutes a major part of their workload (Wilson et al., 2008), many do not feel equipped to engage parents in systematic treatment programmes (Hutchings and Nash, 1998). Prior to the development of the Enhancing Parenting Skills course, there have been a number of initiatives to provide training in the UK through the provision of courses and workshops (e.g. Davis et al., 1997; Hewitt and Crawford, 1988) and the development of a consultation service which enabled health visitors to consult with a specialist about specific problems and learn skills to manage many relatively straightforward cases without consultation (Stallard, 1991). Evaluation of these training strategies and their benefit for families has been mainly positive, suggesting a clear role for community professionals in providing a preventive treatment approach for families with young children. But, to work effectively with families, practitioners need to have an appropriate level of theoretical knowledge and skills in assessing child behaviour problems and engaging parents in behavioural interventions.

It is important that the role of primary care professionals in this work is enhanced through appropriate training and support. A skilled workforce at the primary care level will help to ensure that vulnerable families get appropriate help before the difficult behaviours of preschool children turn into severe child mental health problems.

Conclusion

This chapter briefly described behavioural family interventions for the management of childhood behaviour problems. Some of the factors affecting treatment outcome were described, as well as the specific and common factors associated with effective interventions. The evidence suggests that a combination of both specific and common factors, along with a collaborative delivery method, are key to ensuring effective treatments.

Several parenting programmes incorporating these factors were described, including the Incredible Years and Triple-P programmes. The chapter then summarised the role of primary care staff, including health visitors, in delivering evidence-based programmes to families of children with challenging behaviour.

References

Allen, G. (2011). *Early intervention: The next steps. An independent report to Her Majesty's Government*. London, UK: The Smith Institute and the Centre for Social Justice. Retrieved from: http://dera.ioe.ac.uk/14161/1/graham%20 allen%20review%20of%20early%20intervention.pdf

Bandura, A. (1977). *Social learning theory*. Englewood Cliffs, NJ: Prentice-Hall.

Barth, R. P. & Liggett-Creel, K. (2014). Common components of parenting programs for children birth to eight years of age involved with child welfare services. *Children and Youth Services Review, 40*, 6–12. doi:10.1016/j.childy outh.2014.02.004

Baydar, N., Reid, M. J., & Webster-Stratton, C. (2003). The role of mental health factors and program engagement in the effectiveness of a preventive parenting program for Head Start mothers. *Child Development, 74*, 1433–1453. doi:10.1111/1467-8624.00616

British Medical Association [BMA] Board of Science (2013). *Growing up in the UK: Ensuring a healthy future for our children*. Retrieved from: www.bma.org.uk/ working-for-change/improving-and-protecting-health/child-health/growing-up-in-the-uk

Chamberlain, P. (2003). Multidimensional treatment foster care program components and principles of practice. In: P. Chamberlain (Ed.), *Treating chronic juvenile offenders: Advances made through the Oregon multidimensional treatment foster care model* (pp. 1–22). Washington, DC: American Psychological Association.

Chorpita, B. F., Daleiden, E. L., & Weisz, J. R. (2005). Identifying and selecting the common elements of evidence based interventions: A distillation and matching model. *Mental Health Services Research, 7*, 5–20. doi:10.1007/s11020-005-1962-6

Corrigan, P. (2004). How stigma interferes with mental health care. *American Psychologist, 59*, 614–625. doi:10.1037/0003-066X.59.7.614

Cowan, C. P., Cowan, P. A., & Barry, J. (2011). Couples' groups for parents of preschoolers: Ten-year outcomes of a randomized trial. *Journal of Family Psychology, 25*(2), 240–250. doi:10.1037/a0023003.

Cummings, E. M. & Davies, P. T. (2010). *Marital conflict and children: An emotional security perspective*. New York: Guilford Press.

Davis, H. & Day, C. (2010). *Working in partnership with parents*. London: Pearson.

Davis, H., Spurr, P., Cox, A., Lynch, M. A., Von Roenne, A., & Hahn, K. (1997). A description and evaluation of a community child mental health service. *Clinical Child Psychology and Psychiatry, 2*, 221–238. doi:10.1177/1359104597022004

DeGarmo, D. S. & Forgatch, M. S. (2007). Efficacy of parent training for stepfathers: From playful spectator and polite stranger to effective stepfathering. *Parenting: Science and Practice, 7*, 331–355. doi:10.1080.15295190701665631

Dumas, J. E. & Wahler, R. G. (1983). Predictors of treatment outcome in parent training: Mother insularity and socioeconomic disadvantage. *Behavioral Assessment, 5,* 301–313.

Eddy, J. M., Reid, J. B., & Fetrow, R. A. (2000). An elementary school-based prevention program targeting modifiable antecedents of youth delinquency and violence: Linking the Interests of Families and Teachers (LIFT). *Journal of Emotional and Behavioral Disorders, 8,* 165–176. doi:10.1177/106342660000800304

Farrington, D. & Welsh, B. C. (2007). *Saving children from a life of crime: Early risk factors and effective interventions.* New York: Oxford University Press.

Fernandez, M. A. & Eyberg, S. M. (2009). Predicting treatment and follow-up attrition in Parent–Child Interaction Therapy. *Journal of Abnormal Child Psychology, 37,* 431–441. doi:10.1007/s10802-008-9281-1

Fettig, A. & Ostrosky, M. M. (2011). Collaborating with parents in reducing children's challenging behaviors: Linking functional assessment to intervention. *Child Development Research, 2011,* 1–10. doi:10.1155/2011/835941

Flay, B. R., Biglan, A., Boruch, R. F., Castro, F. G., Gottfredson, D., Kellam, S., . . . Ji, P. (2005). Standards of evidence: Criteria for efficacy, effectiveness and dissemination. *Prevention Science, 6,* 151–175. doi:10.1007/s11121-005-5553-y

Forehand, R. & Long, N. (1996). *Parenting the strong-willed child: The clinically proven five-week program for parents of two- to six-year-olds.* Chicago, IL: Contemporary Books.

Forehand, R. & Long, N. (2002). *Parenting the strong-willed child,* 2nd edition. Chicago, IL: McGraw-Hill.

Forehand, R. L. & McMahon, R. J. (1981). *Helping the noncompliant child: A clinician's guide to parent training.* New York: Guilford Press.

Forgatch, M. S., DeGarmo, D. S., & Beldavs, Z. G. (2005). An efficacious theory-based intervention for stepfamilies. *Behavior Therapy, 36,* 357–365. doi:10.1016/S0005-7894(05)80117-0

Furlong, M., McGilloway, S., Bywater, T., Hutchings, J., Smith, S. M., & Donnelly, M. (2012). Behavioural and cognitive-behavioural group-based parenting programmes for early-onset conduct problems in children aged 3 to 12 years (Cochrane review). *Cochrane Database for Systematic Reviews, 2,* 1–362. doi:10.1002/14651858.CD008225.pub2

Gardner, F., Hutchings, J., Bywater, T., & Whitaker, C. J. (2010). Who benefits and how does it work? Moderators and mediators of outcome in an effectiveness trial of a parenting intervention. *Journal of Clinical Child and Adolescent Psychology, 39,* 568–580. doi:10.1080/15374416.2010.486315

Hartman, R. R., Stage, S. A., & Webster-Stratton, C. (2003). A growth curve analysis of parent training outcomes: examining the influence of child risk factors (inattention, impulsivity, and hyperactivity problems), parental and family risk factors. *Journal of Child Psychology and Psychiatry, 44,* 388–398. doi:10.1111/1469-7610.00129

Hewitt, K. & Crawford, W. (1988). Resolving behaviour problems in preschool children: evaluation of a workshop for health visitors. *Child: Care, Health, and Development, 14,* 1–9. doi:10.1111/j.1365-2214.1988.tb00559.x

Hobbs, S. A., Walle, D. L., & Hammersly, G. A. (1991). The relationship between child behavior and acceptability of contingency management procedures. *Child and Family Behavior Therapy, 12*(4), 95–102.

Hutchings, J. & Nash, S. (1998). Behaviour therapy: What do health visitors know? *Community Practitioner, 71*(11), 364–367.

Hutchings, J., Bywater, T., & Daley, D. (2007). Early prevention of conduct disorder: How and why did the North and Mid Wales Sure Start study work? *Journal of Children's Services, 2*, 4–14. doi:10.1108/17466660200700012

Hutchings, J., Gardner, F., & Lane, E. (2004). Making evidence-based interventions work. In: C. Sutton, D. Utting, & D. Farrington (Eds.), *Support from the start: Working with young children and their families to reduce the risks of crime and anti-social behaviour.* Nottingham, UK: Department for Education and Skills.

Kaminski, J. W., Valle, L. A., Filene, J. H., & Boyle, C. L. (2008). A meta-analytic review of components associated with parent training program effectiveness. *Journal of Abnormal Child Psychology, 36*, 567–589. doi:10.1007/s10802-007-9201-9

Kendrick, D., Elkan, R., Hewitt, M., Dewey, M., Blair, M., Robinson, J., . . . & Brummell, K. (2000). Does home visiting improve parenting and the quality of the home environment? A systematic review and meta analysis. *Archives of Disease in Childhood, 82*, 443–451. doi:10.1136/adc.82.6.443

Knapp, P. A. & Deluty, R. H. (1989). Relative effectiveness of two behavioral parent training programs. *Journal of Clinical Child Psychology, 18*(4), 314–322.

Lambert, M. J. (1992). Psychotherapy outcome research: Implications for integrative and eclectic therapies. In: J. C. Norcross & M. R. Goldfried (Eds.), *Handbook of psychotherapy integration* (pp. 94–129). New York: Basic Books.

Lavigne, J. V., LeBailly, S. A., Gouze, K. R., Binns, H. J., Keller, J., & Pate, L. (2010). Predictors and correlates of completing behavioural parent training for the treatment of oppositional defiant disorder in pediatric primary care. *Behavior Therapy, 41*, 198–211. doi:10.1016/j.beth.2009.02.006

McMahon, R. J., Forehand, R., & Griest, D. L. (1981). Effects of knowledge of social learning principles on enhancing treatment outcome and generalization in a parent training program. *Journal of Consulting and Clinical Psychology, 49*(4), 526.

National Collaborating Centre for Mental Health [NCCMH] (2013). *Antisocial behaviour and conduct disorders in children and young people: The NICE guideline on recognition, intervention, and management* (No. 158). Leicester, UK: RCPsych Publications.

Nock, M. K. & Ferriter, C. (2005). Parent management of attendance and adherence in child and adolescent therapy: A conceptual and empirical review. *Clinical Child and Family Psychology Review, 8*, 149–166. doi:10.1007/s10567-005-4753-0

Ogden, T. & Hagen, K. A. (2008). Treatment effectiveness of Parent Management Training in Norway: A randomized controlled trial of children with conduct problems. *Journal of Consulting and Clinical Psychology, 76*, 607–621. doi:10.1037/0022-006X.76.4.607

Patterson, C. H. (1984). Empathy, warmth and genuineness in psychotherapy: A review of reviews. *Psychotherapy, 21*, 431–438.

Patterson, G. R. (1974). Interventions for boys with conduct problems: Multiple settings, treatments, and criteria. *Journal of Consulting and Clinical Psychology, 42*, 471–481. doi:10.1037/h0036731

Patterson, G. R. (1982). *Coercive family process.* Eugene, OR: Castalia.

Patterson, G. R., Chamberlain, P., & Reid, J. B. (1982). A comparative evaluation of a parent-training program. *Behavior Therapy, 13*, 638–650. doi:10.1016/S0005-7894(82)80021-X

Patterson, G. R., Reid, J. B., Jones, R. R., & Conger, R. E. (1975). *Families with Aggressive Children: A Social Learning Approach to Family Intervention*, Vol. 1. Eugene, OR: Castalia Publishing Company.

Reid, J. B., Eddy, J. M., Fetrow, R. A., & Stoolmiller, M. (1999). Description and immediate impacts of a preventive intervention for conduct problems. *American Journal of Community Psychology, 27*, 483–518. doi:10.1023/A:1022181111368

Reyno, S. M. & McGrath, P. J. (2006). Predictors of parent training efficacy for child externalizing behaviour problems – a meta-analytic review. *Journal of Child Psychology and Psychiatry, 47*, 99–111. doi:10.111/j.1469-7610.2005.01544.x

Sanders, M. R., Turner, K. M., & Markie-Dadds, C. (2002). The development and dissemination of the Triple P – Positive Parenting Program: A multilevel, evidence-based system of parenting and family support. *Prevention Science, 3*(3), 173–189.

Sanders, M. R., Markie-Dadds, C., Tully, L. A., & Bor, W. (2000). The Triple P – Positive Parenting Program: A comparison of enhanced, standard, and self-directed behavioural family intervention for parents of children with early onset conduct problems. *Journal of Consulting and Clinical Psychology, 68*, 624–640. doi:10.1037/0022-006x.68.4.624

Sandler, I. N., Schoenfelder, E. N., Wolchik, S. A., & MacKinnon, D. P. (2011). Long-term impact of prevention programs to promote effective parenting: Lasting effects but uncertain processes. *Annual Review of Psychology, 62*, 299–329. doi:10.1146/annurev.psych.121208.131619

Stallard, P. (1991). The development and evaluation of a health visitor consultation service. *Clinical Psychology Forum, 35*, 10–12.

Taylor, T. K. & Biglan, A. (1998). Behavioral family interventions for improving child-rearing: A review of the literature for clinicians and policy makers. *Clinical Child and Family Psychology Review, 1*(1), 41–60.

Taylor, T. K., Webster-Stratton, C., Feil, E. G., Broadbent, B., Widdop, C. S., & Severson, H. H. (2008). Computer-based intervention with coaching: An example using the Incredible Years program. *Cognitive Behaviour Therapy, 37*, 233–246. doi:10.1080/16506070802364511

Thomas, R. & Zimmer-Gembeck, M. J. (2007). Behavioral outcomes of parent–child interaction therapy and Triple P – Positive Parenting Program: A review and meta-analysis. *Journal of Abnormal Child Psychology, 35*, 475–495. doi:10.1007/s10802-007-9104-9

Webster-Stratton, C. (1990). Enhancing the effectiveness of self-administered videotape parent training for families with conduct-problem children. *Journal of Abnormal Child Psychology, 18*, 479–492. doi:10.1007/BF00911103

Webster-Stratton, C. (1998). Parent training with low-income families. In: J. R. Lutzker (Ed.), *Handbook of child abuse research and treatment* (pp. 183–210). Boston, MA: Springer.

Webster-Stratton, C. & Hancock, L. (1998). Training for parents of young children with conduct problems: Content, methods, and therapeutic processes. In: J. M. Briesmeister & C. E. Schaefer (Eds.), *Handbook of parent training: Parents as co-therapists for children's behavior problems* (pp. 98–152). Hoboken, NJ: John Wiley.

Webster-Stratton, C. & Herbert, M. (1994). *Troubled families – problem children: Working with parents: A collaborative process*. West Sussex, UK: John Wiley & Sons.

Webster-Stratton, C., Reid, M. J., & Hammond, M. (2001). Preventing conduct problems, promoting social competence: A parent and teacher training partnership in Head Start. *Journal of Clinical Child Psychology, 30*, 283–302. doi:10.1207/S15374424JCCP3003_2

Webster-Stratton, C., Mihalic, S., Fagan, A., Arnold, D., Taylor, T., & Tingley, C. (2001). *The Incredible Years: Parent, teacher and child training series: Blueprints for violence prevention.* Book 11 in Blueprints for Violence Prevention Series, ed. D. S. Elliott. University of Colorado, Boulder: Center for the Study and Prevention of Violence.

Werba, B., Eyberg, S. M., Boggs, S. R., & Algina, J. (2006). Predicting the outcome of Parent–Child Interaction Therapy: Success and attrition. *Behavior Modification, 30*, 618–646. doi:10.1177/0145445504272977

Wilson, P., Furnivall, J., Barbour, R. S., Connelly, G., Bryce, G., Phin, L., & Stallard, A. (2008). The work of health visitors and school nurses with children with psychological and behavioural problems. *Journal of Advanced Nursing, 61*, 445–455. doi:10.111/j.1365-2648.2007.04505.x

Wiltz, N. A. & Patterson, G. R. (1974). An evaluation of parent training procedures designed to alter inappropriate aggressive behavior of boys. *Behavior Therapy, 5*(2), 215–221.

3 The EPaS programme, an early intervention for families at home

Programme rationale and overview

The Enhancing Parenting Skills (EPaS) programme was developed to support health visitors and other people that work with the parents of young children who present with behavioural challenges due to developmental and other problems. It recognises the importance of both early intervention and the need to focus on parents as the change agents because they have the most contact with, and impact on, their children.

Every child and family situation is unique, and thorough assessment leading to individualised support is the cornerstone of effective work with families that are experiencing such challenges with their children. That is the premise on which the EPaS programme is based. It provides a structured and systematic, evidence-based approach with a detailed step-by-step process for assessment, case analysis and intervention. This is organised into three sections within this manual. Chapters 4–7 introduce a set of tools for assessment, Chapters 8 and 9 describe a process for case analysis and the identification of relevant and achievable goals, and Chapters 10–12 provides examples of intervention strategies used with a number of common problems.

The assessment, case analysis and intervention strategies are based on a programme, developed by the first author (Judy) over 20 years ago, for parents of children aged between three and ten who had been referred to a Child and Adolescent Mental Health Service (CAMHS) for treatment of severe behaviour problems. This was an intensive coaching programme for parents that included several days in a domestic-style unit in which parents and children were videotaped in a range of situations. Using this video to give feedback, parents were coached in more effective ways to help their child to learn more appropriate behaviour and to manage their child's problem behaviour. The key components were the careful assessment of interactions that provided feedback and then led to extensive practise of alternative strategies. A paper reporting the outcomes of this programme showed it to be superior to standard CAMHS treatment that involved only behaviour management advice at both six-month and four-year follow-up, demonstrating long-term improvements in both child behaviour and maternal mental health only for participants in the intensive treatment programme (Hutchings, Appleton, Smith, Lane and Nash, 2002; Hutchings, Lane, and Kelly, 2004).

A number of factors prompted redesign of the intensive treatment programme as an early intervention strategy for health visitors. Named the EPaS programme, this was designed to give health visitors additional tools to support families with younger, preschool, children with a range of developmental and behavioural problems. The rationale for the development of the programme was that there were increasing numbers of children experiencing behavioural problems that could be identified at a young age and for whom, without help, the long-term prognosis was poor (Allen, 2011). The inability of specialist services to address this growing need was also becoming increasingly recognised (Griffiths, 2001) and at the same time there was growing evidence, particularly over the last 20 years, demonstrating the effectiveness of, and supporting the case for, early intervention (Bywater and Utting, 2012; Glover and Sutton, 2012; Hutchings and Gardner, 2012; Sutton, Murray and Glover, 2012).

The EPaS course built on what had been learned from the intensive CAMHS-based programme and was initially researched with two cohorts of health visitors. Health visitors delivered weekly home-based, one-to-one family interventions and achieved excellent outcomes (Lane and Hutchings, 2002). The initial trial with health visitors provided the basis of the EPaS programme described in this manual. A later evaluation of this programme, funded by the Waterloo Foundation, enabled its further development for wider dissemination. The assessment, case analysis and intervention strategies have their foundation in over 40 years of evidence-based behavioural work with parents of children with developmental and/ or behavioural problems. They draw in particular on the work of Forehand and McMahon (1981), Herbert (1987), Patterson (1982) and Webster-Stratton et al. (2001).

The programme includes a standardised assessment procedure and structured formulation process to facilitate the identification of problem behaviours and their functions and the necessary replacement behaviours. It also emphasises the importance of identifying the family's assets and skills that will support the desired changes and goals for intervention. The interventions themselves are not standardised and, although based on behavioural principles, work undertaken with families is extremely varied. Every family is unique and, whilst there are shared challenges among families that have children with developmental and other difficulties, there are many differences between them, their children and the problems that they bring to the intervention situation. Our goal as professionals is to help to engage families in shared problem-solving aimed at empowering them to meet achievable goals. To do this, professionals need skills in engaging and retaining families and the knowledge upon which to identify effective intervention strategies.

The EPaS programme supports parents and carers as change agents. Parents of young children are with them for much of the time, and what happens in the child's everyday environment has the biggest effect in terms of both contributing to problems and in helping children to learn adaptive behaviours. Throughout this manual, the term *parent* is used to refer to whoever has significant caring responsibilities for a child. The programme has been used effectively with parents, step-parents, grandparents and foster carers.

Recently, the EPaS programme was evaluated using a randomised controlled trial design (Williams, 2017). Fifty-eight families were randomly assigned to either receive the EPaS programme from their health visitor, either immediately or after six months. The results showed significant reductions in children's behaviour problems for those who received the programme, compared to the control group, especially families who completed all three phases of EPaS. Health visitors rated the programme highly, including the content, methods and trainer, and all reported that they would continue to use the methods taught during the course (Williams, 2017).

Working collaboratively with families

Establishing a collaborative relationship with families is essential if we are to engage parents in effective behavioural family interventions for children with developmental, behavioural or emotional problems (Webster-Stratton and Herbert, 1994). Spitzer, Webster-Stratton and Hollinsworth (1991) explored the process of change in interviews with 16 therapists, 77 mothers and 60 fathers of conduct-problem children (ages three to seven years). Using a constant comparison method, they identified the steps involved in gaining knowledge, control and competence. This process comprised five phases that included: the need to acknowledge the family's problem, supporting them through a process of alternating despair and hope, helping the family to have realistic and achievable expectations (tempering the dream), adapting parenting principles and tools for their own specific needs (making the shoe fit), and effective coping for the longer term.

Effective work with families depends on engaging the parent/s or other primary carers as willing partners. This means working with them to identify their own goals and empowering them to use effective strategies to achieve them. This is the collaborative approach that has been shown to be critical in engaging and retaining families (this is described in more detail in Chapter 4, which describes the setting up of the intervention).

The focus on establishing new behaviours

The constructional approach to therapy (Goldiamond, 1974, 1975) describes a collaborative process for helping people to establish new behaviours that also informs this programme. This was developed by Goldiamond as an alternative to the more common approach at that time, which focused on removing problems. Its goal is to develop new replacement behaviours rather than to eliminate unwanted problematic behaviours. Goldiamond saw behaviours or symptoms that caused distress as functional or serving a purpose, in that they successfully produced a desirable or rewarding consequence, but often at a distressing cost. He described the therapeutic task as helping people to construct new adaptive ways of producing the same consequences or rewards. In this approach, people are encouraged to identify what they want to achieve, rather than what problems they want to eliminate, and to build on their own strengths and skills to take them in the direction in which they would like to go.

A structured questionnaire was developed by Goldiamond for use during the initial interview with clients. It was designed to obtain information to establish the outcomes that the client wanted and to identify their strengths and social history. Goldiamond's work was mainly with adults, and his Constructional Questionnaire was adapted by the first author as a Parent–Child Questionnaire. This is described in detail in Chapter 5, as part of the EPaS assessment process.

Conclusion

This chapter has briefly described the history of the development of the EPaS programme and summarised the key components of effective interventions with families on which EPaS was built. These include developing a collaborative relationship that takes parents' concerns as the starting point, helping them to identify goals that build on their existing strengths and skills and to establish the replacement behaviours that will achieve their desired outcomes.

After 30 years of research, we now have a clearer understanding about how behaviour problems develop, the specific skills parents need to promote children's social competence (Hutchings, Gardner and Lane, 2004) and the intervention strategies and techniques that are a necessary part of the intervention process. The evidence suggests a need for evidence-based early interventions that are accessible to all families.

The EPaS programme described in this book is a home-based programme of support for parents of young children who are already demonstrating significant challenging behaviour. Individualised interventions, based on a standardised detailed assessment that is implemented through collaborative work with parents, enable parents to develop a flexible toolkit of parenting skills to promote positive social behaviour, compliance and increased self-esteem in their child (Lane and Hutchings, 2002).

The programme described in this book has been researched with health visitors and subsequently delivered successfully to mixed groups of health visitors, school nurses, primary care and CAMHS workers and social workers dealing with families of children up to the age of 11. These children have had a range of difficulties, usually including non-compliance and other behaviour management difficulties but also other developmental difficulties. Feedback from those who have undergone this training has been extremely positive and many have gone on to become specialists in this work. Part II of this manual provides a step-by-step guide to the assessment, case analysis and intervention process, while Part III describes some typical problems and strategies used to address them.

References

Allen, G. (2011). *Early intervention: The next steps. An independent report to Her Majesty's Government.* London, UK: The Smith Institute and the Centre for Social Justice. Retrieved from: http://dera.ioe.ac.uk/14161/1/graham%20 allen%20review%20of%20early%20intervention.pdf

Bywater, T. & Utting, D. (2012). Support from the start: Effective programmes for nine to 13 year-olds. *Journal of Children's Services*, 7, 41–52. doi:10.1108/17466661211213661

Forehand, R. L. & McMahon, R. J. (1981). *Helping the noncompliant child: A clinician's guide to parent training.* London, UK: Guilford Press.

Glover, V. & Sutton, C. (2012). Support from the start: effective programmes in pregnancy. *Journal of Children's Services*, 7, 8–17. doi:10.1108/17466661211213634

Goldiamond, I. (1974). Towards a constructional approach to social problems. *Behaviourism*, 2, 1–84.

Goldiamond, I. (1975). A constructional approach to self control. In: A. Schwartz & I. Goldiamond (Eds.), *Social casework: A behavioral approach* (pp. 67–130). New York: Columbia Press.

Griffiths, L. (2001). *Everybody's business: The first annual report into the delivery of services for the emotional health and wellbeing of children and young people.* Cardiff: Welsh Government.

Herbert, M. (1987). *Behavioral treatment of children with problems: A practice manual.* London, UK: Academic Press.

Hutchings, J. & Gardner, F. (2012). Support from the Start: Effective programmes for three to eight year-olds. *Journal of Children's Services*, 7, 29–40. doi:10.1108/17466661211213652

Hutchings, J., Gardner, F., & Lane, E. (2004). Making evidence-based interventions work. In: C. Sutton, D. Utting & D. Farrington (Eds.), *Support from the start: Working with young children and their families to reduce the risks of crime and anti-social behaviour.* Nottingham, UK: Department for Education and Skills.

Hutchings, J., Lane, E., & Kelly, J. (2004). Comparison of two treatments for children with severely disruptive behaviours: A four-year follow-up. *Behavioural and Cognitive Psychotherapy*, 32, 15–30. doi:10.1017/S1352465804001018

Hutchings, J., Appleton, P., Smith, M., Lane, E., & Nash, S. (2002). Evaluation of two treatments for children with severe behaviour problems: Child behaviour and maternal mental health outcomes. *Behavioural and Cognitive Psychotherapy*, 30, 279–295. doi:10.1017/S1352465802003041

Lane, E. & Hutchings, J. (2002). Benefits of a course in behavioural analysis for health visitors. *British Journal of Nursing*, 11, 702–714. doi:10.12968/bjon.2002.11.10.702

Patterson, G. R. (1982). *Coercive family process*. Eugene, OR: Castalia.

Spitzer, A., Webster-Stratton, C., & Hollinsworth, T. (1991). Coping with conduct-problem children: Parents gaining knowledge and control. *Journal of Clinical Child Psychology, 20*, 413–427. doi:10.1207/s15374424jcpp2004_10

Sutton, C., Murray, L., & Glover, V. (2012). Support from the Start: Effective programmes from birth to two years. *Journal of Children's Services, 7*, 18–28. doi:10.1108/17466661211213643

Webster-Stratton, C. & Herbert, M. (1994). *Troubled families – problem children: Working with parents: A collaborative process*. West Sussex, UK: John Wiley & Sons.

Webster-Stratton, C., Mihalic, S., Fagan, A., Arnold, D., Taylor, T., & Tingley, C. (2001). *The Incredible Years: Parent, teacher and child training series: Blueprints for violence prevention*. Book 11 in Blueprints for Violence Prevention Series, ed. D. S. Elliott. University of Colorado, Boulder: Center for the Study and Prevention of Violence.

Williams, M. E. (2017). *Evaluation of the Enhancing Parenting Skills 2014 programme*. PhD thesis, Bangor, UK, Bangor University.

Part II
The EPaS programme

4 Assessment session 1

Setting up an effective working relationship with parents

The assessment phase of the EPaS programme takes place over three visits. This chapter describes some of the things that needs to be done at the start of the first visit and Chapter 5 covers the specific information to be gathered in that first session. Parenting programmes based on social learning theory have been developed and researched for over 50 years, and, whilst most programmes work quite well, those that are based on collaborative relationships with parents, and address parents' goals, work best (Hutchings, Gardner and Lane, 2004; Webster-Stratton and Herbert, 1994). This is particularly the case with families that are most disadvantaged and hardest to engage and whose children are at greatest risk of poor outcomes (Gardner, Hutchings, Bywater and Whitaker, 2010; Hartman, Stage and Webster-Stratton, 2003). This collaborative approach is critical to both engaging and retaining families and underpins the EPaS programme. It draws on the work of Lambert (1992), Davis, Day and Bidmead (2002) and Duncan, Miller, Wampold and Hubble (2009), who describe the common factors that influence outcomes across a wide range of interventions. In terms of working with families, these include:

- *The family*: learning about their strengths, beliefs, values, skills, experiences, ability to enlist the help and support of others, their circumstances, their potential for change and the desired changes that are already happening in their lives. Effective support enlists the family's resources in a way that fits with their beliefs and values.
- *The parent/carer–practitioner relationship*: the parent's perception of empathy, acceptance and warmth of the practitioner, the classic counselling skills (Patterson, 1984). This therapeutic alliance is enhanced by:
  - accepting parents' goals at face value
  - tailoring therapeutic tasks and suggestions to the parents goals
  - collaborating with parents rather than dictating to them
  - exploring material that is relevant to the family.
- *Parents' expectation of positive outcome*: their hopes and expectations of change as a result of taking part in the programme. This is harnessed when practitioners:

  - convey an attitude of hope and possibility without minimising the difficulties that accompany it
  - encourage parents to focus on present and future possibilities instead of past problems.

What parents do outside therapy sessions matters most, because it is the changes that they make in their everyday interactions with their children that predict lasting benefits. The intervention goal is that changed parental behaviour will be maintained because it is reinforced by changes in their children's behaviour. However, initially parents need support to maintain their change efforts, since it may take time for them to see the desired changes in their children and for them to learn about the impact of their own behaviour on that of their children. The strength of their relationship with you, the therapist, is a key factor in supporting parents through the initial stages of the process of change.

The initial session – establishing a working relationship and starting to collect information

Session 1 sets the scene during which the intervention process is explained and initial data gathering is undertaken. Your family may have already unsuccessfully tried a variety of strategies to solve their problems and, as professionals, we cannot afford to let them fail again. Giving advice without having sufficient understanding of the problem, and in particular its function, can result in a family experiencing further failure or our advice being rejected because "I have tried that already and it didn't work". So the need for a thorough assessment is explained. The EPaS process – involving three sessions spent collecting information prior to case analysis and intervention – is an important part of this.

It is important to clarify what families can expect from the intervention and from you. The process involves helping families to help themselves. In particular, their cooperation in completing assignments must be established from the outset. They need to see you as a consultant, advising, prompting and teaching to help them to find their own solutions. This is probably not what families have previously experienced in relationships with professionals and it can take time for them to recognise this. Prior contact with the NHS, for example, generally involves the patient describing the problem (briefly) and the doctor diagnosing the cause and prescribing the solution.

Ideally children should not be present during the first session, although this is not always possible. When you make the appointment, it is worth exploring whether it can be arranged for a time when the children are in school or playgroup. If you do not mention this, parents are likely to keep children home or bring them to the clinic. There are several benefits to having the initial session without the children present:

1   It enables the parents to concentrate fully on the session.
2   If the parents talk negatively about their child, the child is not present to hear it.
3   It provides the opportunity for you to clearly demonstrate that you are in a "team" with the parents, helping them to find ways to support their child.

There is always a danger when the children are present – especially if they are not receiving much positive attention from the parents – that professionals establish rapport with the children rather than the parents. This can result in the parent feeling resentful or excluded. They may say, or feel, that "You are not seeing the problems because my child is not normally like this when you are not there." If the children are present, it is important not to take too much notice of them, as it is *essential* that your partnership is with the parent, not the child. The goal is to strengthen the parent's relationship with their child not yours. Hopefully you will not be around in the child's life for all that long, and they do not need another disrupted attachment.

Working with partners

If there are two parents or two adults in the family, maybe a step-parent or partner, there may be stresses in the relationship that can include differences in their understanding of the child's problem, their management of (and goals for) the child. Ideally you can work with both adults, but even if this is not possible it is useful to try to touch base with partners. It can be helpful to explain the plan to the partner, to ask for their view of the problem, to praise the parent that is working with you for their commitment to the child and to ask their partner to support them in the process. This can be done by phone if it is not possible to meet the partner. Differences between partners in what they see as the problem/s and how to deal with them can often be reframed as both of them recognising that they want change and are trying to find a solution. Therefore, it is often the same goal, but different strategies to deal with it, that have caused the disagreement. The intervention goal is to find solutions that will improve things for the child and the adult/s. However, regardless of whether a partner will engage with you, you need to support the parent that you are working with and let them know that their child will learn to recognise their consistency regardless of how others behave towards them. It is not uncommon for partners to come on board later when they see changes occurring.

Introducing the plan

The first step is to give the parents a description of the process and agree some ground rules. It is important that you start by congratulating/praising parents for the commitment that they are making to their child by seeking solutions, especially if their prior efforts to solve the problems have not been successful. This emphasis on solutions is essential from the start, since – although the assessment process will explore the history of the difficulties – the emphasis is on changing things for the future. Praising the parents is extremely important, since the more that parents are praised in therapy, the more they are subsequently observed to praise their children (Eames et al., 2010). The other key therapist skill identified in the same study was active listening, picking up and reflecting back the things that parents were saying: "So, let me check that I understood what you said . . ." Praising and reflecting back what parents say are two core engagement strategies.

The three phases of the intervention are explained to parents:

i) information gathering/assessment, a process taking probably three meetings
ii) case analysis and agreement on realistic targets for intervention (one session)
iii) implementation of the intervention plan (likely to be between four and eight sessions) but determined by goal achievement.

The EPaS process generally takes place over a series of weekly meetings. A week usually works well, allowing time for what has been discussed to be reflected on and for parent assignments to be undertaken. It is also easier for parents to remember appointments if they occur at the same time each week. The assessment phase generally takes three sessions, although if you decide to do a developmental assessment it could take longer. This is followed by the session in which the case analysis is shared with the parent/s and intervention goals agreed. The length of the intervention is harder to specify, but generally, with realistic goals, six to eight sessions are sufficient to achieve changes in most targeted behaviours with young children, with sessions possibly becoming fortnightly towards the end.

Parents are given an assignment at every EPaS session, including the first. This is their contribution to the partnership. Initially, they help by providing information that will lead to an understanding of the problem/s and their functions, as well as goals and strategies to use with their child. Once the intervention phase is under way, the parental contribution is to work on implementing the intervention plan. Generally, at the end of the first session, assuming the necessary literacy skills, the first assignment for the parents is to complete one or more of the standardised parent report measures.

Ground rules

Having explained the intervention process, the next step is to agree some ground rules. These are introduced as working out together the things that will make our sessions comfortable and productive. Making the process predictable is important – for example, by planning appointments in advance. Parents need to know that sessions will take place on a regular basis, ideally at the same time each week. A session should never end without the parent knowing when the next session will be and having this information both verbally and in written form. Families feel respected when they are given a clear plan. Many parents in socio-economically challenging circumstances live in the present, responding to immediate demands, and may not have diaries or calendars. It can be helpful to provide a calendar and/or to ring up or send a text the day before (or on the day of) the appointment to remind parents of the session. Appointment cards are easier for people to deal with than letters – they can be put on the wall or the fridge (and providing a fridge magnet is useful).

It is important to let parents know that if an emergency arises, and you have to change an appointment, you will give them as much notice as possible. This also provides the opportunity to ask the parents to do the same and to be clear about how they do this. When these issues are discussed at the outset, it is rare to have a failed appointment and when parents cannot make appointments they invariably send apologies.

Families need to know how to get messages to you if problems arise between sessions, particularly if they relate to parental assignments. They need a contact phone number, generally an office number. Ideally you should tell them that you will try to respond within 24 hours, although this may not always be possible. The key is making your commitment predictable.

Another ground rule to negotiate is the length of the session. Generally, an hour is agreed, as people can find it hard to concentrate for longer than that. If the session is scheduled for an hour, you must stick to it, as that respects parents' time and recognises their other commitments.

Keeping notes or records of sessions

Information that you collect needs to be written down at the time. You need to explain to parents the purpose of keeping notes and what happens to them. Some therapists feel uncomfortable about keeping notes, thinking that it can destroy the relationship, but if the purpose is explained, this is not the case. Parents can feel uncomfortable that things they say are written down, so they need to know why. You need to tell parents that you will not remember everything they say and that, at the time, you may not know what information is most relevant. The notes hold the information that the parents give you to make the case analysis, to plan your work together and to work out which information is important – they are not subjective judgements. They are used to make the case analysis and negotiate intervention goals.

Therapists have child protection responsibilities that need to be acknowledged. It can be helpful at the outset to say something like "Although our discussions are confidential, if you tell me things that suggest that the programme that we are working on is not going to be sufficient to solve the problems or I feel that I must involve other services, I will explain to you what I am going to do and why."

I have never referred a family to child protection services without explaining first. On occasions, when this became necessary, I have said, "I am concerned for your child, but I am also concerned for you. You are not in a very good place at the moment and may need to be helped in a different way and I need to discuss this situation with colleagues." This leaves open the possibility of working together subsequently (which I have, on occasion, been able to do, because honesty is recognised and does not necessarily destroy the relationship with the parents).

Intervention location

Some considerations apply whether you are working in a clinic or in parents' homes, and some are venue-specific. The one-to-one EPaS programme, as delivered by health visitors, was mainly delivered at home; however, the CAMHS-based intensive treatment programme from which it was derived was initially clinic-based and generally followed up at home.

Clinic-based services

Issues to be considered in relation to clinic appointments are mostly practical. They include timing, location, transportation and cost for the family in attending. There may be child-care issues to be resolved for the target child or other children in the family. You need to check whether funding can be offered to cover transport costs – as is the case for NHS appointments for families on low incomes – and ideally be able to offer a drink and biscuit/ snack.

Home visits

Rules for sessions in family homes include: negotiating having the television off, and asking the parents to ask phone callers to ring back or for visitors to come back later.

Parents should be asked to try to arrange that they don't have visitors at the time of the appointment and that, when possible, telephone callers will be asked to ring back a little later. When seeing patients in the clinic or surgery these things are taken for granted, but in home visits these issues need to be raised politely and expectations made explicit, bearing in mind that home visits are for the convenience of the family. These need to be respectful requests with the rationale explained, such as "Please could you switch the TV off because I want to really concentrate on the information that you will be giving me and I find it distracting." A further prompt, when the volume is turned down on the TV rather it being switched off, is: "I still find that I am a little distracted by the TV, would you mind turning it off please."

It may be necessary to discuss smoking. Parent/s would not smoke if attending a clinic or surgery. You can politely ask that, if they wish to smoke, they take a break and go to a different room. Generally parents decide that they can manage for an hour without a cigarette, but giving them that choice makes it their decision.

Realistic outcome expectations

Before starting to collect information, it is helpful to remind the parents that children who present challenges are more difficult to parent and need special parenting, and that it is good that they are working with you. This establishes that you are not blaming the parents for their child's difficulties, but instead seeing that they face a difficult task in supporting their child and want to explore new ways of doing this. It is worth reiterating that they are in the best position to help their child, both because they know their child so well and because they spend the most time with them. This helps to establish you as a partner, working with the parents to achieve a positive outcome. It is also important that you help the parents to have realistic expectations of the outcome. Parenting is a lifelong commitment, with changing demands, and your work together is not going to solve all of their parenting challenges. However, it can support the parents in helping their child to achieve some of their goals. It can useful to say something like, "Our work together will not solve all of your problems, but I am sure that, if you stick with the programme, some things will improve." Hopefully your work together also gives the parents some tools with which to approach future parenting challenges.

Overview of the assessment components

The assessment process includes seven data sources (or nine, if developmental assessment or external sources of information are included) and the case analysis may require making use of all of them. Session 1 contains: the modified Personal Development and Health Questionnaire (Hutchings, 1996), the Three-Problem Rating Scale (Miller, Duncan, Brown, Sparks and Claud, 2003; Scott, 2001) and the Parent–Child Constructional Questionnaire (Goldiamond, 1974, 1975, as modified by the author for work with families). Parents are then asked to complete standardised parent report questionnaires as their first home activity.

In session 2, you will check in on parents' home activity, complete a typical day interview and design an individual record sheet (to be kept by parents and brought to the next session).

In session 3, you will check in on parents' home activity records and undertake an observation of parent–child interactions. Following this, parents will be asked to complete two questionnaires – "Things your child enjoys" and "Things your child can do" (Hutchings 1996) – as homework assignments.

Additional information sources

You may decide that a developmental assessment of the child would be useful. This can be done using a parent report measure such as the Ages and Stages Questionnaire (Squires, Potter and Bricker, 1999) or you or a colleague can administer an assessment such as the Schedule of Growing Skills (Bellman, Lingam and Aukett, 1996, 2008) or Denver Developmental Scale (Frankenburg, Dodds, Archer, Shapiro and Bresnick, 1992).

Sometimes it is useful, with parental agreement, to obtain other information about a child from health records, a visit to the child's nursery or school to talk with the child's teacher and/or to observe the child in school. However, it is the problems that the parent is experiencing at home that are the focus of the intervention. The later stages of the intervention involve the development of a case analysis to share with the parents, the negotiation of a contract and an implementation phase.

Having covered these issues, you are now ready to start collecting information. The checklist at the end of this chapter covers the things you need to do to set up the programme.

The programme has three phases. The first session is an information-gathering phase to make sure that you learn about the challenges that parents are experiencing with their child and also to establish what are the important goals that you can work on together. This normally takes three one-hour weekly sessions.

The following is an example of words I tend to use.

Phase 1: Assessment

Session 1 focuses on collecting background information and at the end you will be asked to complete some questionnaires before our next session.

Session 2 is about the present situation. Information is gathered using a "typical day" interview. At the end, we will design a record sheet for you to complete with the focus on one specific problem.

Session 3 has an opportunity for us to observe you and your child generally during a play situation. This helps us to learn more about your child. After this, you will be asked to complete two questionnaires about "Things your child can do" and "Things your child enjoys".

Phase 2: Case analysis

During this session, we will present you with our understanding of the information that you have provided and check that we have understood correctly. Then we will make suggestions about why any problems might be occurring. After this, we will discuss and agree with you some goals to work on in the next phase: intervention.

Phase 3: Intervention

During this phase we will agree weekly targets leading toward the goals that we have agreed to work on. This can generally take between four and eight sessions, but it is based on achieving the goals that we have agreed together.

References

Bellman, M. H., Lingam, S., & Aukett, A. (1996). *Schedule of Growing Skills II: Reference manual.* London: NFER Nelson Publishing Company Ltd.

Bellman, M. H., Lingam, S., & Aukett, A. (2008). *Schedule of Growing Skills II: User's guide*, 2nd edition. London: NFER Nelson Publishing Company.

Davis, H., Day, C., and Bidmead, C. (2002). *Working in partnership with parents: The parent adviser model*. London: The Psychological Corporation.

Duncan, B. L., Miller, S. D., Wampold, B. E., & Hubble M.A. (Eds.) (2009). *The heart and soul of change: Delivering what works in therapy*. Washington, DC: American Psychological Association.

Eames, C., Daley, D., Hutchings, J., Whitaker, C. J., Bywater, T., Jones, K., & Hughes, J. C. (2010). The impact of group leaders behaviour on parents' acquisition of key parenting skills during parent training. *Behaviour Research and Therapy*, 48, 1221–1226.

Frankenburg, W. K., Dodds, J., Archer, P., Shapiro, H., & Bresnick, B. (1992). The Denver II: A major revision and restandardization of the Denver Developmental Screening Test. *Pediatrics*, 89, 91–97.

Gardner, F., Hutchings, J., Bywater, T., & Whitaker, C. J. (2010). Who benefits and how does it work? Moderators and mediators of outcome in an effectiveness trial of a parenting intervention in multiple "Sure Start" services. *Journal of Clinical Child and Adolescent Psychology*, 39, 568–580.

Goldiamond, I. (1974). Towards a constructional approach to social problems. *Behaviourism*, 2, 1–84.

Goldiamond, I. (1975). A constructional approach to self control. In: A. Schwartz & I. Goldiamond (Eds.), *Social casework: A behavioural approach*. New York: Columbia University Press.

Hartman, R. R., Stage, S. A., & Webster-Stratton, C. (2003). A growth curve analysis of parent training outcomes: Examining the influence of child risk factors (inattention, impulsivity, and hyperactivity problems), parental and family risk factors. *Journal of Child Psychology and Psychiatry*, 44, 388–398.

Hutchings J. (1996). *The personal and parental characteristics of preschool children referred to a child and family mental health service and their relation to treatment outcome*. PhD thesis, Bangor, University of Wales.

Hutchings, J., Gardner, F., & Lane, E. (2004). Making evidence based interventions work in clinical settings: Common and specific therapy factors and implementation fidelity. In: C. Sutton, D. Utting & David Farrington (Eds.), *Support from the start: Working with young children and their Families to reduce the risks of crime and antisocial behaviour*, Research Report 524. London: Department for Education and Skills.

Lambert, M. J. (1992). Implications of outcome research for psychotherapy integration. In: J. C. Norcross & M. R. Goldstein (Eds.), *Handbook of psychotherapy integration* (pp. 94–129). New York: Basic Books.

Patterson, C. H. (1984). Empathy, warmth and genuineness in psychotherapy: A review of reviews. *Psychotherapy*, 21, 431–438.

Miller, S. D., Duncan, B. L., Brown, J., Sparks, J. A., & Claud, D. A. (2003). The Outcome Rating Scale: A preliminary study of the reliability, validity, and feasibility of a brief visual analog measure. *Journal of Brief Therapy*, 2(2), 91–100.

Scott, S. (2001). Deciding whether interventions for antisocial behaviour work: Principles of outcome assessment, and practice in a multicentre trial. *European Child and Adolescent Psychiatry*, 10(1), S59–S70.

Squires, J., Potter, L., & Bricker, D. (1999). *The ages and stages user's guide*. Baltimore, MD: Paul H. Brookes Publishing.

Webster-Stratton, C. & Herbert, M. (1994). *Troubled families – problem children: Working with parents: A collaborative process*. West Sussex, UK: John Wiley & Sons.

EPaS set-up activity checklist

	Activity	Completed (Yes/No)
1	Clarify with the family that this is a collaborative relationship – "I am here to help you to help yourself"	
2	Explain that you will be working on parent goals	
3	Explain that the parent/s will have home activities between sessions	
4	Clarify whether you are working with one or both parents (if two)	
5	If appropriate, make contact with a second parent who will not be part of the session	
6	Clearly describe the three-stage EPaS process	
7	Negotiate time, place, etc. for the weekly meeting	
8	Negotiate ground rules, including those specifically linked to the home visits	
9	Clarify how to make contact with you between sessions	
10	Explain the purpose of your written notes	
11	Give realistic expectations of the intervention – that it will focus on specific goals	

Note: This is completed at the end of session 1 to check that you covered everything!

Parent/s: *Sue Smith*   Service provider: *Judy Hutchings*
Location: *1, Smith Street*

Appointment	Date	Time
1	Monday 12 September	10.00–11.00 a.m.
2		
3		

If this is not convenient, please telephone or text 07777-777777 to arrange a more suitable date/time.

5   Assessment session 1
Initial information gathering

Having set up a working relationship, as described in the previous chapter, you are now ready to start collecting information.

Obtaining history, current circumstances and goal information

This first session uses two interview tools, a short version of the Personal Development and Health Questionnaire (PDHQ; Hutchings, 1996) and the Parent–Child Constructional Questionnaire (PCCQ; Goldiamond, 1974, 1975, as modified by the author – Hutchings, 2014) and one short parent report measure asking parents to identify the three most challenging problems, the Three-Problem Rating Scale (Miller, Duncan, Brown, Sparks and Claud, 2003). Copies of these three tools are included at the end of the chapter.

The PDHQ is a brief interview guide. Whilst it is important for families to know that they only need to share information about which they feel comfortable, it is helpful to start with the family and child's history – finding out who lives in the house, children's names and ages, schools attended, how long they have lived there, etc. This lets the parents realise that you are interested in them and their circumstances and want to hear their story in their own words.

The PDHQ was originally developed as a research tool (Hutchings, 1996) but the shortened version contains only the most relevant questions about the child and family history and circumstances. It can also be helpful to find out who else has contact with the child.

Risk factors for poor outcomes for children were described previously (Chapter 1) and, if the parent seems comfortable and it feels appropriate, you can ask about some of these, such as income and other social circumstances that might present challenges to parenting. However, it is important to keep focused, and the Parent–Child Constructional Questionnaire will also give you relevant information about family circumstances, skills, goals, etc.

In asking about background information, you are showing genuine interest in the parent. Questions like "Your accent is not local – what brought you here?" (or other questions that help you to build a picture of the family's and child's background and circumstances) are useful. If the parent has concerns about the child's behaviour in playgroup or school, you can suggest that there may be things that they can work on together at home that will help to give the child skills that will help them to be successful in other situations. It is important not to agree to work on a goal that is not within the parent's ability to achieve, such as something related to a situation where the parent is not present, or a goal for a partner with whom you are not working. The parent may be able to work on a goal at home that may help the child in playgroup or to improve their own relationship with their partner, but goals must only be related to (and achievable by) the person or persons with whom you are working.

The Three-Problem Rating Scale

(Adapted from Scott, 2001)

For the second step of the initial interview, you ask the parents to identify up to three problem areas that are causing them the most distress, by asking them to complete the Three-Problem Rating Scale. This asks parents to list three problems and rate them on a 10 cm line marked "Not a problem" at one end and "Couldn't be worse" at the other. This indicates the severity of the problems with regard to how much distress they cause for the parent, and the score is the point's measurement on the 10 cm line. A copy of this rating scale is at the end of the chapter.

Scott (2001) argues that it is important to measure the concerns of parents and whether they have improved with the intervention. An intervention might be unpopular with families if the child did not improve in the areas the parents were concerned about (even though, on scientific measures of antisocial behaviour, the child actually *has* improved). In Scott, Spender, Doolan, Jacobs and Aspland's (2001) study, maternal concerns included "jealousy", "possessiveness with toys" and "fighting in the supermarket", and changes in parent-defined problems had a large intervention effect size of 1.11 – as large as, or larger than, the other reported measures of behavioural problems from their study, including the Strengths and Difficulties Questionnaire (Goodman, 1997) and the Child Behaviour Check List (Achenbach and Edelbrock, 1983).

The Parent–Child Constructional Questionnaire (PCCQ)

(Goldiamond 1974, 1975)

Once you start working through the Constructional Questionnaire questions, you will ask the parent to translate problems into the replacement target behaviours that they need to teach the child. Before proceeding with this interview, you need to clarify that, whilst the information given so far (including an understanding of the child's history) is important, the work that you will do together will focus on the current problem behaviour or behaviours that are causing concern, what might be maintaining it/them, and the achievement of parents' goals by identifying the strategies that will enable the child to develop more appropriate behaviours. The Parent–Child Constructional Questionnaire (PCCQ) will give you information that will help you to start identifying the functions of problematic behaviours, realistic replacement goals and family assets and skills that build a picture of family functioning, and will contribute to solutions. This provides the baseline from which you can build an effective intervention and helps you to be realistic in your own expectations of what can be achieved with the family. The background information and context feed into the case analysis and intervention plan and provide a possible understanding of why problems have developed – which is often different from what is currently maintaining them.

The PCCQ starts with a question about goals. Parents' initial responses are likely to be about the cessation or reduction of problem behaviour, possibly those that they identified on the Three-Problem Rating Scale. However, from the outset, you need to help them to become more specific and goal-focused. Goldiamond (1974, 1975) describes how adults with mental health problems often enter therapy with a global and negative view of their situation. They cannot describe the problem accurately and do not have positive goals. He sees the goal of intervention as helping people to become their own behaviour analysts, and to do this they need accurate observation skills and achievable targets or goals for which they develop workable plans. Our work with parents of children with behavioural difficulties has identified the same problems. Over half of the mothers of children with significant behavioural problems score themselves in the clinical range on the Beck Depression Inventory (Beck, Steer and Brown, 1996). Both the intensive treatment study (Hutchings, Appleton, Smith, Lane and Nash, 2002) and our Sure Start study of the Incredible Years group parenting programme (Hutchings et al., 2007) reported significant improvements in parental depression, with similar clinical effect size changes to the improvements in child behaviour, and these effects were sustained (Bywater et al., 2009; Hutchings, 2004). Key parental skill deficits among parents of children with challenging behaviour are: inaccurate observation skills, poor problem-solving skills and having unrealistic goals. Effective parenting interventions improve both the mental health challenges faced by parents and problematic child behaviour by helping parents to develop the three core skills: accurate observation, problem-solving and realistic goal setting (Hutchings et al., 2012). Furthermore, programmes that teach these components also demonstrate effectiveness for those familes at greatest risk of poor outcomes: single parents, young parents, parents with mental health problems and parents of children with the greatest level of difficulties (Gardner, Hutchings, Bywater and Whitaker, 2010; Hartman, Stage and Webster-Stratton, 2003).

Goals for children

In terms of work with children, the first PCCQ question is "Assuming we were successful, what would the outcome be for your child?" If a parent says that the child would not have so many tantrums, the next questions ask for specific examples of the alternative to tantrums: "What would others observe if the successful outcome was obtained?", "How does this differ from the present state of affairs?", "Can you give an example?" These questions help to identify target replacement behaviours, but to get to this you might need to ask about the circumstances in which tantrums occur. It may be that the child's tantrum is positively reinforced by getting an ice cream or other reward, or it may be negatively reinforced by achieving the removal of a command, such as the parent not following through with an instruction to switch off the TV. In another situation the child may be frustrated because they cannot do something, or their Lego tower falls down, and their tantrum produces help. During the case analysis session, you will set out tentative problem functions for the parent, but at this stage it is important to identify some possible target replacement behaviours.

Goals might be general, such as "Johnny will follow instructions quietly", but then have some specific examples; for example, "He will be in bed by 7.30 with the light out and will remain in bed throughout the night", "He will stay calm when told that he cannot have an ice cream now but can have one after dinner" or "He will stay calm and ask for help to build the castle". This process helps to emphasise that the intervention involves establishing alternative behaviours rather than eliminating problem behaviours, but parents may need lots of scaffolding to be able to do this.

Parent goals

Having established some potential child goals, the next set of questions are similar, but relate to the parent. They ask about how achievement of child goals might change things for the parent. The questions are: "Assuming we were successful, what would the outcome be for you?", "What would others observe if a successful outcome was obtained?", "How does this differ from the present state of affairs?", "Can you give an example?" Parents again often give fairly global responses, such as "Well, I won't be so stressed." This needs prompting in terms of how the parent will behave when less stressed to get goals, such as "If Johnny is following instructions, I will be speaking to him in a friendly manner", "I will be going out to visit friends with Johnny", "I will go to the shops with him once a week", "I will be able to leave him with my mum or a babysitter and have a night out." These can be important goals for many parents. Exploring these goals with parents helps them to realise that you recognise the significant restrictions placed on their life by the child's problems.

Partner goals

The final area to explore during goal setting is in relation to others in the child's environment. The question asks "In what way would this change things for you and your partner or other significant people in your child's life?" Ideally, if there are other adults in the home, work with all of them but if this is not possible try to include the other adult from time to time through phone calls or an occasional evening visit. In any event, you can prompt the parent with whom you are working to think of a goal that relates to their partner. You may say, "We often find, when parents have a child with challenging behaviour, that they tell us that the problems can cause disagreements between them. They may disagree about how to handle them or there may just not be enough time together to meet their own and each other's needs. Is this a problem for you?" If the parent says "Yes", as many do, *although you cannot set a goal for the person who is not present,* you may be able to discuss a goal with the parent that you *are* working with that they will try to work on ways to improve their communication with their partner about how to help the child.

The goals identified at this stage may not, necessarily, be those that are worked on later, when the case analysis is formulated and discussed and the intervention goals agreed with the parents. At this stage, parent goals may be developmentally inappropriate or not achievable in the short term for other reasons. However, the important thing about introducing discussion about goals at the start of the intervention is that it helps to focus the parent on the idea that the process is future-oriented. Things will be different in the future and your work together is focused on achieving solutions to problems faced by the parent with their child.

The next set of questions helps to give a broader description of the current situation. They ask about what is going well for the child and parent and anything else that might change indirectly. The questions ask: "What is going well for your child now and what areas of your child's life would not be affected by our work?", "What areas of your own life are going well and would not change?", "Are there any areas of your life, other than those that we would directly work on, that would change?"

Helping parents to identify things that are going well for either their child or themselves can require some prompting, as this is not something that they are often asked to think about. However, it is important that the agreed intervention will not interfere with things that are going well. So it is worth spending a little time exploring, for example, other positive relationships in either the child's or parent's life or things that occupy the child successfully, particularly games or activities. It may be that the parent has taught the child some good routines for meals or bedtimes, that the child enjoys playgroup or nursery, that the parent has some good friends. One parent said, "I would still be a full-time mum and I enjoy being at home and spending time with friends and people that I know well, but I would be more confident about speaking to other people without feeling that I was being judged."

The next questions ask about the onset of the problems and any attempted solutions: "Why do you want to work on these problems now? Has there been any recent trigger?", "When did it first occur to you that there was a problem? What was going on?", "What was happening in your life at that time?", "What did you do? How did it work out?" The first questions explore the parents' motivation for seeking help now. You may be told, "Well, the playgroup have said that they might have to exclude her because she is hurting other children." The onset of a problem can give some clues as to its possible function. For example, it might occur when a toddler becomes mobile, at the departure of a parent or the arrival of a younger sibling. It is important that every attempt to deal with the problem is viewed as a strength, although the parent may not perceive it in this way. They had identified a problem and tried to do something about it. Moreover, even though what they tried did not seem to have worked, they are still working on finding a solution, so this is also an asset – that they are persistent in seeking a solution. It is also important to find out how parents have tried to solve problems, as it will give clues about possible solutions that might or might not be successful. You might be told, "I was advised to ignore it but it got worse and he started hitting himself." When you start the intervention, you may want to use components of the solutions that parents have previously tried – but in combination with other strategies – to establish an alternative behaviour, and you will need to help the parent to understand why they did not work previously.

The next questions explore the parents' strengths and general problem-solving skills: "What skills or strengths do you have that are related to what you would like to achieve?", "What other skills do you have?", "In the past, what related problems with your child have you tackled successfully?" Parents are often not good at recognising their own assets and skills. In relation to their child, these can include anything from getting them to school on time, toilet training or any other skills that the child has learned. More generally parents can be encouraged to recognise their sense of humour, loyalty to a friend, care for a relative, budgeting, preparing meals on a small budget, their ability to plan for things in the future, etc. We then explore other problem-solving skills and strategies with the question "What other problems have you personally tackled successfully?" This question helps parents to recognise that they are problem-solvers and help to establish the intervention as a solution-focused approach. You may need to prompt the parent with questions about handling relationship break-ups, house moves, bereavement, changes in habits (such as smoking or drinking), weight loss, managing debt or more general problems. One parent told us that, having been orphaned at 6 years of age, she had coped with many things, she could decorate a house, had been a union representative in order to support others and also did everything for her husband, including buying his clothes, socks and shoes because he refused to go into shops.

The next questions relate to things that might be rewarding the problem behaviour and also other problems arising from the difficulties. They start with "In relation to your child's problem(s), has it brought you or your child any additional support?" Responses can include support from statutory, family and social network sources. It is important to know this, as these may be the people that will be needed to support the changes that the parents want to make. You may have already covered the next question, "How is your child's present problem difficult for your child or yourself or what does it stop either or both of you from doing?" The answers may already be obvious at this stage in terms of the responses to prior questions about what will be happening when the problem is dealt with. This question continues by exploring "What does your child really like to do? What makes him or her happy?" This is important in terms of identifying reinforcers for the child that could be linked to new behaviour, and in assessment session 3 parents are given an additional questionnaire to complete, the "Things your child enjoys", which further explores this. The remaining questions in this section are: "Who else is interested in the changes you are after?" and "Which people have been helpful in the past? What help did they give you? How did you obtain this from them?" These questions can add information on the parent's problem-solving and social support networks. For example, one parent said "I didn't ask for help, but my neighbour noticed that I was having difficulties getting Peter to walk to school and offered to take him with her children."

The final set of questions conclude the PCCQ interview with a check in on whether the parents feel that they have given an accurate picture of the situation or left anything out, and whether they have any questions about the intervention process. These questions provide an opportunity to restate the intervention process that will involve further information gathering, case analysis and agreement to an intervention plan.

Once you have completed the three assessments, you can introduce the first homework assignment: the parents need to complete three standardised self-report questionnaires before the next session.

Parent self-report measures

If you are working with both parents, you should provide two copies of these measures and ask them to complete them independently. The three suggested measures cover child behaviour, parental mental health and parenting skills. These are described below and all are free to use. The Strengths and Difficulties Questionnaire (SDQ) and Warwick–Edinburgh Mental Wellbeing Scale (WEMBWS) can be downloaded, whereas the Arnold–O'Leary Parenting Scale has been reproduced as Figure 5.1 on pp. 65–68 with permission of the American Psychological Association. None of them take more than about five to ten minutes to complete, so it is not a lengthy first assignment. There are many other standardised self-report tools, most of which are copyrighted and require payment of a fee. You could also use any tools that you already have and have found useful.

At the end of the initial session, these parent report measures are introduced as a between-session activity for the parents. It is important to establish whether the parents have the literacy skills to complete this assignment. If there are difficulties, you should ask them if they can identify someone who can help them. Completing them yourself, with the parents, is the last resort, since this is their first homework assignment and sets up the pattern for future work they will do when you are not present. It is better to help them to find their own support – a relative or friend. If there are major literacy problems, or the parents cannot identify someone to help them, you may have a student, assistant or volunteer who could help parents to complete the questionnaires. In any event, you need to be sure that they can either complete them unaided, that they have a support structure to help them to achieve this, or that you can provide help to facilitate this.

The three measures are:

- The Strengths and Difficulties Questionnaire (Goodman, 1997), a parent report screening measure on their child's emotional and behavioural health.
- The Parenting Scale (Arnold, O'Leary, Wolff and Acker, 1993), a self-report assessment of parenting behaviour.
- The Warwick–Edinburgh Mental Well-being Scale, an adult mental well-being measure (http://wrap.warwick.ac.uk/543/1/WRAP_Stewart_Brown_Warwick_Edinburgh.pdfUser guide).

A brief description of these scales follows. Further information on scoring, interpretation and access can be found in Appendices 1 to 3.

The Strengths and Difficulties Questionnaire (SDQ)

(Goodman, 1997; www.sdq.info)

This well-established 25-item inventory contains four problem subscales: conduct problems, hyperactivity, emotional symptoms and peer problems. These add together to give a Total Problem score, and there is also a pro-social subscale. For children with identified problems, there is an impact scale that assesses the extent to which problems impact on the child's everyday functioning and can contribute to the motivation of parents to seek help for their child.

It was designed as a behavioural screening measure to assess the occurrence of problem and prosocial behaviours in children. Various scoring ranges are published for the Total Problem and subscale scores (see Appendix 1). Care must be taken in their interpretation, particularly the subscale scores, as this is a screening measure with only five items per subscale. Nevertheless, it has been extensively used in national and international research studies, including in many of our own trials in Wales (e.g. Hutchings et al., 2007) and is sensitive in identifying post-intervention therapeutic gains.

There are two age versions: for children aged 2–4 years, and for children and young people aged 4–17 years. Both versions are intended for completion by parents and/or for self-report by young people of at least secondary school age. There are versions for teachers, follow-up versions and almost 100 different language versions, including Welsh. Appendix 1 contains sample items and further information about the scoring and interpretation of the SDQ. The author asks that users *download the most relevant version from the website* (at www.sdqinfo.org).

The Parenting Scale

(Arnold et al., 1993)

This 30-item inventory is a self-report measure of dysfunctional discipline practices. It is completed by parents and takes approximately 10 minutes. The three subscales ask parents to report on their use of three specific aspects of their discipline practise: Laxness, Over-reactivity and Verbosity and the sub-scales also sum into a Total score. Responses are made on a 7-point scale, where seven represents the most ineffective response and one the most effective. Care must be taken when scoring as the direction of scoring changes with different items.

Subscale examples

An example from the Laxness subscale is: *When I say my child can't do something*, (situation) *I let my child do it anyway* (most ineffective response, score 7), or *I stick to what I said* (most effective response, score 1).

An example from the Over-reactivity scale is: *When my child misbehaves* (situation) *I usually get into a long argument with my child* (most ineffective response, score 7) or *I don't get into an argument with my child* (most effective response, score 1).

An example from the Verbosity scale is: *I threaten to do things which* . . . (situation) *I am sure I can carry out* (most effective response score 1) or *I know I won't actually do* (least effective response score 7).

It has been used in many studies (including several of our own in Wales), showed baseline problematic scores on all subscales with clinical and high-risk groups, and was sensitive to intervention changes, distinguishing between intervention and control samples at follow-up (e.g. Hutchings et al., 2007).

A copy of the Parenting Scale is included as Figure 5.1 and scoring details are included in Appendix 2.

Parenting Scale

Child's Name: _____   Today's Date: _____

Sex: Boy _____   Girl _____   Child's Birthdate: _____

Instructions:
*At one time or another, all children misbehave or do things that could be harmful, that are " wrong",
or that parents don't like. Example include:*

hitting someone	*whining*	*not picking up toys*
forgetting homework	*throwing food*	*refusing to go to bed*
having a tantrum	*lying*	*wanting a cookie before dinner*
running into the street	*arguing back*	*coming home late*

*Parents have many different ways or styles of dealing with these types of problems. Below are items
that describe some styles of parenting.*

**For each item, fill in the circle that best describes your style of parenting during the past two
months with the child indicated above.**

SAMPLE ITEM:

At meal time…
   I let my child decide   **0---0---● ---0---0---0---0**   I decide how much
   how much to eat.   my child eats.

---

1. **When my child misbehaves…**

   I do something   **0---0---0---0---0---0---0**   I do something
   right away.   about it later.

2. **Before I do something about a problem…**

   I give my child several   **0---0---0---0---0---0---0**   I use only one
   reminders or warnings.   reminder or warning.

3. **When I'm upset or under stress…**

   I am picky and on my   **0---0---0---0---0---0---0**   I am no more picky
   child's back.   than usual.

4. **When I tell my child not to do something…**

   I say very little.   **0---0---0---0---0---0---0**   I say a lot.

Figure 5.1 The Parenting Scale: A measure of dysfunctional parenting in
           discipline situations

(continued)

5. **When my child pesters me...**

   I can ignore   0---0---0---0---0---0---0   I can't ignore
   the pestering.   pestering.

6. **When my child misbehaves...**

   I usually get into a long   0---0---0---0---0---0---0   I don't get into
   argument with my child.   an argument.

7. **I threaten to do things that...**

   I am sure I can   0---0---0---0---0---0---0   I know I won't
   carry out.   actually do.

8. **I am the kind of parent that...**

   set limits on what   0---0---0---0---0---0---0   lets my child do
   my child is allowed to do.   whatever he/she wants.

9. **When my child misbehaves...**

   I give my child   0---0---0---0---0---0---0   I keep my talks short
   a long lecture.   and to the point.

10. **When my child misbehaves...**

    I raise my voice   0---0---0---0---0---0---0   I speak to my child
    or yell.   calmly.

11. **If saying "No" doesn't work right away...**

    I take some other   0---0---0---0---0---0---0   I keep talking and try
    kind of action.   to get through to my child.

12. **When I want my child to stop doing something...**

    I firmly tell my   0---0---0---0---0---0---0   I coax or beg
    child to stop.   my child to stop.

13. **When my child is out of my sight...**

    I often don't know what   0---0---0---0---0---0---0   I always have a good
    my child is doing.   idea of what my child is
                                                                  doing.

14. **After there's been a problem with my child...**

    I often hold a grudge.   0---0---0---0---0---0---0   things get back to
                                                                  normal quickly.

15. When we're not at home…

I handle my child the   0---0---0---0---0---0---0   I let my child get
way I do at home.   away with a lot more.

16. When my child does something I don't like…

I do something about it.   0---0---0---0---0---0---0   I often let it go.
every time it happens.

17. When there is a problem with my child…

things build up and I do   0---0---0---0---0---0---0   things don't get out
things I don't mean to do.   of hand.

18. When my child misbehaves, I spank, slap, grab, or hit my child…

never or rarely.   0---0---0---0---0---0---0   most of the time.

19. When my child doesn't do what I ask…

I often let it go or end   0---0---0---0---0---0---0   I take some other
up doing it myself.   action.

20. When I give a fair threat or warning…

I often don't carry it out.   0---0---0---0---0---0---0   I always do what I
said.

21. If saying "No" doesn't work…

I take some other   0---0---0---0---0---0---0   I offer my child
kind of action.   something nice
so he/she will behave.

22. When my child misbehaves…

I handle it without   0---0---0---0---0---0---0   I get so frustrated or
getting upset.   angry that my child
can see I'm upset.

23. When my child misbehaves…

I make my child tell me   0---0---0---0---0---0---0   I say "No" or take
why he/she did it.   some other action.

24. If my child misbehaves and then acts sorry…

I handle the problem   0---0---0---0---0---0---0   I let it go that time.
like I usually would.

(continued)

(continued)

25. When my child misbehaves...

I rarely use bad   0---0---0---0---0---0   I almost always
language or curse.   use bad language.

26. When I say my child can't do something...

I let my child   0---0---0---0---0---0   I stick to what I said.
do it anyway.

27. When I have to handle a problem...

I tell my child   0---0---0---0---0---0   I don't say I'm sorry.
I'm sorry about it.

28. When my child does something I don't like, I insult my child, say mean things, or call my child names...

never or rarely.   0---0---0---0---0---0   most of the time.

29. If my child talks back or complains when I handle a problem...

I ignore the complaining 0---0---0---0---0---0   I give my child a talk
and stick to what I said.   about not
                                                         complaining.

30. If my child gets upset when I say "No"...

I back down and   0---0---0---0---0---0   I stick to what I said.
give in to my child.

The Warwick–Edinburgh Mental Well-being Scale (WEMWBS)

The WEMWBS was developed to:

- monitor well-being both nationally and locally (England, Scotland and Iceland are currently using the scale for these purposes)
- evaluate projects and programmes that could have an influence on mental well-being
- investigate the determinants of mental well-being.

It has 14 items, with five response categories for each item. The items are all worded positively and cover both feeling and functioning aspects of mental well-being. Item scores are summed to provide a score of between 14 and 70. It is a short and psychometrically robust scale, with no ceiling effects in a population sample, and offers promise as a tool for monitoring mental well-being at a population level. Tennant et al. (2007) report that it has moderate to high levels of construct validity with nine other comparable scales (median .73, range .42–.77) and a national median score from a population of 1,749 parents of 51 (inter-quartile range 45–56). See the user guide (at http://wrap.warwick.ac.uk/543/1/WRAP_Stewart_Brown_ Warwick_Edinburgh.pdfUserguide).

Warwick and Edinburgh Universities were commissioned to develop the WEMWBS in 2006, and it is free to use, but users must register their use by completing the registration form on the WEMWBS website. Details of how to download the form and additional information are included in Appendix 3.

It is recommended that this is used as a tool for discussion with parents as part of the case analysis process, contributing an understanding of the parents' well-being. It was not designed to detect mental illness –however, very low scores indicate the need for clinical support. It was used in the large Pathfinder Early Intervention Project (Lindsay, Strand and Davis, 2011) and shown to be sensitive to intervention change in mental well-being. Data from this trial are also reported in Hutchings, Bywater, Williams, Whitaker, Lane and Shakespeare (2011). Advice is available on NHS Direct and other public access databases, where scores are interpreted to offer clinical advice.

WEMWBS does not have a cut-off point that signifies mental well-being. However, national surveys have been published, giving population norms for Scotland (2008) and England (2013). These show WEMWBS scores by age, gender and for various other demographic groups. The English report also has some longitudinal data from population studies. The population means and distribution for the WEMWBS are summarised for the 2011 Health Survey for England (at www2.warwick.ac.uk/fac/med/research/ platform/wemwbs/).

Ending the first session

Having agreed a plan for the parents to complete the self-report measures, the final step is to close the session and arrange for your next visit. End the session by letting the parents know that you will phone or text to ask how they are getting on with the assignments and to confirm the next appointment. You can also let them know that you will be asking them to go through their typical day in fine detail in the next session.

It can be helpful to end by reminding the parent that they are parenting a child with challenges, who probably needs more thoughtful parenting to help them learn the skills that some other children might learn more easily. You should thank them again for their commitment to their child and express the realistic hope that things will improve as a result of working together. It can be helpful to say something like "There is no magic wand for helping children, but having worked with other parents with similar children I know that if we work together we will find some ways of helping your child to do some of the things that you would like him/her to do."

After concluding the session, you should look at the session checklist included at the end of the chapter.

References

Achenbach, T. M. & Edelbrock, C. S. (1983). *Manual for the Child Behavior Checklist and Revised Child Behavior Profile*. Burlington: University of Vermont, Department of Psychiatry.

Arnold, D. S., O'Leary, S. G., Wolff, L. S., & Acker, M. M. (1993). The parenting scale: A measure of dysfunctional parenting in discipline situations. *Psychological Assessment, 5*, 137–144.

Beck, A. T., Steer, R. A., & Brown, G. K. (1996). *Manual for the Beck Depression Inventory-II*. San Antonio, TX: Psychological Corporation.

Bywater, T., Hutchings, J., Daley, D., Whitaker, C. J., Yeo, S. T., Jones, K., Eames, C., & Edwards, R. T. (2009). Long-term effectiveness of a parenting intervention in Sure Start services in Wales for children at risk of developing conduct disorder. *British Journal of Psychiatry, 195*, 318–324.

Gardner, F., Hutchings, J., Bywater, T., & Whitaker, C. J. (2010). Who benefits and how does it work? Moderators and mediators of outcome in an effectiveness trial of a parenting intervention in multiple "Sure Start" services. *Journal of Clinical Child and Adolescent Psychology, 39*, 568–580.

Goldiamond, I. (1974). Towards a constructional approach to social problems. *Behaviourism, 2*, 1–84.

Goldiamond, I. (1975). A constructional approach to self control. In: A. Schwartz & I. Goldiamond (Eds.), *Social casework: A behavioural approach*. New York: Columbia University Press.

Goodman, R. (1997). The Strengths and Difficulties Questionnaire: A research note. *Journal of Child Psychology and Psychiatry, 38*, 581–586.

Hartman, R. R., Stage, S. A., & Webster-Stratton, C. (2003). A growth curve analysis of parent training outcomes: Examining the influence of child risk factors (inattention, impulsivity, and hyperactivity problems), parental and family risk factors. *Journal of Child Psychology and Psychiatry, 44*, 388–398.

Hutchings, J. (1996). *The personal and parental characteristics of preschool children referred to a child and family mental health service and their relation to treatment outcome*. PhD thesis, Bangor: University of Wales.

Hutchings, J. (2014) *The Enhancing Parenting Skills (EPaS) 2014 programme: A behavioural intervention to support families in developing children's social competencies and dealing with common childhood problems*. Children's Early Intervention Trust, Bangor.

Hutchings, J., Lane, E., & Kelly, J. (2004). Comparison of two treatments for children with severely disruptive behaviours: A four-year follow-up. *Behavioural and Cognitive Psychotherapy, 32*, 15–30.

Hutchings, J., Appleton, P., Smith, M., Lane, E., & Nash, S. (2002). Evaluation of two treatments for children with severe behaviour problems: Child behaviour and maternal mental health outcomes. *Behavioural and Cognitive Psychotherapy, 30*, 279–295. doi:10.1017/S1352465802003041

Hutchings, J., Bywater, T., Williams, M. E., Lane, E., & Whitaker, C. J. (2012). Improvements in maternal depression as a mediator of child behaviour change. *Psychology, 3*, 795–801.

Hutchings, J., Bywater, T., Williams, M. E., Whitaker, C. J., Lane, E., & Shakespeare, K. (2011). The extended school aged Incredible Years parent programme. *Child and Adolescent Mental Health, 16*, 136–143.

Hutchings, J., Bywater, T., Daley, D., Gardner, F., Whitaker, C. J., Jones, K., Eames, C., & Edwards, R. T. (2007). Parenting intervention in Sure Start services for children at risk of developing conduct disorder: Pragmatic randomised controlled trial. *British Medical Journal, 334,* 678–685.

Lindsay, G., Strand, S., & Davis, H. (2011). A comparison of the effectiveness of three parenting programmes in improving parenting skills, parent mental well being and children's behaviour when implemented on a large scale in community settings in 18 English local authorities: The parenting early intervention pathfinder (PEIP). *BMC Public Health 2011, 11,* 963. Retrieved from www. biomedcentral/1471-2458/11/962

Miller, S. D., Duncan, B. L., Brown, J., Sparks, J. A., & Claud, D. A. (2003). The Outcome Rating Scale: A preliminary study of the reliability, validity, and feasibility of a brief visual analog measure. *Journal of Brief Therapy, 2*(2), 91–100.

Scott, S. (2001). Deciding whether interventions for antisocial behaviour work: Principles of outcome assessment, and practice in a multicentre trial. *European Child and Adolescent Psychiatry, 10*(1), S59–S70.

Scott, S., Spender, Q., Doolan, M., Jacobs, B., & Aspland, H. (2001). Multicentre controlled trial of parenting groups for childhood antisocial behaviour in clinical practice. *British Medical Journal, 323,* 194–197.

Tennant, R., Hiller, L., Fishwic, R., Platt, S., Joseph, S., Weich, S., . . . Stewart-Brown, S. (2007). The Warwick-Edinburgh Mental Well-being Scale (WEMWBS): Development and UK validation. *Health and Quality of Life Outcomes, 5,* 63–75.

Abbreviated PDHQ

(Hutchings, 1996)

There are a number of questions to which answers can be sought during initial interview:

1 Where were you living at that time that he/she was born, and with whom?
2 Were there any problems during the pregnancy or the birth?
3 Was he/she a healthy/easy baby?
4 Has he/she had any significant health problems since he/she was born?
5 Has he/she ever been in hospital?
6 Have you had health problems or been in hospital since he/she was born?
7 Was his/her development generally normal or did it cause you concern?
8 When did you first realise that he/she had the problems that you are now experiencing with him/her?
9 Does he/she have difficulties in other situations, such as playgroup or school?
10 Who else lives here and/or has contact with him/her, and what relation are they to him/her?

The Parent–Child Constructional Questionnaire (PCCQ)

(Adapted by the author from Goldiamond 1974, 1975)

Question 1: OUTCOMES

Question 2: AREAS CHANGED/UNCHANGED

Question 3: CHANGE HISTORY

Question 4: ASSETS

Question 5: CONSEQUENCES

Question 6: ADDITIONAL INFORMATION

Question 7: QUESTIONS YOU WANT TO ASK US

Question 1: OUTCOMES

a. Assuming we were successful, what would the outcome be for your child?
b. What would others observe if the successful outcome was obtained?
c. How does this differ from the present state of affairs?
d. Can you give an example?
e. Assuming we were successful, what would the outcome be for you?
f. What would others observe if the successful outcome was obtained?
g. How does this differ from the present state of affairs?
h. Can you give an example?
i. In what way would this change things for you and your partner or other significant people in your child's life?

Question 2: AREAS CHANGED/UNCHANGED

a. What is going well for your child now and what areas of your child's life would not be affected by our work?
b. What areas of your own life are going well and would not change?
c. Are there any areas of your life, other than those that we would directly work on, that would change?

Question 3: CHANGE HISTORY

a. Why do you want to work on these problems now? Has there been any recent trigger?
b. When did it first occur to you that there was a problem? What was going on?

c. What was happening in your life at that time?
d. What did you do? How did it work out?

Question 4: ASSETS

a. What skills or strengths do you have that are related to what you would like to achieve?
b. What other skills do you have?
c. In the past, what related problems with your child have you tackled successfully?
d. What other problems have you personally tackled successfully?

Question 5: CONSEQUENCES

a. In relation to your child's problem(s), has it brought you or your child any additional support?
b. As a result of your child's problem, has your child been excused from anything?
c. How is your child's present problem difficult for your child or yourself, or what does it stop you from doing?
d. What does your child really like to do? What makes him or her happy?
e. Who else is interested in the changes you are after?
f. Which people have been helpful in the past? What help did they give you? How did you obtain this from them?

Question 6: ADDITIONAL INFORMATION

a. Is there anything we left out or did not get enough information about?
b. Was there something we overlooked, or made too much of?
c. Are there any impressions you would like to correct?
d. Are there any questions you would like to ask? Any comments?

Question 7: QUESTIONS YOU WANT TO ASK US

a. Are there any questions you would like to ask? Any comments?

Three-Problem Rating Scale

Name of child _____ Age_____

Please list below, in order of priority, up to three problems you have with your child's behaviour that you would most like help with at the moment, then rate the problems on the line from "Not a problem" to "Couldn't be worse".

For example, "temper tantrums at bedtime" scored at the end of the line as it couldn't get any worse.

Concern 1 ....

Not a problem _____ Couldn't be worse

How long have you had this concern/problem? _____

Concern 2 ....

Not a problem _____ Couldn't be worse

How long have you had this concern/problem? _____

Concern 3 ....

Not a problem _____Couldn't be worse

How long have you had this concern/problem? _____

EPaS checklist for assessment session 1

	Activity	Completed (Yes/No)
1	Get a complete history, including a PDHQ	
2	Get parents to identify three main problems and rate them on the 10 cm scale	
3	Complete the Parent–Child Constructional Questionnaire interview and generate some target behaviours	
4	Explain the three parent self-report measures as a home activity	
5	Give copies of the three questionnaires: Strengths and Difficulties Questionnaire, Arnold-O'Leary and Warwick-Edinburgh	
6	Explain what will happen next time: the typical day interview	
7	Arrange the next appointment	
8	Close the session by praising the parents' commitment to helping their child	

6 Assessment session 2

The typical day interview and parent record keeping

Hopefully you have managed to catch up with the parent/s by phone before the second appointment. In which case, you will probably know whether they have managed to complete their assignment. The first thing to do at the start of assessment session 2, after greeting the parents, is to ask about the questionnaires. If the parents have completed them, they need to receive immediate positive feedback for this. You need to thank them and look at the parent to ensure that all of the questions have been answered and then explain that you will be using them in your case analysis and giving feedback on them at that stage. If they have not completed them, some troubleshooting is needed to establish what made it difficult and how they *can* be completed before the next session. Having done this, the main activity for this session is to complete the typical day interview and to establish some specific record keeping in relation to an identified problem.

The typical day interview

This an interview strategy has been used for over 25 years and its origins are not really known. It formed an important part of the initial intensive treatment programme (Hutchings, Lane and Kelly, 2004) and health visitor EPaS trials (Lane and Hutchings, 2002; Williams, 2017), and, two decaders on from the first trial, health visitors say that they still use it. Its purpose is to get a clear picture of the current situation. It establishes what is happening at the present time within the family situation, and helps to establish the pattern of family life, including the pressure points.

Many parents' descriptions of their children's behaviour tend to be global and problem-focused (Hutchings, Nash, Williams and Nightingale, 1998; Hutchings, Bywater, Williams, Lane and Whitaker, 2012). They describe problems as happening "all the time" and fail to spot the triggers that prompt problems or to be aware of their own responses to them. The typical day interview helps parents to examine and describe specific events in detail, a skill that they need in order to both identify specific problems and work on effective solutions.

It takes time to establish the current patterns of behaviour by prompting parents to describe what actually happens. The global labels and descriptions that parents use can be followed up with questions such as "Tell me exactly what he does and says when you ask him to get dressed, clean his teeth, etc." and "Can you give me some examples of what happens at bedtime and how you respond?"

The typical day interview is a powerful tool for establishing the pattern of family activity, because you can learn about the responses of other family members to the target child and their difficulties. It is used to decide on which behaviours to ask parents to keep records that will help to provide an objective measure of the extent and context of problem behaviours. This record keeping is an essential aspect of the development of the collaborative relationship, which is necessary for successful work and the building of parental observation skills.

You should explain that you want the parents to describe what happens in their family on a typical day. You can initiate the description and give the parents some idea of the content and detail expected by asking, "Who gets up first?" and "What time is that, usually?" Then guide the parents through the day, taking them back if parts are missed, and asking for more detail as necessary. This process can take most of an hour to do thoroughly and is the only activity for this session, apart from agreeing on a record-keeping assignment. You are trying to tease out the *Antecedents* (things that might be triggering the problem), *Behaviours* (exactly what the child does) and *Consequences* (the response to the child's behaviour and how it works out). This *ABC* model is described in more detail in Chapter 8, on developing a case analysis, but involves establishing exactly who is present, the time of day, the location, what is happening and any other circumstances associated with problem behaviour, as well as the consequences that follow the problem behaviour for both child and parents.

Extracts from a typical day interview follow. These show how this strategy helped to build a picture of family functioning and the pressure points in their everyday life through detailed questions about the daily pattern, and who does and says what at different times in the day. The extracts are part of an interview with a family that were participants in the initial intensive treatment study (Hutchings, Lane and Kelly, 2004). The family comprised a single mother with three children: a girl aged 8 and two boys aged 4 and 1 year. The referred child (Simon) has a sister (Jenny) and a baby brother (Peter).

Typical day extracts

The first question about the structure of the day identified that the older two children were sharing a bed because the referred child had broken his sister's bed: "They're sharing a bed as well, cos hers was a big solid pine and he's broken it all to bits". Not surprisingly the mother later reported that there were also night time problems.

The next incident shows how important it is to question the parent in detail to find out what actually happens.

Mother:	If he's had the toothpaste and its on the sink and things I'll make him clean it . . . you know whatever mess he's made I make him tidy it up and clean it.
Interviewer:	And does he resist when you make him clean it?
Mother:	Yeah, he won't do it.
Interviewer:	So what do you do then when he is resisting?
Mother:	Well, because he won't do it in the end I'll have to do it because I've got to get three of them ready and get to school by 9 o'clock.
Interviewer:	So when you say that you make him clean it up, what you do is you try and make him clean it up?
Mother:	Yeah, sometimes he will and sometimes he won't, you know, he'll start and then "I don't want to . . .", you know.

The next example starts to identify a problem in terms of the child's self-help skills:

Interviewer:	So will the children get dressed quite quickly?
Mother:	No, he'll [S] take his pyjamas off and that'll be it, he'll just sit there.
Interviewer:	Is the TV on?
Mother:	Yeah.
Interviewer:	So S will sit there, so will J get dressed quite quickly?
Mother:	She, yeah, and then I'll do P [the baby] and in the meantime I'm sayin', "S get dressed, please get dressed, we're not getting anywhere."
Interviewer:	OK, and will you have to end up helping S as well?
Mother:	I have to dress him altogether then.
Interviewer:	Are either of them [S or P] at all resistant when you are trying to dress them?
Mother:	Yeah, if he [S] doesn't wanna have his socks or his underpants on he won't and he sits there and I really have to lift his legs up, put them on, stand him up and, you know, as I'm trying to lift him I'm trying to put his socks on him, its really hard with him, but these two are no problem.

The description of breakfast time provides further evidence of S's problematic and controlling behaviours. Mum describes how S has to have his own special bowl for breakfast in a special place on a cupboard by the TV, how the milk has to be filled to a certain level or he throws it at his mother or tips it on the floor. Other problems are also identified in relation to breakfast, including the lack of suitable table space where the children can eat.

A few minutes later, in response to a question about whether there are problems between the children in the mornings, Mum reports that S, having chosen his cereal, then demands his sister's toast. Mum says "No", at which point he starts hitting his sister and pulling her hair for her toast. At this point Mum reports that she puts S in his room for five minutes but adds that she can only leave him there for five minutes in the morning because they have to get to school; at other times he could be there for "hours".

At this stage, the interviewer clarifies that the mum clearly recognises that she wants to find some solutions to these challenges.

The interview moves on to getting the children to school and the problems associated with that. The next problem is the "walk" to school, during which S's sister often ends up pushing baby P in the pushchair whilst Mum carries S. As the interview continues, more about Mum's life, and the restrictions imposed on it by S's behaviour, become apparent. She describes her good fortune in meeting her brother on her last trip to town with S and how he "had" to carry S home from town for her.

Problems continue throughout the afternoon and evening with S having a special meal cooked for him. Mum allows S out to play even though he gets into trouble "all the time. I've always got somebody knockin', you know the door." Mum also describes the problems of getting S to come in: "Yeah, I have to go chasing him round the street an everythin' to get him to come back in. People laugh at me, yeah."

Bedtime

S refuses to put on his pyjamas after his bath and, when he is finally put to bed, refuses to stay there, getting up throughout the night, often until about 4 a.m., when he finally falls asleep.

Detailed information such as this allows an opportunity to express sympathy with the parents for the problems that they are having with the child. It also provides an opportunity to explain how useful this information will be in tackling the problems and to reinforce the parents' decision to seek help. It is already clear that the functions of S's behaviour are both that it enables him to avoid doing things that he is being asked to do and that it obtains things for him, attention or crisps, staying up later or physical contact from Mum. Mum's behaviour is also reinforced, in that it gets things done, like getting S to school on time. It also gets help from other family members, such as her brother. Giving in to S's requests avoids having to endure his tantrums, but at a cost, such as people laughing at her when she has to chase him around the neighbourhood to get him to come in from play. Her behaviour is, in Goldiamond's terms, "logical but costly" (see Chapter 3, p. 38), which is why she is seeking help.

Whilst it may not be necessary to complete a full typical day interview, it is clear from the above examples that a lot can be learned about the circumstances surrounding problem situations by this very thorough approach. The information gathered then informs the next task, which is to ask parents to keep records about a particular problem. This will be the parental assignment for completion before the next session.

Establishing parental record keeping

During the assessment phase, the parental contribution to the partnership is their expert knowledge of the child, which is recognised by asking them to collect information and to have it available for the next session. This also confirms the collaborative nature of the relationship in which we are helping the parents to help themselves. The record-keeping task has to be designed with care to ensure that it is within the capabilities of the parent, but all parents are capable of simple frequency records and many can do much more.

Parents are asked to keep records on a specific problem that they have already reported and/or may have been identified during the typical day interview. After deciding on the behaviour to be recorded, a record sheet can be drawn up by hand and given to the parents. You may decide to use a basic ABC chart – Antecedents (triggers), Behaviour, Consequences (what happens next). This helps to establish the actual conditions under which the problem occurs, who is present, where the problem occurs, time of day and what triggers it, an instruction from the parent or a demand from the child, for example. Tables 6.1 and 6.2 are record sheets showing examples of Antecedent, Behaviour, Consequence charts relating to a shopping and a nappy-changing situation (a blank copy is included at the end of the chapter).

The next record (Table 6.3) highlights the escalating coercive cycle that the child and parent often engage in. This was originally described by Patterson (1982), and describes how child and parent are each intermittently reinforced by escalating their behaviour. When the child's demand was not met, his mum shouted at him and his problem behaviour escalated, throwing the juice, etc., until (on this occasion) he realised that it was impossible for his demand to be met.

Table 6.1 ABC chart: shopping

Antecedents	Behaviour	Consequences
This can be what is happening, people, places, time of day, type of demand	This can be appropriate or inappropriate (it may be an appropriate request but made in an inappropriate way)	The consequence predicts the likelihood that the behaviour will or will not happen again
Mum, child, other people in the supermarket	Tantrum for sweets (other people are watching)	Child gets sweets, Mum gets peace and quiet

Table 6.2 ABC chart: nappy change

Antecedents	Behaviour	Consequences
This can be what is happening, people, places, time of day, type of demand	This can be appropriate or inappropriate (it may be an appropriate request but made in an inappropriate way)	The consequence predicts the likelihood that the behaviour will or will not happen again
Mum is changing the baby's nappy	Older child is demanding sweets and baby is crying	Child gets sweets, Mum gets peace and quiet to change the nappy

Table 6.3 ABC chart: L's record of difficult times involving clothes

Antecedent	Behaviour	Consequence
Where you were, what was happening, who was present, time, what you wanted or asked him to do	What L did	What L did and how it worked out
Friday morning, Dad in work		
L was very slow in getting ready for school, same as day before.	L had a tantrum.	I shouted at him.
At 8.30 he said "I have got football today" and there was a man coming to the school to teach them, so he demanded his football top. I told him it was in the wash, I could not get it ready in time.	He went mad and started to thump me in my stomach. He threw his football boots and tipped all the blackcurrant juice all over the sink (it was full)	Time was getting on so he realised he had to make up his mind.
I wanted him to wear another top for football, so I got another red top.	He reluctantly put it on	It was only because time was getting on he decided to wear it. He said to me at school "Don't tell Dad that I spilt the pop over."

Individualised charts

You can make a more detailed chart about a specific behaviour. It is a good idea to make a copy of any written information that is left with parents. In the EPaS trials we gave health visitors carbonated pads, which gave them a copy. In the original intensive treatment programme, we used a sheet of carbon paper. Copies of the record sheet can be made into a neater typed version and then sent by post to the parents. Individualised record sheets that have the name of the child on them can encourage parents to complete them, as in 'Charlie's bedtime record' example (see box). They are devised to clarify further the information gained during the typical day interview. It may be helpful to record the frequency of a particular behaviour problem (such as tantrums) and can, as in the boxed example, include what else was going on at these times.

This record was helpful in understanding the pattern of the problem bedtime behaviour. When this was kept each night for a week, it showed the roles of both Mum and Dad in the bedtime routine and their different strategies for getting Charlie to bed. It also showed his pattern of waking and successfully demanding food.

Charlie's bedtime record

Date__*May 5th*_____

Who is at home? *Mum, Dad, Charlie & Iwan*

What time did the bedtime routine start? *7.00pm*

What happens first? *Dad says – "ok bedtime Charlie"*

Any problems? *C says "No it's not bedtime, I'm busy"*

What time did C go to bed? *7.15. Dad said if you go now I will read you a story*

Who goes up to bed with him? *Dad reads with him.*

What time do you leave him? *7.45.*

Any problems leaving? *No. He said he wanted to be alone*

What happened after that? Does he get up, how many times, when? *He came down at about 10.30 and said he was hungry*

What do you do, how does it work out? *Let him stay downstairs for a bit and watch TV while he had a yogurt. He went back to his room at 11.15 when I told him I was going to bed.*

It can be particularly useful to identify a problem for record keeping that is unlikely to occur during your observation session (assessment session 3) or would be hard for the practitioner to observe – for example, a problem that generally arises at bedtime, during the night, or in the morning in preparation for school.

Parental record keeping is an important part of the intervention process. It makes use of their valuable knowledge and experience. It helps them to focus on specific behaviours, to see the pattern of behaviours, to see their own role in the pattern and to see themselves as agents of change. It is not unusual for parents to solve problems themselves, either following a typical day interview or as a result of being asked to keep detailed records.

The following guidelines will help to ensure that parents successfully complete their record keeping task:

1   The rationale for the records must be explained clearly. The need for this information from the parent, the expert, must be emphasised. It is their contribution in the collaborative alliance that will provide detail about problems.
2   The records sheets must be clear and well laid out, targeted on the particular child and one specific problem, and easy to fill in.
3   The task must be clearly stated, such as "Record one incident each day that leaves you feeling cross with yourself about the way you dealt

with Johnny" or "Record with a cross or a tick every morning whether Mary's bed is wet or dry".

4   Parental ability to complete the task should be considered: for example, "Have you ever kept any records before?" or "Do you do the football pools or the lottery?" or "Do you have to fill in any forms for school about your child, such as whether they have done any reading?" Some of the information will already be known, following the standardised questionnaire activity and the constructional questionnaire information.

Keeping records can be very empowering for parents, helping them to become more accurate in their understanding of their child's abilities and challenges. The typical day interview provides descriptions of situations that might be suitable for record keeping, but this is also something to discuss with parents in terms of their own priorities.

Before finishing the session, you need to explain that you wish to undertake an observation of the parent and child together in the next session, and that it will probably be your final information-gathering session prior to starting to develop and work together on a plan. You need to obtain parents' permission and prepare them for this. Explain that you would like to observe how they and their child behave together, that you will observe and take notes, and will not talk to them during the observation, so as to make it as natural as possible. It can be a good idea to suggest a task, or the parents could suggest one themselves.

You should finish the session by reminding the parents of the record-keeping assignment, and that you will try to speak with them before the next session and confirm details of the next appointment. Conclude the session by thanking them for their commitment to the child and for working with you to achieve their goals.

A checklist of the key activities for assessment session 2 is included at the end of the chapter.

References

Hutchings, J., Lane, E., & Kelly, J. (2004). Comparison of two treatments for children with severely disruptive behaviours: A four-year follow-up. *Behavioural and Cognitive Psychotherapy, 32*, 15–30. doi:10.1017/S1352465804001018

Hutchings, J., Nash, S., Williams, J. M. G., & Nightingale, D. (1998). Parental autobiographical memory: Is this a helpful clinical measure in behavioural child management? *British Journal of Clinical Psychology, 37*, 303–312. doi:10.1111/j.2044-8260.1998.tb01387.x

Hutchings, J., Bywater, T., Williams, M. E., Lane, E., & Whitaker, C. J. (2012). Improvements in maternal depression as a mediator of child behaviour change. *Psychology, 3*, 795–801. doi:10.4236/psych.2012.329120

Lane, E. & Hutchings, J. (2002). Benefits of a course in behavioural analysis for health visitors. *British Journal of Nursing, 11*, 702–714. doi:10.12968/bjon.2002.11.10.702

Patterson, G. R. (1982). *Coercive family process.* Eugene, OR: Castalia.

Williams, M. E. (2017). *Evaluation of the Enhancing Parenting Skills 2014 programme.* PhD thesis, Bangor, UK, Bangor University.

EPaS checklist for assessment session 2

	Activity	Completed yes/no
1	Greet parents and ask for the home activities	
2	Check that they have completed them by looking briefly through to see if they are complete.	
3	Thank the parent and ask how the parent found completing them.	
4	Trouble-shoot with parents that have not completed assignments.	
5	Complete the typical day interview.	
6	Design and agree record sheets for one problem situation.	
7	Leave a copy with the parents.	
8	Decide on the structure of the observation for next session.	
9	Explain what will happen next time (the observation).	
10	Arrange next appointment.	
11	Thank the parent for working with you to help their child, and conclude session.	
12	If appropriate, make further copies of the record sheet and send to the parent.	

Antecedents	Behaviour	Consequences

7 Assessment session 3

Observing the parent–child interaction and other information sources

As with the previous session, you should start the session by checking on the assignments that you agreed with the parents (in this case, the individualised record sheets). If parents' initial record keeping is to be maintained, it is essential that they receive attention for their efforts and feedback on it – for example, "How did you get on with your record sheets?" or "Can I have them, please?" You should look at them briefly to be sure that they have been completed with the relevant information, thank the parents, and then set the record sheets aside for later discussion, reminding the parents that you will be using them to build your case analysis. If the parent has had a problem keeping the records, it needs to be dealt with immediately and the record-keeping requirement may need to be changed. If you cannot get a parent to keep records of some sort, even if it is only a tick on a calendar for a dry bed, it is unlikely that you will successfully help them to implement other changes that will be essential to the solution of the presenting problems.

The main purpose of this session is to undertake some direct observation of parent–child interactions. This is likely to be helpful even if it does not directly relate to the problems described by the parent. This may be the first time that you have seen the child. What you are looking for is the pattern of interactions between the parent and child. While interview and parent-kept data are useful, direct observation has many additional advantages. It provides an opportunity to:

- become acquainted with the child in his or her natural environment
- collect information that is not overlaid with interpretation – you can record actual events at the time and reflect on their meaning and function later
- check on the accuracy of the parent or caretaker reports
- identify controlling variables and functional relationships
- observe parenting behaviour
- have a baseline against which to assess the effects of the intervention
- identify child and parent assets.

Observing realtime parent–child interactions will help you to understand the pattern of, and possible reasons for, the child's behaviour. You need to look at all of the components of the events that you observe, triggers or Antecedents, Behaviours and Consequences. Careful observation of how parents interact with their children will contribute to your analysis and provides a check on the accuracy of parental reports regarding both their children's and their own behaviour. Parents may not notice things, they may misperceive events, be unaware of the impact of their own actions or may have unrealistic expectations.

Setting up the observation

As discussed earlier, at the end of the previous session, you need to obtain parents' permission to undertake an observation and to prepare them for this. We have never known permission to be withheld if you explain the purpose of the observation. You want to observe how their child behaves with them. You also need to explain the process, and that you will observe and take notes and will not talk to them during the observations, so as to make it as natural as possible. It can be a good idea to suggest a task or invite the parent to suggest one. You are not particularly looking at a problem situation. You are likely to get examples of levels and quality of parental praise and encouragement, quality of parental instructions, etc. You will also hopefully see examples of parental behaviours that you can feed back as assets – for example, staying calm, etc. In the intensive treatment version of the programme (Hutchings, Lane and Kelly, 2004; Hutchings, Appleton, Smith, Lane and Nash, 2002), we observed parents and children in five different situations: child-led play, toys tidy-up, a competitive game, a parent-led activity (preparing a meal) and a mealtime. You probably cannot do all of this, but based on the information that you already have you can decide on a task – observing child-led play is often quite revealing of interaction patterns. After the observation, ask the parent: "Is this what he or she is normally like? Worse? Better?"

As an observer, it is important that you blend into the background as much as possible. You want the parent and child to behave as though you were not there. Try not to interact with children or their parents during the observations. You can busy yourself with note taking to avoid being drawn in. Children's approaches or questions should be ignored or answered briefly before returning to your notes. Generally, it takes only a few minutes for the child to start to behave typically and for parents to respond as they usually would.

There are some extremely complex and detailed coding systems. However, when working with individual families in their own homes the simplest way of recording is to use an ABC chart and record events as they occur. Examples of ABC charts were included in Chapter 6 (along with a blank ABC chart at the end of the chapter). Another simple way to record is to count the frequency of specific behaviours. One mother gave 67 instructions in an hour, but her extremely active 3-year-old child did not follow any of them. In fact, she was often teaching him other things that he could do, by predicting what he would do next and asking him not to do it. For example, when he ran near to the TV, she said, "Don't touch the TV," and he immediately turned and touched it. You can capture this sort of information with a combination of ABC and frequency recordings. Also, since non-compliance with instructions is a frequently occurring challenging behaviour, it is useful to record examples of the type of instructions that parents give, and children's responses. Often these will be *negative* instructions that ask the child to stop doing something rather than *positive* instructions that tell the child what to do. You will return to these problems when developing the case analysis and intervention strategies, but it is useful to notice whether an instruction is to "Stop shouting!" or "Please speak quietly", since the words themselves affect the way that we speak. Most people when they give the instruction "Stop shouting!" do this in a loud and possibly angry way, whereas the alternative – "Please speak quietly" – is more likely to be said quietly.

Two examples of behaviour recordings are presented below.

In the first example, a recording is made of the number of instructions given in 20-second intervals. The number of negative comments, such as "You are a naughty boy", as well as the number of instructions that were (not) followed, are also shown. For this kind of recording, a 20-second bleep can be useful. (This can generally be set on a digital watch.)

Observation of James (age 3) and Suzy (mother)
Observer: Mary P, Health Visitor   Date: _____

	Parent			Child		
	Instruction	Praise/ smile	Negative comment	Complies with instruction	Other positive behaviour	Negative behaviour
0.20	✓✓					
0.40	✓		✓			✓
1.00	✓✓✓			✓		
1.20		✓✓			✓	✓
1.40	✓✓		✓			✓✓✓
2.00	✓	✓			✓✓	
2.20	✓			✓	✓	
2.40		✓✓	✓		✓✓	✓✓
3.00	✓✓	✓		✓		
3.20		✓			✓✓	
3.40	✓		✓			✓

(continued)

(continued)

	Parent			Child		
	Instruction	Praise/ smile	Negative comment	Complies with instruction	Other positive behaviour	Negative behaviour
4.00						
4.20			✓			✓✓
4.40	✓					✓
5.00	✓✓✓			✓		✓
5.20		✓				
5.40		✓			✓✓	
6.00	✓					✓

This mother gives a lot of instructions – 18 in 5 minutes – and there were only four compliances (22 per cent), which were followed by praise within the following 20 seconds. Against this, all five negative parental comments are associated with negative child behaviour, and overall there are 13 recorded problem child behaviours. ABC records of some of these incidents would add further detail in terms of how many of the instructions were repetitions (something often experienced by challenging non-compliant children), how the parent responded to compliance, the quality of the instructions and the feasibility of compliance – for example, whether the child was developmentally capable of complying. It is also important to record examples of child compliance and effective parental responses, as this may later help parents to see things that work better and build on strengths.

The next example lasts for only 3 minutes, but is probably a fairly typical example of the behaviour of a non-compliant child.

Minute 1

Interval	10	20	30	40	50	60
Child	Watching TV	Watching TV – no response	Watching TV – "Mm"	"Yes" – shouts "Can't ye see I'm busy" – louder	Watching TV	Turns briefly, screams, "No"
Mother	"Tea's ready"	"Do you want it there?"	"Are you listening?"	"The chips will get cold"	"I think the TV needs to go off!"	Mum leaves the room

Minute 2

Interval	10	20	30	40	50	60
Child	Watching TV	Child starts eating	Child continues eating	Child asks for a drink "I want a drink"	Child "Coca-Cola"	Child stops eating and is watching TV
Mother	Mum brings food	Mum says "Say thank you"	Mum watches	Mum asks "What drink would you like?"	Mum leaves the room	

Minute 3

Interval	10	20	30	40	50	60
Child	Watching TV	Watching TV	Child continues watching TV and takes drink	Child starts to drink	Child says "I don't want any more to eat"	Child watching TV
Mother		Mum returns with Coca-Cola	Mum watches	Mum says "Be careful with that drink"	Mum asks "Why not, you asked for it?"	

The fact that this mother was being observed probably did not stop this from being a typical interaction. She brought the food to the child, who remained in front of the TV and was unresponsive to her comments or instructions, while he briefly ate some of his tea before demanding a drink and abandoning his tea. If the mother had carried out her threat to switch off the TV, she would probably have had a tantrum to deal with. This observation would provide an opportunity, during the case analysis presentation, to discuss with the mother what she wanted and how it could be achieved.

It is particularly helpful if you can film an observation: it both allows you to analyse it at a later time and can be used in the intervention to look at with the parent. Video Interaction Guidance (VIG) (see Rusconi-Serpa, Rossignol and McDonough, 2009) involves filming and showing parents examples of their positive interactions with their child or children and has been shown to increase positive parent behaviours. Whether you video-record parent–child interactions or simply write down what you see, it is important that you work from a strengths-based approach and include feedback about effective parent behaviours.

If you decide to film, you need to explain the reason to the parent and you may find that many parents are not as resistant to the idea as you would expect. You need to clarify what will happen to the film, when it will be destroyed and who will see it – generally only yourself and the parent, but you need to check out any agency requirements for filming interactions and the storing of such data. A sample consent to video-record an interaction is included at the end of the chapter. If you use this and/or any other letters that you write, you should use the headed paper of the organisation for whom you work.

Based on what you have observed, you can complete the EPaS Observation Checklist that was developed as part of this programme. This prompts you to think about parental assets that can be included in the case analysis, and is included at the end of the chapter.

Developmental assessment

Depending on what else is known about the child and their general level of functioning, it can be useful to get a snapshot of the child's developmental level. This can help to establish the extent to which parental expectations are realistic. There are a number of developmental assessment and screening tools, and it would be useful to establish which ones are in use in your area. Many health visitors use the Denver Developmental Scales (Frankenburg, Dodds, Archer, Shapiro and Bresnick, 1992). In Wales, the Schedule of Growing Skills (Bellman, Lingam and Aukett, 1996, 2008) was specified by the Welsh Government as an assessment tool for children living in severely socio-economically disadvantaged Flying Start areas. This is a developmental screening tool which, when used with a sensitive scoring system (Williams, Hutchings, Bywater, Daley and Whitaker, 2013), can provide useful information about possible delay in a number of developmental areas. Another approach is to ask parents to assess their child's developmental status using the Ages and Stages Questionnaire (ASQ; Squires, Potter and Bricker, 1999). This gives a parental report on developmental assessment and can be useful in helping parents to focus on observing their child's behaviour.

Data from external sources

The final assessment issue to consider is whether it would be useful to obtain data from health records, the school or other sources. You need to think about whether this will be helpful, because you cannot solve problems that occur in other settings when you are working only with the parents. Your goal is to help parents to work on issues that are within their control. However, it can be useful to know whether the same or similar problems occur in other situations. Furthermore, if the issue at school is lack of friendship skills, for example, this may be something that can be worked on with home-based goals.

Parent records for this session

The home activity for parents for this week is to complete two questionnaires about their child: the "Things your child enjoys" questionnaire and the "Things your child can do" record. Both of these questionnaires were developed for the EPaS programme and continue to build parents' observation skills and knowledge about their children. The "Things your child enjoys" questionnaire also provides information about possible reinforcers for the child that could be useful in the intervention phase. The "Things your child can do" record helps parents to focus on what their child can actually do, and what they will be able to build on. Blank and completed examples of both are included at the end of the chapter.

It can be helpful to give the parent a stamped, addressed envelope and ask them to post these questionnaires back to you, so that you can use them in your case analysis. It can also be useful to leave a fortnight until the next appointment, so that you have time to work on your case analysis and this can then be explained to the parent. You may also consider giving the parent a reading assignment from the booklet *The Little Parent Handbook* (Hutchings, 2013), which you might wish to give to the parent at this stage.

It could be that you find that your family has already started to make changes that address some of their goals, because the assessment process itself builds parental observation skills and understanding about their child's and their own behaviour, which can help them to identify relevant functional relationships. This is not uncommon, as the EPaS assessment process has similarities to the Family Check-Up programme developed by Dishion and colleagues as an early intervention. Although the check-up process could lead to further support, for some families it was also found to be of therapeutic value in its own right (Dishion, Brennan, Shaw, McEachern, Wilson and Jo, 2014; Dishion, Shaw, Connell, Gardner, Weaver and Wilson, 2008). In relation to the EPaS process, any changes that parents are making should be praised, but they may still need help to ensure that the appropriate replacement behaviours are identified and taught.

At the next session you will present your understanding of the problem(s) and help the parents to agree intervention goals and the first stage of a plan to achieve them. You now have the information needed to build a picture of the child and their family and to tentatively identify some of the functions of problem behaviour and possible goals.

At the end of the chapter, there is a table containing an EPaS checklist of items that are covered in this assessment session.

References

Bellman, M. H., Lingam, S., & Aukett, A. (1996). *Schedule of Growing Skills II: Reference manual*. London: NFER Nelson Publishing Company.

Bellman, M. H., Lingam, S., & Aukett, A. (2008). *Schedule of Growing Skills II: User's guide*, 2nd edition. London: NFER Nelson Publishing Company.

Dishion, T. J., Brennan, L. M., Shaw, D. S., McEachern, A. D., Wilson, M. N., & Jo, B. (2014). Prevention of problem behaviour through annual family check-ups in early childhood: Intervention effects from home to early elementary school. *Journal of Abnormal Child Psychology, 42*, 343–354. doi:10.1007/s10802-013-9768-2

Dishion, T. J., Shaw, D., Connell, A., Gardner, F., Weaver, C., & Wilson, M. (2008). The Family Check-Up with high-risk indigent families: Preventing problem behaviour by increasing parents' positive behaviour support in early childhood. *Child Development, 79*, 1395–1414. doi:10.1111/j.1467-8624.2008.01195.x

Frankenburg, W. K., Dodds, J., Archer, P., Shapiro, H., & Bresnick, B. (1992). The Denver II: A major revision and restandardization of the Denver Developmental Screening Test. *Pediatrics, 89*, 91–97.

Hutchings, J. (2013). *The Little Parent Handbook*. Bangor, UK: Children's Early Intervention Trust.

Hutchings, J., Lane, E., & Kelly, J. (2004). Comparison of two treatments for children with severely disruptive behaviours: A four-year follow-up. *Behavioural and Cognitive Psychotherapy, 32*, 15–30.

Hutchings, J., Appleton, P., Smith, M., Lane, E., & Nash, S. (2002). Evaluation of two treatments for children with severe behaviour problems: Child behaviour and maternal mental health outcomes. *Behavioural and Cognitive Psychotherapy, 30*, 279–295. doi:10.1017/S1352465802003041

Rusconi-Serpa, S., Rossignol, A. S., & McDonough, S. C. (2009). Video feedback in parent-infant treatments. *Child Adolescent Psychiatric Clinical North America, 18*, 735–751.

Squires, J., Potter, L., & Bricker, D. (1999). *The ages and stages user's guide*. Baltimore, MD: Paul H. Brookes Publishing.

Williams, M. E., Hutchings, J., Bywater, T., Daley, D., & Whitaker, C. J. (2013). Schedule of Growing Skills II: Pilot study of an alternative scoring method. *Psychology, 4*, 143–152.

Enhancing Parenting Skills (EPaS) observation checklist

The EPaS programme is a strengths-based programme

The observation provides an opportunity to identify *positive* parenting behaviours that you see during the observation, and which you might want to ask the parent to do more of. Note *Yes/No* or *not applicable (N/A)* to the observation situation and note any examples linked to the behaviours you have observed that you could use in your case analysis.

	Behaviour observed	*Yes/No/N/A*
1	The parent used positive strategies to get the child's attention.	
2	The child gave appropriate attention to the parent.	
3	The parent gave clear and specific instructions.	
4	The parent explained the reasons for the instructions.	
5	The child followed the instructions.	
6	The parent remained calm if the child did not follow the instructions.	
7	The parent gave specific labelled praise for the child's activities with words (building, sorting, etc.).	
8	The parent shared their own feelings with the child.	
9	The parent's praise was given enthusiastically.	
10	The parent gave appropriate attention to the child with non-verbal responses, eye contact, body language . . .	
11	The child responded positively to parental attention.	
12	The parent labelled the child's behaviours (working quietly, concentrating).	
13	The parent labelled the child's feelings ("you look happy", "you look frustrated").	
14	The parent prompted the child with suggestions of things to do (problem-solving).	
15	The parent ignored minor challenging behaviour.	
16	The parent redirected problem behaviour towards constructive behaviour.	
17	The parent gave the child time to change activity.	
18	The environment was free of distractions (TV off etc.).	
19	The home had appropriate toys and books for the child.	
20	The parent and child treated each other respectfully.	

Things your child enjoys

Name of child _____ Age _____

Please fill this in when you actually see the child doing something they enjoy, not from memory.

Food	Sweets/snacks	Drinks
_____	_____	_____
_____	_____	_____
_____	_____	_____
_____	_____	_____

Toys	Activities	TV programmes
_____	_____	_____
_____	_____	_____
_____	_____	_____
_____	_____	_____

People	Things that calm him/her when upset
_____	_____
_____	_____
_____	_____
_____	_____

Anything special at bedtime or other times, e.g. stories, cuddles

_____

_____

Any other observations

_____

Things your child enjoys

Name of child   *S*   Age   *26 months*

Please fill this in when you actually see the child doing something they enjoy, not from memory.

Food	**Sweets/snacks**	**Drinks**
Fish fingers	*Milky bars*	*Milk*
Peas	*Chocolate buttons*	*Orange squash*
Alphabites	*Assorted crisps*	*Lemon squash*
_____	_____	*Mixed squash*

Toys	**Activities**	**TV programmes**
Telephone	*Jigsaws*	*Disney Club*
Teddies Books	*Playing with ball*	*Tots TV*
Stickle Bricks	*Crayons and books*	*TaleSpin*
_____	_____	*Children's Ward*

People

D_____
M
Sh_____
J S_____

Things that calm him/her when upset

Cuddles with Mum
(acts as dad)   *Cuddles with teddy*_____
_____
_____

Anything special at bedtime or other times, e.g. stories, cuddles
Cuddles and kisses her teddies, doll and dummy
_____

Any other observations
Loves looking at her books on her own or with anyone who will sit with her to look at them
_____

Things your child can do

(This will help you to be sure that your expectations about your child are realistic and achievable and build on his or her strengths)

Name of child: _____ Age: _____

Social skills
Examples: getting on with others, helping other people, showing interest in others, negotiating for things, asking for help, waiting for something.

Physical skills
Examples: riding a bike, walking, climbing, swimming.

Fine motor skills
Examples: holding a crayon, doing a puzzle, posting box.

Language
Examples: making sounds, naming objects, making requests for things, explaining things, listening to or telling a story.

Toileting
Examples: dry at night, going independently to the toilet in the day, asking when they need help, showing when they are wet or dirty.

Eating
Examples: sitting at the table, using a knife and fork independently, feeding themselves with help, finger feeding.

Playing skills
Examples: imitating others, playing alone for a few minutes, make-believe play.

Things your child can do

Name of child _____ Age _____

Social skills

Examples: getting on with others, helping other people, showing interest in others, negotiating for things, asking for help, waiting for something.

Likes to help do washing up, clearing. If it's a new person, she becomes very shy. She likes to see what other people are doing, does not ask for help, then gets frustrated, she is very impatient, does not wait for something, has to have things done straight away – if not, goes into a temper.

Physical skills

Examples: riding a bike, walking, climbing, swimming.

Can sit on a bike and push with her feet, does quite a bit of walking with reins on, likes climbing, has not been swimming but imitates in the bath.

Fine motor skills

Examples: holding a crayon, doing a puzzle, posting box.

Holds a crayon and can do squiggles and tries to copy what you do, can do puzzles if supervised.

Language

Examples: making sounds, naming objects, making requests for things, explaining things, listening to or telling a story.

Can repeat the alphabet, and make sounds of animals, of a car, etc. can name most objects, finds it hard to explain things, gets frustrated if I do not understand. Likes listening to stories or trying to read herself.

Toileting

Examples: dry at night, going independently to the toilet in the day, asking when they need help, showing when they are wet or dirty.

Is not at this stage yet although she will tell me when she is dirty. And has just started to ask for the potty when nappy is being changed.

Eating

Examples: sitting at the table, using a knife and fork independently, feeding themselves with help, finger feeding.

Will sit at the table on her little chair, uses spoon and fork, is feeding herself really well now.

Playing skills

Examples: imitating others, playing alone for a few minutes, make-believe play.

Is very quick to pick new things up – for example, toy with different shapes and movements to pop the toys up. Was shown once, then she went and did it on her own, tends to have someone with her rather than on her own.

Consent for video-recording of parent–child interaction

I, ..., agree that my child and I will be video-recorded during a brief interaction between us.

I understand that the purpose of the recording is to contribute to the formulation of intervention goals. I understand that the recording will be destroyed as soon as we have agreed our intervention package.

I AGREE to the recording, which will be available to me to view should I so desire.

Signed: ....

Date: ....

EPaS checklist for assessment session 3 activities

	Activity	Completed (Yes/No)
1	Collect the records completed by parents since the last session or trouble shoot to find record keeping solutions	
2	Explain the observation plan and the activity that had been agreed with the parent	
3	If relevant. get the completed consent to video	
4	Undertake the observation	
5	Set up the parent record keeping activity – the "Things Your Child Enjoys" and "Things Your Child Can Do"	
6	Provide a replied paid envelope for the parent to return them to you for inclusion in the case analysis	
7	Explain what will happen next time: presentation of the case analysis	
8	Arrange the next appointment	
9	Close the session by praising the parent's commitment to helping their child	
10	Complete the EPaS observation checklist after the session	

8 Developing a case analysis

Many interventions fail through lack of sufficient information about the current situation and failure to identify why problem behaviour is occurring and to agree realistic, achievable targets. This chapter describes the tools for analysing the functions of problem behaviour and identifying new adaptive behaviour, and the process of developing a case analysis to share with a parent or parents. Chapter 9 includes a case example.

It is helpful if parents can return the two questionnaires that they were given as a home activity at the end of the observation session, the "Things your child can do" and "Things your child enjoys". These may contain information that will be useful in the case analysis. It is usually effective to leave a stamped, addressed envelope with the family, so they can return the questionnaires to you.

Throughout the process of collecting information about the child and their circumstances, you have been engaging the parent collaboratively. This is fundamentally important, as the intervention goal (at a general level) is to build parents' skills in observing their child's behaviour accurately, identifying the functions of problem behaviour and being able to support their child in developmentally achievable goals. It is this process that will enable parents to tackle future problems and ensure both the maintenance of any changes and the generalisation of the learned skills to future situations and challenges.

The EPaS case analysis is based on the framework developed by Goldiamond (1974, 1975) and makes use of all of the information that has been gathered during the assessment phase that you and the parents have collected together. The case analysis provides an understanding of the child and their history, the problem history and current function(s), the skills and strengths of the child and parents, previous solutions to problems that the parents have achieved, the assets available in the situation that will support change, and some potential short- and longer-term goals. It will give a clear description of the problem, a functional description of why it is likely to be occurring, and will identify the target parent and child behaviours that will help to establish developmentally achievable alternative behaviours.

The assessment process has provided information about the specific problem (or problems) in terms of when and where it occurred, who was present when it occurred, whether it occurred at a particular time of day (when a child might be hungry or tired) or whether the child was worried about what was going to happen next. These records enable you to identify the frequency and intensity of the problem, and whether the same problem behaviour functions to achieve different outcomes for the child in different situations.

The key step is to identify the events occurring around each problem behaviour that will help to explain it. This will clarify what is triggering and maintaining it and whether the behaviour achieves some positive consequence, enables the child to avoid a demand, is developmentally unachievable or results in avoidance of an anxiety-provoking situation. This step is needed to formulate potential goals and to develop a plan to achieve them.

If the problem involves disputes between siblings, it is not unusual for one child to be seen as having the problem – for example, hitting another child – when some aspect of the other child's behaviour may be triggering the problem but be less obvious to the parent. This could be, for example, behaviours such as teasing, taking a toy, name-calling or other provocative behaviour. This is another important reason for analysing the behaviour within the situation in which it occurs. Hitting is not acceptable and the child needs to learn a different response to provocation. However, without an understanding of the triggers, when the child does learn to handle the situation differently the problem can sometimes shift from one child to another child in the family. In this situation, one of the goals may include encouraging the development of friendship skills between siblings.

It is important to help parents to see problem behaviour as a skill deficit, an alternative behaviour that the child has not yet learned. Therefore, identifying the necessary and achievable replacement skills and behaviours is essential. For some children, maybe more noticeably in children with autistic spectrum problems, social skills deficits and an inability to understand how other people are feeling are probable. This can be associated with anxiety in social situations. This is why the case analysis needs to be very detailed – to build on the knowledge obtained through the assessment process and to identify (with the parents) small, developmentally achievable goals that will enable the child (and parents) to experience success.

Current life circumstances are an important factor that might affect parents' capacity to implement changes – for example, adult relationships or housing problems, neighbourhood challenges or mental health or financial difficulties. However, Patterson, Forgatch, Yoerger and Stoolmiller (1998) have shown that, although parenting capacity can be compromised by a variety of stresses, these things affect the parents and only indirectly the child. It is parenting behaviour that predicts child behaviour, not the environmental stresses per se. Many parents of children with challenging behaviour do a great job meeting their children's needs, despite environmental stresses. Our own studies, and others, have shown that parents of challenging children who live in socially disadvantaged circumstances and/or are dealing with other stressful events can develop positive parenting skills when engaged in collaborative programmes, and achieve positive outcomes for their children, despite their other difficulties (Gardner, Hutchings, Bywater and Whitaker, 2010; Hartman, Stage and Webster-Stratton, 2003).

It is essential to distinguish between current and historic contributions to problems. Historic factors may – indeed, almost certainly will – have contributed to the present pattern of behaviour and may explain how it has been learned but may no longer be directly relevant. For example, night-time problems may have initially been established when a child was unwell but now be maintained by attention. What has happened in the past and how the child has behaved in the past are strong predictors of how children will behave in the future. However, the case formulation is based on the current circumstances and reinforcement contexts, whilst acknowledging how developmental challenges and previous learning history have contributed.

The information gathered during the assessment phase provides evidence about parental cognitions or understandings about their child's behaviour and also about how realistic their expectations are. The assessment phase has been helping parents to become more accurate in their observation of their children's behaviour, and their motivation to support their child is clearly evidenced by their willingness to work with you on a programme.

The principles that we encourage parents to apply to their children are also important for us to model in working with families. Our own research has shown that, in parent groups, the extent of leader praise and encouragement of parents predicts the extent to which parents then praise their children at home (Eames et al., 2010). The principle that parents are models for their children's behaviour applies equally to ourselves when we are working with parents.

Using an adapted Goldiamond (1975) structure, developing the case analysis is a four-step process. There is a blank case analysis sheet and intervention agreement form at the end of this chapter. Chapter 9 contains a worked example.

Step 1: Background information

This is a brief summary of the information gathered, including the child's history, child and parent assets and skills. Goldiamond suggests that the first step is to feed back information to the parents that they have given to you. Then they have the opportunity to see that you have fully understood the situation and the problem and/or to correct any errors or misunderstandings.

Step 2: The problem

This is a clear description of the problem(s) and the associated circumstances.

Step 3: The function

This is a tentative understanding of why the problem(s) are occurring. The various information sources should be used to provide a clear enough description of the problem to enable a tentative understanding of why it is occurring.

Step 4: Targets

This is the identification of a developmentally achievable target behaviour, or behaviours, that will replace the problem behaviour(s) and the assets and resources that will help to achieve this.

Presentation of the case analysis to the parents

This involves sharing your tentative case analysis with the parents, agreeing a contract, specifying the goals that you will work on together and establishing the first intervention activities. The weekly intervention plan is described in Chapter 10. This involves agreement on the short-term work plan for the coming week, the assets that you have observed (or learned about) that demonstrate that the weekly targets are achievable and how the short-term targets relate to the intervention goals.

Step 1: Background

In introducing the case analysis, it is helpful to remind parents about the successes that they have had in teaching things to their children, and about their motivation for seeking help at the present time. Then feed back a general summary of the information provided, including what you have learned of the child's general history, their specific developmental challenges, etc. This should include reference to other sources of support, skills and assets that the parents have evidenced, and to problems previously solved. Responses to questions on the constructional questionnaire are useful here because they specifically explore parental problem-solving strategies.

This is also the time when you can feed back the results of the three standardised parent report questionnaires: the SDQ, the Arnold-O'Leary Parenting Scale and the Warwick-Edinburgh Mental Well-being Scale that were introduced in Chapter 5. If the parents reported the child as being in the high or clinical range on the SDQ (Goodman, 1997) on either the Total Scale or any of the subscales, you can discuss this in terms of their having a child who is harder to parent than most children. Also, it is unlikely that the child will be in the clinical range on all of the subscales, so you can reflect on areas where the child does or does not need more help. There is also an impact scale for assessing the extent to which problems impact on the child's everyday functioning and may have contributed to the parents' motivation to seek help for their child.

The results from the Arnold-O'Leary Parenting Scale (Arnold, O'Leary, Wolff and Acker, 1993) enable you to discuss parenting strategies in general with the parent, although you can return to this in more detail when you have completed the functional analysis. The three subscales of Laxness, Over-reactivity and Verbosity provide evidence of the parent's style and whether they find it difficult to set limits (Laxness), engage in too much debate (Verbosity) or have a tendency to respond to problems with anger (Over-reactivity). This can help to identify patterns of parenting that are challenging and those that are not. It is important that positive results are fed back first, but where parents' responses have suggested a problematic pattern in one of these areas this can generally be framed as a learned response to the challenges presented by their child that has occasionally been successful.

You have collected a lot of information about the parents, their parenting style and their specific responses to problem behaviours. One way to assess parental behaviour is to relate it to the five key parenting skills described in *The Little Parent Handbook* (Hutchings, 2013). These five key areas are relationship building skills, praising and rewarding positive behaviour, clear instruction giving, the ability to ignore minor misdemeanours and problems, and consistent handling of the management of problem behaviour. These are aspects of parenting behaviour that promote positive outcomes and where parenting skill deficits tend to reinforce problematic child behaviour. It will be important to feed back to parents their parenting skills, and this – together with feedback from the Arnold O'Leary Parenting Scale – will give you a framework for deciding which parenting behaviours to focus on.

All 14 items of the Warwick–Edinburgh Mental Well-being Scale (WEMWBS) ask about positive aspects of mental well-being, so higher scores indicate positive mental health. There is no clinical cut-off, as it was designed as a population screening tool but, as described earlier, it has been shown to demonstrate clinically significant changes in parenting trials (scores for mean and clinical groups are included in Appendix 3). If the parents have a low score, they should be thanked for their honesty in sharing how they feel. This could also be fed back in a positive way in terms of the challenges that the parents face, with reassurance that, as parents start to find solutions to problems, this is likely to have a positive impact on their well-being (http://wrap.warwick.ac.uk/543/1/WRAP_Stewart_Brown_Warwick_Edinburgh.pdfUserguide). If parents report a very low score, you also probably need to suggest that they contact their GP and consider addressing this as a separate problem. However, all of our parenting trials, individual and group, have shown significant improvements in parental mental health.

The information from the "Things your child can do" assessment is helpful in identifying the child's developmental level and likely short-term achievable targets. The "Things your child enjoys" information is used again in setting up intervention strategies because it provides information on possible reinforcers.

Step 2: The problem

Here you are only offering an accurate description of the child's behaviour at the present time and the circumstances surrounding it. You will need to draw on a number of information sources, the constructional interview, the typical day interview, the problems identified on the Three-Problem Rating Scale, any records that the parents have kept and your observations. This description includes all of the circumstances associated with the problem situation, who is present, what is asked of the child, etc. A bedtime problem might only occur when one parent gives the instruction, in the presence of particular people or when the child is tired or hungry. It might only occur when there is a particular programme on the TV that the child wants to watch.

Step 3: The function

This step involves sharing with the parents an understanding of why the problem is occurring, what its function is for the child and what might be maintaining it (in terms of both the child's behaviour and that of the parents and others). It can be helpful to draw in some of the history information as a way to understand why the child may have developed the difficulties. This can include any specific developmental challenges or skill deficits that a child has and it will be important to be very clear about these in defining intervention goals. History information may also help to explain some of the reasons why parents, at times, may have allowed children to persist with problem behaviour rather than helping them to develop more socially acceptable behaviour. Often this is because parents recognise that their child has special needs. Sometimes parents of children with developmental challenges can be overprotective, for good reasons. However, assuming that the child's developmental challenges ("It's because of his autism or ADHD") explain the behaviour can be a barrier to helping a child towards independence and social acceptability in other situations, and with other people. The child may have developmental challenges, but our recent autism parenting trial demonstrated that it was the associated behavioural challenges that parents found most difficult to deal with, and could be addressed despite the other difficulties (Hutchings, Pearson-Blunt, Pasteur, Healy and Williams, 2016)

The parents' behaviour might have been both logical and appropriate at the time, but may have resulted in the development of a problem, and the current situation. For example, a bedtime problem can develop because, at one time, the child was ill and the parent needed to spend time with them and nurse them to sleep or provide them with drinks or other care during the night. However, this may have become a persistent problem, reinforced in other ways when the initial reason for the parental response no longer exists. Why the behaviour is occurring must be considered in terms of what function the behaviour is achieving for the child at the current time and how the behaviour of parents, or others, might be contributing to this.

Functions of child behaviour – general principles

A framework for identifying possible functions is presented below and summarised in the Functional Assessment Checklist at the end of the chapter. (Examples of functions of a range of typical problems are described in the case analysis example in Chapter 9 and in the intervention examples in Chapters 13–18.)

The same problem behaviour can serve different functions

The function of problem behaviour must be clearly identified and each behaviour must be understood in its own context. The same problem behaviour, e.g. a tantrum, can serve several different functions for the same child. It can be a way of avoiding an instruction, such as to go to bed; a way of getting a demand met, such as for sweets or a drink; and/or a way of dealing with frustration and generating help when things go wrong. A problem behaviour may get attention, but it might also be because the child cannot avoid the problem because the alternative behaviour is developmentally beyond them. This is why focusing on problems will fail, because the replacement behaviours are not related to the problem behaviour per se, but to its function. Therefore, it is important to look at each of the situations where problems occur, because each of these different situations may need to be dealt with in different ways and problems will need to be prioritised.

The same behaviour can serve different functions for different children. One child's refusal to go to school might be because they are being teased and have become anxious about school; another child may refuse to go to school because they are afraid that their mother might be hurt if they are not there to protect her or they may have a sick parent that they do not want to leave; another child might find being at home more reinforcing than school, because they can play computer games all day; another child can get reinforcement from meeting other truanting friends and engaging in risky, adrenalin-inducing activities, such as shoplifting.

What follows is a summary of possible functions of problem behaviours. These are also further explored (with additional examples) in Chapters 13–18. For a more detailed understanding of functional analysis, see Malott and Shane (2014).

i) Attention

One of the most frequently used explanations for problem behaviour is that it is for attention. This may be the case, and it may be the only function. Young children particularly need attention and if they cannot get it in positive ways they can escalate problem behaviour, because at one level "any attention is better than none". However, the need for attention may only be part of the explanation. The analysis also needs to identify why a child might use problem behaviour to get attention. It may be due to lack of attention for appropriate behaviour and/or lack of skills to get attention in a different way. Can the child achieve the required alternative behaviour? A key question to ask is whether teaching is needed to establish the required behaviour, or whether is it developmentally unachievable for the child. Getting attention for problem behaviour is, in any case, a risky strategy, since it can get inconsistent responses from adults and be alternately rewarded and punished (as in the coercive cycle described by Patterson, 1982), in which both parents and child escalate their behaviour and are alternately and intermittently rewarded. The attention that rewards the behaviour may not be particularly pleasant, but, in the environment of a young child where the child gets insufficient positive attention, it may suffice in the short term.

In some cases, children can provoke negative attention from parents, because when the parents become calm and regret their response, they then give the child affection. In this case, it is a chain of responses that is reinforced. I first observed this pattern working with child protection cases in the 1970s.

ii) The problem behaviour may achieve a tangible reward

Although negative parental attention may have established problem behaviours, it is likely, over time, to cease to be reinforcing, or even become aversive, and children are likely to use problematic behaviour to achieve short-term tangible reinforcers instead.

Problem behaviour can result in the child's demand for something being met. Parents may "give in" to avoid confrontation, such as giving a child a biscuit or sweets at the supermarket till. The problem behaviour may be a threat that achieves a reward, for example saying to another child "give me that toy or I will hit you" or the child may engage in an aggressive behaviour that ceases when the demand for the biscuit is met.

Particularly in the case of children with developmental challenges, problematic behaviour can be rewarded by people other than the parents. One mother described how her daughter, who had a severe developmental disability, would grab a bar of chocolate in the local shop, put it in her mouth and bite into it (without taking off the wrapping). The mother was trying to be consistent, both offering to pay for the item and get her daughter to give it back. However, the shopkeeper did not want to be paid, nor to take the item back – her behaviour suggested that she believed that the child could not help it. However, reinforcing such behaviour doubly handicaps a child, since the likely response from the mother is to stop taking her daughter to the shop, to avoid both the embarrassment and the inadvertent reinforcement of the child's behaviour. Unfortunately, this then further restricts the child's everyday experiences.

iii) The child's demand is immediately complied with by the parent

Sometimes the child does not have tantrums because the parent has learned to comply with the child's demands immediately, so avoiding a tantrum. Identifying this pattern of reward is harder, because the parent has learned to pre-empt problem child behaviour by meeting the demand before the child has a tantrum. We worked with one 13-year-old child with a significant developmental difficulty who demanded that cola and crisps were on the table when he arrived home from school in a taxi. His past very aggressive tantrums had led his mother to avoid any confrontation by providing what he wanted before he asked for it. Teaching him to greet his mum, and wait for his cola and crisps, took some time.

iv) Avoiding or resisting following an instruction

Non-compliance with instructions is a feature of children with behavioural problems. There are a number of reasons why children fail to follow instructions:

a. The child may not have been taught what to do (it may be developmentally appropriate but needs teaching). It may be that the child needs to learn earlier skills like paying attention and giving eye contact.
b. Refusal could be because the child cannot do what is being asked (the instruction is not developmentally appropriate, so a different target behaviour is needed).
c. It could be because what the child is doing at the time – playing with Lego, watching TV, etc. – is more reinforcing than what they are being asked to do, such as getting ready for bed, and their problem behaviour is reinforced because they get more play time, etc.
d. The child may not have been given sufficient time to process the instruction. It could be that the child's need for time to adjust to a change has been ignored. This need for transition time from one activity to another can be a particular challenge for children with developmental difficulties.
e. Sometimes the problem occurs because the child has not understood what is required of them. The task is developmentally appropriate, but not explained clearly enough. This is a particular challenge for children whose language skills may not be sufficient to correctly interpret what is required of them.
f. Sometimes parental behaviour is so inconsistent that the child does not know what is expected of them at any particular time.

v) The child's behaviour generates support

Some problem behaviours generate help to deal with frustration. Sometimes children are frustrated by their own failure at some activity and a tantrum is a call for help. The child may have been doing a puzzle, building a tower or trying to get dressed. This can often be a problem for inattentive children, such as those diagnosed as having ADHD (who tend to rush at tasks) or those with developmental challenges (who may have communication difficulties).

vi) The behaviour removes an aversive situation

Aggressive responding to a perceived or actual threat or aversive situation can remove the threat – for example, when a child behaves aggressively towards someone who has been unkind to them, maybe in response to teasing or being excluded.

vii) The behaviour avoids a threatening or aversive situation

Some behaviours serve to reduce stress through avoidance of what appear to be problem situations. This can be one of the reasons for non-compliance associated with some school refusal where school is associated with bullying or with demands to do things that the child finds challenging or situations where the child is afraid of making a mistake or being punished but it can also occur in a number of other situations that generate anxiety, such as social situations or transitions from one activity to another for children with autistic spectrum problems. This could also apply to children with other specific difficulties, such as dyslexia, who can avoid situations that demand the skills that they find challenging. More severe forms of avoidance that produce severe physiological responses can sometimes be described as phobias.

These examples should help to guide you in deciding some tentative functions for the problem behaviours and the next step is the identification of alternative behaviours that will achieve the same or similar goals for the child. A checklist of these possible functions is included at the end of the chapter and remember that many times a behaviour can achieve more than one function.

Step 4: Targets – identifying the developmentally achievable alternative target behaviours

Decisions about the identified function(s) of problem behaviour(s) leads to tentative identification of the overall intervention goal for that problem behaviour.

i) **Behaviour that functions to get attention.** If this is the only function of the behaviour, then the goal will be to increase attention for pro-social behaviour. In order to reliably reduce attention-seeking behaviour the child needs to get at least four times more attention for positive behaviour than for problem behaviour (Hutchings, 2013). Encouraging child-led activities that strengthen the parent–child relationship will often also be included as part of the intervention plan even if the behaviour also serves other functions, such as avoiding following instructions. This is because pairing praise with other reinforcers that children enjoy helps to strengthen the reinforcing power of parents' positive attention. This is particularly important for children for whom the key reinforcers are tangible rather than social.

ii) **Problems that result in children achieving tangible rewards**. Problem behaviours involving rewards are telling you what the reinforcers are for the child and can be used in helping the child to achieve things that the parent wants. This could be a biscuit or being allowed to stay up and watch TV. Addressing these problems involves deciding if, and when, the child can have the reward – for example, television after finishing their homework, or an ice cream after eating a meal. The goal might be helping the child to learn to wait for the reward. Possibly the behaviour means that the child stays up later than the parents want. This may involve helping the child to accept that they can only stay up later on a night when there is no school the next day, or it may involve the parent recording a favourite TV programme for viewing the next day.

iii) **The child's demands are immediately complied with by the parent**. This describes situations where the parent gives the child the reward that they want without the child behaving badly, because they know what will happen if they do not do this and they want to avoid a tantrum. The example described earlier of the child requiring cola and crisps took time to deal with, as he was 13 and could be extremely violent. His single-parent mum was afraid of him, and changing this pattern of behaviour required a lot of home-based support for her, which eventually resulted in him achieving the goal of greeting his mum and asking politely for the cola and crisps.

These problems can occur particularly in public places like supermarkets, where other people are present. Interventions generally involve ensuring that the parent can teach the required skills at home before exposing themselves and the child to public situations. It is generally agreed that it is OK for the child to choose something in the supermarket, but that to achieve this the child needs to comply with a series of tasks, such as helping to find items for the parents' trolley, holding the trolley, etc. All of this needs to be practised and discussed prior to arriving at the supermarket.

iv) **The child is non-compliant, refuses to follow instructions.**

a) If the behaviour is achievable but has not been taught, this will require a clear teaching strategy and – particularly if it has been associated with conflict – this might be a situation where a small incentive would help.

b) If the behaviour required is developmentally inappropriate, evidence about the child's current level of functioning will be needed to decide on a developmentally appropriate achievable goal. Mealtime goals associated with getting a child to sit at the table may need to be made much smaller, such as sitting for five minutes at the table or ensuring that food is only eaten at the table. Allowing the child initially to come and go from the table at will, but only eat when at the table, may be a first step. This problem behaviour might also be achieving attention, so you might need to included in the plan that no attention is ensured when the child is not at the table, and only to give attention at other times unrelated to mealtimes.

c) If the behaviour that the child is currently engaged in is more reinforcing than following the instruction, then making the reinforcing behaviour contingent on following the instruction is likely to be the goal. For example, part of the solution might be teaching the child that when they follow the instruction they can play on their PlayStation.

d) Sometimes a problem occurs because a child needs time to process an instruction, and the solution may involve considering what sort of transition warnings would be developmentally appropriate and understood by the child. Children who are poor at following instructions can often be bombarded with repeated instructions, which can generate stress for both the parent and the child and add to the child's unwillingness to comply.

e) If the child does not understand what they are being asked to do, the problem is a communication failure. This is an example of a skill deficit and/or of an unrealistic expectation on the part of the parents, and needs addressing through a clearer understanding of the child's communication and comprehension skills, which leads to realistic goals. For some children, particularly those with developmental challenges, learning to attend can be a challenge. They may be surrounded by ongoing stimulation from televisions, etc. that will need addressing, and the goal will be to find effective strategies to gain the child's attention before focusing on giving an instruction. Attention can be prompted in child-led play situations. When asking "Would you like the toy, etc.", holding it near to the face and waiting until the child gives fleeting eye contact before giving it to them.

  f) The child does not know what is expected of them because rules/ expectations are inconsistent. This problem arises as described by the coercive cycle, where the child's behaviour is sometimes reinforced and sometimes punished. It can often depend on other things that are affecting the parents and their energy level at the time. This issue of consistency can involve other adults in the child's life, although it is important if only working with one parent that we focus them on the idea that their child will learn what to expect from them if they are consistent, regardless of how other people behave. It is also important to address one issue at a time, so that both the parents and child experience success in adopting new strategies.

v) **The child's behaviour generates support.** Dealing with frustration can be particularly difficult for children with developmental problems – for example, a child with ADHD who rushes at things and makes mistakes. But our goal is that the child learns how self-calm without adult help, as it is a skill that they will need in lots of situations outside the home. This may involve helping parents to coach children in the self-calming strategies that will help them to stay calm and try again, or it could involve helping the child to learn to ask for help.

  Solutions to many of these functions will include coaching the child in self-calming strategies and self-talk, although this is not effective when the child is disregulated and may only add attention to a problematic behaviour. But this is very helpful at a time when the child is calm and can problem-solve and practise how they will handle the situation.

vi) **The child's behaviour removes an aversive situation.** Aggression can be a response to a perceived or actual threat or a response to being teased, in order to terminate the behaviour of the other person. Sometimes this is provoked by the other child in order to draw attention to the behaviour of the child, who may not be particularly liked. As with the previous category, this requires goals that might include: learning to stay calm and/or to seek the help of someone else; or finding ways of responding assertively rather than aggressively, to let the other child know that their behaviour was unfriendly.

vii) **The behaviour avoids a threatening or aversive situation.** Children can avoid situations or activities that make them anxious. Whatever the cause of the avoidant responses, the goal will generally be very small steps towards the desired behaviour in a process known as desensitization. This is discussed in the case example in Chapter 9, although it is also helpful to see if whatever makes the child anxious can be changed, as well. For the child that did not like to leave his mother to go to school, because he believed that his presence kept her safe from her abusive partner, a plan of support for his mother was needed for him to start going to school again. For a child that worried about failure at school, working with both parents and school to address this problem and ensure that things she was asked to do were developmentally achievable and that in test situations she was allowed to sit in a room away from other children helped her to deal with this situation. For one child who avoided going to school because he was being bullied, the programme involved helping his mother to recognise that, to reduce bullying, his clothes were dirty and smelly and that she needed to address this.

Having tentatively identified the function of the child's behaviour(s) you will also have identified the behaviour of others that might be maintaining the problem. This will have provided a lot of information about the pattern of interaction between the child and the parents, so it should identify the extent to which the parents will need help in learning to give more positive attention generally to the child, in being more specific and clear in instruction giving and in being able to ignore minor problems, etc. The EPaS Parenting Behaviour Observer Rating Scale will have given you an opportunity to reflect on the parenting behaviours you have observed, or learned about, through the interview or other sources, including ABC records and the Arnold-O'Leary Parenting Scale.

Having worked through this process, you are ready to identify possible goals that address both parental concerns and the apparent functions of the problem behaviours, although this remains tentative until it is tested in the intervention. Decisions on goals also need to consider parental assets and skills that will ensure that the goals are achievable. Chapters 13–18 contain brief case examples, suggesting ideas for addressing many of these problems.

Presentation of the case analysis to the parents

Having developed the case analysis, this is then presented to the parents, describing the history, particular challenges and needs of the child, and your understanding of any specific developmental problems that need to be acknowledged in identifying goals for intervention. You will also need to identify the particular challenges to parenting implied by the child's needs.

It is likely to take almost an hour to present and discuss your analysis with the parents. Your case analysis is introduced as a summary of the information that you have gathered and the parents are free at any time to clarify any misunderstandings and add any information. The parents are already collaborating with you, and their contribution in terms of record sheets, questionnaires, etc. should be acknowledged.

When you have discussed your case analysis with the parents, you should complete the Intervention Agreement together (see the end of this chapter). Chapter 9 contains sample case information, the case analysis and Intervention Agreement.

Having shared your understanding of the situation and how and why the problem behaviour may be occurring, it is important that the parents agree to the intervention goals. Your task in working with them is to ensure that their goals are pro-social and developmentally appropriate, and that they understand the need to work on small, realistic and achievable targets that will enable them and their child to achieve these goals successfully.

There is a checklist of session activities at the end of the chapter.

References

Arnold, D. S., O'Leary, S. G., Wolff, L. S., & Acker, M. M. (1993). The parenting scale: A measure of dysfunctional parenting in discipline situations. *Psychological Assessment, 5*, 137–144.

Eames, C., Daley, D., Hutchings, J., Whitaker, C. J., Bywater, T., Jones, K. & Hughes, J. C. (2010). The impact of group leaders behaviour on parents' acquisition of key parenting skills during parent training. *Behaviour Research and Therapy, 48*, 1221–1226.

Gardner, F., Hutchings, J., Bywater, T., & Whitaker, C. J. (2010). Who benefits and how does it work? Moderators and mediators of outcome in an effectiveness trial of a parenting intervention in multiple 'Sure Start' services. *Journal of Clinical Child and Adolescent Psychology, 39*, 568–580.

Goldiamond, I. (1974). Towards a constructional approach to social problems. *Behaviourism, 2*, 1–84.

Goldiamond, I. (1975). A constructional approach to self control. In: A. Schwartz & I. Goldiamond (Eds.), *Social casework: A behavioural approach*. New York: Columbia University Press.

Goodman, R. (1997). The Strengths and Difficulties Questionnaire: A research note. *Journal of Child Psychology and Psychiatry, 38*, 581–586.

Hartman, R. R., Stage, S. A., & Webster-Stratton, C. (2003). A growth curve analysis of parent training outcomes: examining the influence of child risk factors (inattention, impulsivity, and hyperactivity problems), parental and family risk factors. *Journal of Child Psychology and Psychiatry, 44*, 388–398.

Hutchings, J. (2013). *The Little Parent Handbook*. Bangor, Wales: Children's Early Intervention Trust.

Hutchings, J., Pearson-Blunt, R., Pasteur, M.-A., Healy, H., & Williams, M. E. (2016). A pilot trial of the Incredible Years® Autism Spectrum and Language Delays programme. *Good Autism Practice Journal, 17*, 15–22.

Malott, R. W. and Shane, J. T. (2014). *Principles of behaviour*, 7th edition. Oxford: Routledge.

Patterson, G. R. (1982). *Coercive family process*. Eugene, OR: Castalia,.

Patterson, G. R., Forgatch, M. S., Yoerger, K. L., & Stoolmiller, M. (1998). Variables that initiate and maintain an early-onset trajectory for juvenile offending. *Development and Psychopathology, 10*(3), 531–547.

Case analysis sheet

Step 1: Background

This is a brief summary of the information gathered, including the history of the child. Note any information that the parent has given you, so that they have the opportunity to see that you have fully understood the situation and the problem, and also their skills and resources, general problem-solving strategies and previous successes. It forms a picture of the child and their general circumstances.

Step 2: The problem

This is a clear description of the problem and all of the circumstances associated with it, time of day, who present, etc.

Step 3: The function

This is the tentative understanding of why the problem might be occurring.

There may be a number of possible explanations and the various information sources should provide a sufficiently clear description of the problem to enable a tentative understanding of why it is occurring.

Step 4: Targets

This is the identification of developmentally appropriate target behaviour(s) which will replace the problem behaviour(s) and the assets and resources which will help to achieve this.

Intervention agreement

This agreement is made between:

Name: _____ (parent)

Name: _____ (case worker)

The goals relate to: _____ (name of child)

We will work together to achieve the following goal/goals:
(list a maximum of three goal areas)

1

2

3

To achieve these goals:

I, the case worker, agree to visit weekly and to work together to set up weekly targets towards the agreed goals. I will arrange our weekly appointments in advance and try to let you know if for any reason I will be unable to make the appointment.

_____ Signature _____ Date

I, the parent, agree to work together to agreed weekly targets and keep agreed progress records. I will endeavour to notify you if I cannot keep an appointment.

_____ Signature _____ Date

Functional assessment checklist

Possible function	Yes/Maybe/No
i) **Attention** Child is using the behaviour to get attention: a) in the absence of sufficient attention for positive behaviour b) because afterwards when calm the parent gives them positive attention/affection	
ii) **The problem behaviour may achieve a tangible reward** Child uses the behaviour to achieve other tangible rewards: staying up, drinks, etc.	
iii) **The child's demand is immediately complied with by the parent** Child's tantrums have resulted in the parent giving the child what they want to avoid the tantrum	
iv) **Avoiding or resisting following an instruction** a) the child has not been taught the alternative pro-social behaviour b) the child has not got the developmental ability to behave differently/appropriately c) what the child is doing is more reinforcing than what they are being asked to do d) the child is not given sufficient time to process the instruction e) the child could do what is required but does not understand the instruction (communication problem) f) the child does not know what is expected of them because rules are inconsistent	
v) **The child's behaviour generates support** The child uses the behaviour to get help when frustrated	
vi) **The behaviour removes an aversive situation** The child is responding to stop something aversive, such as being teased or bullied	
vii) **The behaviour removes stress through avoidance** a) the child may be afraid of doing the wrong thing/making a mistake and/or being punished b) the child has skill deficits that lead them to avoid the situation	

EPaS checklist for case analysis session 4

	Activity	Completed (yes/no)
1	Greet the parents.	
2	Thank them for returning the questionnaires.	
3	Explain that you want them to tell you whether they agree that you have the correct information as you go though the case analysis.	
4	Explain that it will be in four steps and you will pause to discuss each step.	
5	Confirm parents' agreement with the case analysis or amend as agreed.	
6	Agree some specific goals for intervention (ideally not more than three).	
7	Identify the parent assets that will support the goals.	
8	You and parents sign the contract and leave a copy with the parents.	
9	Agree initial weekly targets and complete weekly target sheet.	
10	Agree record keeping.	
11	Thank the parents.	
12	Arrange next appointment.	

9   Sample case analysis

This chapter gives a brief summary of information gathered from one family and presents the key components of the case analysis. This family consisted of a single-parent mum living with three children: Jenny, a girl aged 8; Simon, a 4-year-old boy; and 18-month-old Peter. The family was living on state benefit and the mother had separated from the children's father shortly after the birth of her third child on discovering that he was in a relationship with another woman. The child for whom she was seeking help was her four-year-old son, Simon, who had recently started school. Some examples from Mum's typical day interview are described earlier in Chapter 6.

Extracts from the PDHQ and constructional interviews suggested that Simon's problem behaviour started shortly after the birth of his baby brother. This also coincided with his starting nursery and with the separation of his parents. His father lived locally but had a new partner and had only intermittent and unpredictable contact with the children.

Finances were limited, but Mum prioritised the needs of her children and managed within her limited income. The family lived in a two-bedroom, privately rented flat. The two older children shared a room and the younger one slept in his mum's bedroom.

Mum described how she was living with her ex-husband when all of the children were born, in the town where she was born and still lived. She had no problems during her pregnancy when carrying Simon, and initially he was an easy baby. Simon was an active toddler and had visited A&E departments due to accidents involving falling and, on one occasion, a scald. Social Services had had previous involvement with the family and there had been a child protection case conference, which Mum had attended with her own mother. However, there was no current involvement.

Mum described how she had become depressed when she learned of her husband's relationship with another woman and that they had separated shortly after Peter's birth. This coincided with the escalation of Simon's problems, at that stage aged 2 years 6 months. She described how there had also been concerns at the nursery about Simon's behaviour and his unwillingness to share toys or to sit and listen to stories, and that he had now started full-time school and she was concerned that he was not settling well.

In terms of her support network, she described how her mother and brother lived locally and both offered her some support. She also had a good friend, but was reluctant to visit with Simon, as his behaviour outside the home was often even more of a problem than it was at home.

Initially, and typically, Mum was concerned to get rid of tantrums and other problem behaviours. At first, she had difficulty in identifying positive goals but, in response to the question "What would others observe if Simon did not have the problem?", and with prompting, she identified instruction-following as a general goal, giving lots of specific examples around getting dressed when asked, staying in bed, etc. Her description of her current situation in the first session was amplified in the subsequent session during the typical day interview.

Mum could identify how her own life would be different if solutions to the problems could be achieved – for example, being able to take the children out and visit her friend with the children and being calmer, particularly with the children.

In terms of her relationship with her mother and brother, she identified that (although they were supportive) at times they were critical of her management of the children, describing her as "too soft". She felt that her relationship with them would change if she was able to help Simon to change. She could offer them more support and they would respect her more.

Mum struggled to identify things going well for her child and herself. She said that Simon had good physical coordination and could already ride a small two-wheeler bike. He liked doing things to help his mum if it was his idea. He could at times be very loving, both towards her and towards his baby brother, Peter. More information about Simon's skills came from the "Things your child can do" assignment. He also played well with his older sister, Jenny, and their relationship was good, although Mum felt that this was because Jenny let him take charge. He had good concentration for things he enjoyed doing, like playing games on his PlayStation.

For herself Mum said that, although finances were limited, she prioritised the needs of her children and was not in debt. She saw herself as a loyal person and as someone willing to recognise a problem and take advice. She had the support of her family and her friend.

Mum had only recently identified that she needed to address the problem, as a result of concerns associated with Simon starting school and recognising that his problems could lead to possible long-term difficulties. Her previous strategy had been to give him time and hope that he would grow out of the problems. For herself, she had coped with the break-up of her relationship with the support of her family. She had dealt with allowing the children access to her ex-husband, although was frustrated that he was unpredictable about it.

Mum did not identify recent situations that had triggered the problem. The problems that Simon experienced in the nursery, and was continuing to have at school, had helped her to realise that she needed to find solutions. She saw his challenging behaviour as having gradually escalated since the arrival of his brother Peter, which also coincided with him starting nursery and his father's departure.

The question about things her child liked to do produced a list of activities, including watching certain TV programmes, particular toys, etc. Responses to this question were also expanded in the "Things your child enjoys" questionnaire.

As was highlighted in the typical day interview (some extracts were included in Chapter 6) and the constructional questionnaire, Mum got support from her family because of her problems, but at a cost. She did not see herself as excused from anything because of the problem; rather, it excluded her from normal social situations. She also recognised that Simon was not invited to other children's homes to play.

Her recent history of problem-solving had been generally passive, in that her family had seen that she was depressed and had stepped in to support her. She had successfully supported her three children and was proud of her daughter, who was doing well in school and whose company she enjoyed. Before having the children, she had worked in a shop and had been given additional responsibilities because she was recognised as being honest and reliable.

Mum kept some useful records of the morning situation, based on her report from the typical day interview and some specific examples of bedtime problems. Together we decided to prioritise bedtimes, as evidence suggests that many children do not get sufficient sleep (Gregory and Sadeh, 2012) and that this can be a contributory factor in daytime behavioural problems. In many cases daytime problems become less problematic when children develop good sleep hygiene, and addressing night-time problems can quite quickly bring about positive changes.

The three problems that Mum identified on the Three-Problem Rating Scale were:

1 Refusal to cooperate with morning routine
2 Hitting his sister and brother, mainly when he wanted things that they had, particularly when Mum was not present
3 Refusing to stay in bed.

Observation showed that Mum was able to remain calm in the face of challenging behaviour, but that she tended to either avoid possible tantrums by acquiescing to Simon's demands, or if a confrontation arose she initially stood firm but then backed off, as in the typical day example of morning dressing. This was also reflected in her self-reported parenting style, which showed that she scored in the problematic range on the Laxness scale (inability to stick at and follow through with instructions) and also on the Verbosity scale (threatening to do things, but then failing to follow through). Her score on the Over-reactivity scale was not in the problematic range.

Mum's report of child behaviour on the SDQ (www.sdqinfo.com) showed that she rated Simon's behaviour in the high/very high range on his total problem score, with the peer problem, hyperactivity and conduct problem subscales all scoring within the high/very high range. Mum had completed a

Beck Depression Inventory (Beck, Steer and Brown, 1996) that showed her to be reporting a clinic level of depression. This is not unusual among parents reporting their children as having clinical levels of problem behaviour. Our work has shown that the deficits associated with problematic parenting and adult depression are similar. They include poor observation skills, global and negative (rather than specific) recall of past events, and poor problem-solving skills (Hutchings, Bywater, Williams, Lane and Whitaker, 2012). Our randomised controlled trial studies on parenting programmes show significant and long-term improvements in parental depression, as well as improvements in child behaviour, as was demonstrated in the initial version of this programme and in our large Sure Start study (Gardner, Hutchings, Bywater and Whitaker, 2010; Hutchings, Lane and Kelly, 2004; Hutchings, Appleton, Smith, Lane and Nash, 2002; Hutchings et al., 2007).

The case analysis was constructed using this and other information supplied by Mum, and is summarised below:

Case analysis summary: Simon

Step 1: Background

This is a brief summary of the information gathered, including the history of the child. Note any information that the parent has given you, so that they have the opportunity to see that you have fully understood the situation and the problem and also their skills and resources, general problem-solving strategies and previous successes. It forms a picture of the child and their general circumstances.

Simon is the second of three children, now aged 4, and attends the local primary school full time. He lives with his mum and two siblings, an 8-year-old sister, Jenny, and a brother of 18 months, Peter, in a two-bedroom privately rented flat. Mum grew up locally and her mother and brother live nearby.

Simon had a normal delivery and was an easy baby, becoming an active toddler. When he was 2½, his younger brother, Peter, was born and shortly after this his parents separated following Mum discovering that her husband was having another relationship. Despite the impact of this separation on herself, Mum coped well, keeping her family together and dealing with intermittent contact for the children from her ex-husband. She has managed her limited income and prioritised her children. She has a good relationship with her daughter, Jenny, whom she finds supportive both generally and in managing Simon's challenges. Simon is an active child with good coordination skills and can at times be very loving and affectionate. Whilst Mum recognised that Simon was presenting challenges, she was, until recently, reassured by friends that it was a "phase" that he would grow out of. She now acknowledges that Simon's behaviour is not developmentally acceptable and is problematic for him, as evidenced by her rating of his behaviour on the SDQ and feedback from his school. She is keen to help him learn alternative ways of behaving.

Mum also recognises how Simon's behaviour is putting restrictions on her own and the family's lives as well as the impact on his own life both within and outside school particularly in his peer relations. She is also concerned that he will act as a role model for his young brother, Peter, and is already beginning to see signs of this. She is motivated to find solutions and has co-operated in the assessment phase, providing valuable information in interviews and by keeping records. She has the support of her family and a local friend and a good relationship with Jenny who is doing well at school, has friends, is very close to her Mum and at times is Mum's helper, for example pushing Peter in the pushchair when Mum had to carry Simon to school.

Step 2: The problem

This is a clear description of the problem and all of the circumstances associated with it, time of day, who present, etc.

This provides an opportunity to feed back the information obtained from the typical day and the records that Mum had kept about morning and evening problems.

Mornings

Breakfast

Simon was generally the first to get up in the morning, often by 6.30 a.m., which was before his Mum was up. He would be watching TV when Mum wanted him to have breakfast and this had developed into a ritual that involved a special bowl with cereal and milk at a certain level. The bowl was put by Mum on a cupboard by the TV and Simon stood and ate some of it, generally not finishing it. Mum complied with his demands to avoid Simon throwing the bowl at her, as had happened in the past. His sister Jenny was also in the room but had a bowl of cereal on a coffee table. Mum would sometimes ask Simon if he wanted toast but he would generally not reply. When Mum brought toast for Jenny, Simon might grab her hair and take the toast and Mum would then try to put him in his room for five minutes, although she had difficulty keeping him there. However, to avoid this problem Mum generally brought toast for Simon without him being asked, even though he often did not eat it.

Dressing

The next problem was getting Simon to wash and dress. Left unsupervised in the bathroom, whilst Mum was dealing with Peter, he would run water and flick it about or squeeze toothpaste out onto the basin. As the typical day had shown, Mum attempted to get him to clear up but generally ended up doing this herself. Dressing was also a problem. On schooldays Jenny dressed in the bedroom, but Mum would bring Simon's and Peter's clothes to the living room. Whilst dressing Peter, Mum would repeatedly ask Simon to dress. Generally, he would take his pyjamas off and sit naked, until Mum struggled to get him dressed whilst he resisted. At weekends he often remained in pyjamas for much of the day but he did have skills to dress himself, and if Mum suggested going to the park or to buy something for him he would dress himself.

(continued)

(continued)

The walk to school

Similar detail was fed back to Mum to confirm the situation regarding the walk to school.

Bedtime routine

Mum had a routine for bedtimes that she tried to stick to. At 6.30 p.m., she would leave Simon and Jenny watching TV whilst she bathed Peter and put him to bed, having him in bed by 7 p.m. Peter had recently transferred from a cot to a bed, but remained in bed in Mum's bedroom with a bottle and generally fell asleep quite quickly.

At 7 p.m. Mum took Simon for a bath, which she did every day. This was no problem, as he enjoyed the bath; the challenge came when he was asked to get out of the bath, which he resisted and Mum struggled to drain the bathwater and eventually to lift him out of the bath. Getting pyjamas on was generally a struggle. Although in her typical day Mum had initially said that he shared a bed with his sister, it transpired that because he had broken her bed Jenny now slept with her mum. Simon demanded that he watched a DVD in the bedroom and that Mum brought him a drink and biscuits in bed. Mum would then leave and he would watch the DVD for a while before getting up. Whilst he was watching the film, Mum organised Jenny to get ready for bed. Generally, within 45 minutes Simon was out of bed and Mum then returned him to his bed, switched off the TV and laid beside him until he fell asleep. This could take anything up to an hour. When she left, he sometimes remained in bed until the morning, but could get up several times during the night. She would try to put him back in bed, but sometimes he ended up in bed with Mum and Jenny. During her record keeping she recorded that during one week he got up an average of three times per night and ended the night in Mum's bed on two occasions.

Step 3: The function

This is the tentative understanding of why the problem(s) might be occurring.
There may be a number of possible explanations and the various information sources should provide a sufficiently clear description of the problem to enable a tentative understanding of why it is occurring.

The circumstances that had precipitated most of the problems lay in the past and this was shared with Mum. Simon presented with a number of problems that had emerged over the last year and a half. Their onset had been associated with significant changes in the life of the family. A new baby had arrived, Dad had left and Simon had started nursery. Mum had struggled to come to terms with the break-up of her marriage and she was still reporting a moderate level of depression. She recognised that she may have been less available to Simon at a time when he was competing for attention with his younger brother, coping with the demands of the nursery and dealing with his father's departure. Prior to this he had been at home with Mum for much of the day, as his sister had been in full-time school since his birth. This escalation of challenging behaviour was also a time when he was becoming increasingly independent but before he had sufficient language to understand what was happening and to enable him to regulate his own behaviour. Mum's depression, triggered by the departure of her husband, probably meant that Simon had to work harder for her attention and, as a result, a number of problematic behaviours had been reinforced. His sister was also rewarded by sleeping in Mum's bed when Simon was presenting challenges at night.

Viewing the world through Simon's eyes, he had experienced a number of significant changes at a young age and before he had the linguistic skills to comprehend and manage his own behaviour. The two-year phase (often referred to in our society as the "terrible twos") is when tantrums are common among children due to their not having the language skills to understand the situation, to negotiate with others to get their needs met and/or not having learned to accept the necessary limits associated with their growing independence. Much of Simon's challenging behaviour was targeted on getting and keeping his mum's attention.

Having shared this understanding of the history, the information gathered regarding the current situation showed that Simon's behaviour was currently being reinforced in several different ways. It is typical for behaviours to have several functions. In Simon's case, these included attention, access to other reinforcers through non-compliance, exerting power and control over others with aggression or the threat of aggression and avoidance of unpleasant tasks, such as cleaning up mess that he had caused.

Simon's non-compliance over dressing forced his mum to engage with him and dress him, giving him the attention that much of his behaviour was demanding. The good coordination that Simon had in other activities, and the fact that he could dress himself at the weekend in order to do something that he wanted, demonstrated that dressing was something that Simon was developmentally capable of doing.

When he made a mess in the bathroom, Mum was aware that he should be held responsible for his behaviour and tried to get him to clean up, for example, the toothpaste, but her efforts gave Simon yet further attention and his aggressive response towards her resulted in her doing the clearing up herself. Mum recognised that she needed to supervise some of these activities in order to avoid such problems, rather than sending Simon to do them alone and then having to deal with problems.

Mum's description of Simon's specific demands in relation to breakfast were an example of how she has learned to avoid his tantrums, allowing Simon to control her behaviour over what he wanted, how and where he wanted it, and included his being able to continue to watch TV whilst having breakfast. This had led to his making ever more specific demands, such as requiring an exact level of milk in his bowl. For Simon this escalation of demands also controlled his mother's attention. The demand to have his sister's toast, which Jenny also complied with to avoid him pulling her hair, was another example of using problem behaviour to gain power over others. This resulted in yet more attention from Mum, and generally Mum made toast for Simon whether he wanted it or not, although he often did not eat it. Simon's aggressive behaviour

(continued)

(continued)

towards Jenny, who to him may have appeared to be Mum's favourite, sharing her bed, etc., resulted in her compliance with his demands as well as gaining yet more of his mother's attention. Simon wanted Mum's attention but had learned to achieve this in high-cost ways. He was also using some of these strategies in peer relationships in school and consequently his transition into school was problematic.

The family lived in a quiet street and the children did play outside their house, but Simon's refusal to come in from playing outside was another example of refusal to follow instructions when what he was doing was more reinforcing than following the instruction. This also resulted in additional attention from, and stress for, Mum, as she had described in her typical day about how she chased him around the neighbourhood, also presenting a potential accident risk for Simon.

Difficult behaviour at bedtime, with Simon avoiding following instructions, gained him a lot of his mum's attention in undressing him, etc. Mum had said that he no longer shared his bed with his sister as he had broken her bed. However, Mum's bedtime records showed a pattern of regularly allowing Jenny to share her bed. Throughout the night,, when Simon got up Mum was initially consistent in putting him back to bed, although she often then sat with him until he fell asleep, giving him yet further attention. On other occasions he ended up in bed with her and Jenny.

Step 4: Targets

This is the identification of a developmentally appropriate target behaviour or behaviours which will replace the problem behaviour(s) and the assets and resources which will help to achieve this.

Mum had become increasingly aware of the patterns of Simon's behaviour through the assessment process and was committed to following through with a plan to help him to develop the necessary instruction following skills that would result in developmentally appropriate and achievable behaviour. She had a supportive family and had shared with them that she was working on a plan to support Simon, and they had offered support. Mum recognised the need for changes and wanted to prioritise helping Simon in order that he would be able to deal more effectively with school. Mum had done a good job supporting Jenny and could see that Simon had experienced a different set of circumstances during his early childhood. Despite the challenges, there were times when Simon could be very loving towards her. Mum recognised the need for some consistent limit-setting and consequences for problem behaviour. She did try to follow through at times – for example, putting Simon in his room if he hit his brother or sister – but this resulted in further challenges in trying to keep him there and did not reduce the problems. Mum recognised that this did not teach Simon an alternative behaviour.

The developmentally appropriate targets suggested for Simon were mainly focused on teaching him to follow instructions, of which the main ones were:

i)   to get up and wash and dress himself in the morning
ii) to sit at a table to have his breakfast cereal

iii) to walk to school holding the pushchair
iv) to come in from play when Mum called him in
 v) to go to bed at 7.30 p.m. and remain in bed until morning.

In order to achieve these goals, Mum would need to decide on, set and
follow through with appropriate limits in relation to the various problem
situations.

Other targets included Simon being able to spend positive time in the presence of
his younger brother and sister when his mum was not present, and creating
opportunities for him to help Mum in tasks around the house that included
meal preparation.

The suggested contract included three overarching goals:

1 Helping Simon to get attention from his mum in appropriate ways
2 Increasing Simon's instruction following
3 Strengthening Simon's relationship with his siblings.

Having presented and discussed this information with Mum, we agreed
to work together on a plan and wrote this into a contract.

The contract agreed with Simon's Mum is set out below.

Intervention agreement

This agreement is made between:

Name: _____ (parent)

Name: _____ (case worker)

The goals relate to: <u>Simon</u>_____ (name of child)

We will work together to achieve the following goal/goals:

(list a maximum of three goal areas)

1 Strengthening Simon's relationship with Mum by creating opportunities
   for Simon to get attention from his mum in appropriate ways
2 Increase Simon's instruction following, particularly in relation to mornings and bedtimes
3 Simon to build positive relationships with his siblings

To achieve these goals:

I, the case worker, agree to visit weekly and to work together to agree
weekly targets towards the agreed goals. I will arrange our weekly appointments in advanced and try to let you know if for any reason I will be unable
to make the appointment.

_____ Signature _____ Date

I, the parent, agree to work together to agreed weekly targets and keep agreed progress records. I will endeavour to notify you if I cannot keep an appointment.

_____ Signature _____ Date

Since attention appeared to be a key driver for several of the problematic behaviours, and many of Mum's instructions were to do things that Simon could developmentally achieve, Mum recognised the need to work on targets to increase Simon's appropriate behaviour in order to eliminate the problem behaviours. Whilst Mum was the key reinforcer, she had also identified a number of other potential reinforcers in the "Things your child enjoys" handout.

The first task suggested by this analysis was to strengthen the relationship between Simon and Mum by giving him attention for appropriate behaviour and special time with Mum. Strengthening their relationship through shared activities would also be likely to increase his willingness to follow her instructions.

References

Beck, A. T., Steer, R. A, & Brown, G. K. (1996). *Manual for the Beck Depression Inventory II*. San Antonio, TX: Psychological Corporation.

Gardner, F., Hutchings, J., Bywater, T., & Whitaker, C. J. (2010). Who benefits and how does it work? Moderators and mediators of outcome in an effectiveness trial of a parenting intervention. *Journal of Clinical Child and Adolescent Psychology, 39*(4), 1–13. doi:10.1080/15374416.2010.486315

Gregory, A. M. & Sadeh, A. (2012). Sleep, emotional and behavioral difficulties in children and adolescents. *Sleep Medicine Reviews, 16*(2), 129–136.

Hutchings, J., Lane, E., & Kelly J. (2004). Comparison of two treatments of children with severely disruptive behaviours: a four-year follow up. *Behavioural and Cognitive Psychotherapy, 32*(1), 15–30. doi: 10.1017/S1352465804001018

Hutchings, J., Appleton, P., Smith, M., Lane, E., & Nash, S. (2002). Evaluation of two treatments for children with severe behaviour problems: Child behaviour and maternal mental health outcomes. *Behavioural and Cognitive Psychotherapy, 30*, 279–295. doi:10.1017/S1352465802003041

Hutchings, J., Bywater, T., Williams, M. E., Lane, E., & Whitaker, C. J. (2012). Improvements in maternal depression as a mediator of child behaviour change. *Psychology, 3*(9A), 795–801. doi:10.4236/psych.2012.329120

Hutchings, J., Bywater, T., Daley, D., Gardner, F., Whitaker, C. J., Jones, K., . . . Edwards, R. T. (2007). Parenting intervention in Sure Start services for children at risk of developing conduct disorder: Pragmatic randomised controlled trial. *British Medical Journal, 334*(7595), 678–684. doi:10.1136/bmj.39126.620799.55

10 The intervention plan

The case formulation session and agreement of a contract leads to the intervention phase. The processes that operate during this phase are similar to those in the assessment phase in terms of parents undertaking assignments and keeping records, except that the targets are now intervention targets. Weekly targets are negotiated and recorded on the Intervention Worksheet so that parents understand exactly what they are agreeing to do and the reasons for the activities in terms of how the weekly targets relate to the intervention goals and the recognition that they have the skills/assets to achieve the targets. As previously, you must also take away a copy of agreed targets and record sheets, because it will be the first thing you look at at the start of the next session. In our own trials we have used carbonated paper, both in the initial information-gathering phase for parent records and in the intervention phase where targets are discussed, agreed and written down during the session. The weekly target sheet also includes a place to record the date and time of the agreed next session.

It is important to clarify with parents that your agreed understanding of the problem is a "working hypothesis" that leads to some suggested target behaviours and goals. However, you must stress the importance of monitoring and keeping records about how any agreed strategies are working because if parents are not achieving the targets or the child is not responding well you need to re-evaluate the plan together. You are learning more about the function of any problematic behaviours throughout the intervention phase and may need to refine and modify the case analysis, goals, targets and strategies. If you are clear from the outset that the case analysis is a working hypothesis, parents will continue to work with you even if things do not immediately work out positively.

The intervention strategy has targets that develop alternative behaviours. This is our "constructional" analysis with the aim of establishing new behaviours that achieve positive outcomes for the child and replace problematic behaviours before directly tackling problem behaviour itself, should this still be necessary (which in many cases it is not). This is the rationale for intervention targets that strengthen the parent-child relationship (*The Little Parent Handbook*; Hutchings, 2013, Chapter 1). Attention seeking and non-compliance are frequent challenging behaviours and strengthening the child's relationship with their parent's through joint activities provides attention that does not require problem behaviour to obtain it, and compliance is also increased if this parent–child relationship is strong. For a child for whom the parent's negative attention has ceased to be a reinforcer, pairing positive attention also helps to re-establish the parent as a reinforcer by association (the Premack Principle).

The intervention goals, and more particularly the weekly targets, should be observable so that it is possible to be certain when/whether change has occurred. This is part of the process of helping parents to be better observers of their children's and their own behaviour. Having a child who is happy and being a relaxed and confident parent is what most parents would like, but that will only be achieved by some very specific targets, such as the child learning to relate positively to other children, developing the persistence to try again when things go wrong, or asking for help, etc.

At the end of the case analysis session, written long-term goals and immediate tasks that parents will undertake over the following week are agreed, as well as record-keeping goals in relation to these tasks. As discussed in the assessment phase, record-keeping assignments for parents need to be within their competences. For some parents a detailed ABC record might be possible, while for other parents you may only be asking them to put a tick on a calendar every time they spent five minutes playing with their child or the child has a dry bed.

This chapter includes an example of a weekly intervention plan and a variety of intervention phase records. It is a strength of the EPaS programme that you are working with the parents, not the child, so any changes in child behaviour come from the changes made by the parents, when you are not even present, providing immediate feedback to the parents of the impact of their behaviour and increasing the likelihood that new parent behaviour will be maintained by the child's response.

When setting weekly targets, you must also identify how and why individual target behaviours are feasible, and what is needed in terms of strategies to help to achieve this. (See the completed intervention worksheet, the example worksheet also asks the parents to record their play sessions with their child on an intervention ABC chart (there is a blank play session ABC chart at the end of the chapter)).

Intervention worksheet

Name of child: Joe   Date:

Task	Reason for task	Existing skills/assets that will enable this task to be completed
Both parents to spend 5 minutes each day with J in one-to-one time and record what happens on the ABC charts	To strengthen relationship and contribute towards the instruction-following goal	Parents are keen to help J. They can create time in early evening and have already kept ABC records

Get J's attention before giving an instruction. Give clear, specific, positive instructions. Notice and praise any instructions that J follows	Working on the goal of getting J to stay in bed by increasing instruction following generally	J does follow some instructions and parents can give clear instructions
Give J a bedtime drink before taking him to the bedroom	This will help J to learn that the bedroom is where he sleeps	Parents want to solve this problem and recognise the need to help J to learn to sleep in his bedroom
Read Chapter 1 of *The Little Parent Handbook* and the bedtime problem handout	Chapter 1 describes principles for child-led play and the bedtime problem handout suggests some ideas for solutions	Parents are happy to undertake reading assignments to provide them with ideas
Develop a possible bedtime routine plan that should ensure that J is calm at bedtime for discussion next week	Getting J to bed at 7 p.m. is the goal	Parents can work well together. We can plan the bedtime routine at the next session using their proposed routine

The case analysis had already defined the longer-term goal or goals, such as to help Joe to sit through a mealtime so that the family could to go to a restaurant or to another place outside the home and know that he could behave appropriately. The short-term, immediately achievable, goals might include only that the child is rewarded for sitting at the table for five minutes or that all food and drink is consumed at the table, even though the child may remain only briefly at the table and return several times to eat or drink. It may include rewarding the child with a choice of pudding for sitting at the table for a certain amount of time. The decision regarding the short-term target(s) will be based on what is happening at the present time and on building the replacement behaviours in small steps. If a child can only sit at the table for two minutes, then probably an initial goal of remaining at the table for three minutes will be set with some discussion around the use of specific labelled praise and a small incentive for achieving this. You can use the "Things your child enjoys" record to discuss and agree small incentives.

Short-term goals should be what are achievable by the parent, and hopefully the child, by the next meeting, which is generally within a week. In the example of sitting at the table, the short-term goals might include thinking about how you can arrange things so that you allow the child to leave the table before they do it without permission – for example, by asking them to fetch something. This is using the shaping process described in Chapter 11 and in *The Little Parent Handbook* (Hutchings, 2013, Chapter 7).

Many parent goals for younger children are likely to target eating, toileting, bedtime or sleeping problems. Several of these problems may restrict what a child can do, such as go for a sleepover with a friend or grandparent, and it is helpful to have these outcomes in the longer-term goals. The initial part of the intervention will need to focus on the things that will help to establish the alternative behaviours, and once they are in place it will then be possible to consider whether it will be necessary to provide any consequences for the problem behaviour itself. In many cases this may not be necessary at all.

Your strategies for short-term targets can draw on the ideas in Chapters 13–18. As discussed above, you will probably decide together to include some more general activities for parents that will strengthen their relationship with their child as well, identifying specific behaviours to praise and reward, and specific and clear instructions associated with behaviours that are not highly challenging. You will have to justify these targets to the parent. These are covered in the first three chapters of *The Little Parent Handbook* (Hutchings, 2013). The focus in initial weekly targets is on increasing replacement behaviours, using prompting, praising and rewarding, before considering using discipline plans that involve time-out or consequences, although it may include withdrawing attention from some problem behaviour (ignoring). Parents have often been told to ignore so-called "attention seeking" behaviour, but what they describe is ignoring the child rather than the specific behaviour sometimes for long periods of time. Not surprisingly they report that this does not work. Ignoring is only effective if attention is returned to the child as soon as the problem behaviour ceases. At times it also involves teaching replacement behaviours. The specific use of differential attention, giving attention to behaviour the parent wants to see more of and removing attention from behaviour they want to see less of, is generally understood by parents following a case analysis. Any use of consequences and time-out procedures should come later. Parental targets will require a teaching plan using strategies from those identified in Chapter 11, including shaping, prompting, etc. Chapters 13–18 also contain brief case studies of problem behaviours, including night-times, mealtimes, mornings, a shopping trip, a toileting problem, an eating problem, helping children to talk about their day at school, and dealing with fears and phobias. You may find it helpful to read these examples, as they may prompt ideas about useful strategies to discuss with parents when addressing these common problems.

It is generally easier for parents to help children to make changes in their behaviour at home when they are not under the scrutiny of other people, so even if the goal is to help a particular child to behave appropriately in a shop or restaurant, this will not be the initial target, which is likely be to increase compliance and instruction following at home generally. It may also involve discussion with the child about what is required in going shopping and possibly role-play practise of a shopping trip during a play session at home.

Sometimes the trigger for problem behaviour can be events that have occurred prior to the child coming into the problem situation. There may have been a difficulty at school or in some other situation that means that the child is disregulated or that the child is tired or hungry, and if this is not recognised or is handled badly this can trigger problem behaviour in a new situation. Parents have to learn to watch the child for cues about how they are feeling, and particularly to notice when problems occur, time of day, etc. If a child has had a bad day at school, it is important that parents do not exacerbate the problem by telling the child off or punishing them at home. It might be better to help parents to share the idea that they are sad to learn that the day in school did not go well and that they hope that the following day might be better. They can then offer their child an opportunity to talk about problems if they wish to, prompt problem-solving ideas and ensure that problems do not transfer from one situation to another.

Rewards

A basic sticker chart is included at the end of this chapter. There are five golden rules for using rewards.

1   Only target one behaviour at a time with a reward programme.
2   The child must be able to achieve the behaviour required for the reward, or it will cause frustration and resentment. This involves ensuring that the task is within the child's ability, is clearly defined and developmentally realistic.
3   The child must want the reward. Although rewards should be small, it is still important that they are being chosen with care. The "Things your child enjoys" handout can help, but the parent has also been learning from observation of the child what they enjoy. Any high-frequency behaviour is by definition reinforcing.
4   The parent must remember to give the reward once earned, even if the child has behaved badly in some other respect. Rewards for one behaviour cannot be taken away because of a different problem.
5   Rewards are always paired with parental praise, as they can be thought of as a prosthesis, with the longer-term aim to strengthen the value of parental attention in encouraging desired behaviour.

If these rules are followed, rewards make a useful contribution to an intervention programme. For young children, rewards need to be immediate and stars and stickers alone are often sufficient, but older children can earn points or stickers towards a small reward. *Small* is the important word, as parents may have previously offered big rewards or bribes. If a child gets a bicycle for staying in their own bed for a week, it is hard to imagine how they can be persuaded to continue this behaviour the following week. What happens then can be that larger rewards tend to become used as consequences, so the bicycle is removed (causing arguments and tension).

The remainder of this chapter presents some sample intervention record sheets and notes explaining how they were used.

An ABC record on ignoring tantrums

The parent has completed this ABC record sheet during the intervention phase, after being encouraged to ignore tantrums, and she is being effective. However, in discussing this record, a number of issues arise that might help the child.

Mum and Dad's ABC record of L's problem behaviour during intervention

Try to record each event that you ignore as soon as possible after they occur

Date: 3rd October

What was going on? Where were you? Who was there altogether? What time was it?	What started the problem? What did L do and say? What did you do and say?	What happened next? What did you do? How did it work out?
I was talking to a friend at a friend's house Me and my friend and L were the only ones there It was about 4.15 I told her I would not pick her up until I had finished my tea and she had stopped crying.	My friend had just made me a cup of tea but L wanted me to pick her up. I told her that I would pick her up when I had drunk my cup of tea She threw herself onto me then the floor, hit me, head butted the floor, cried, screamed for 15–20 mins	She started crying I picked her up about one minute after she stopped crying

First, it is not clear how the mother prepared her child for the situation. Did she let her know what she was going to be doing? Could she have planned for something for her daughter to do whilst she was talking with her friend, drinking her tea? Could she have offered her daughter a cold drink? This clear description of the situation allows for problem-solving about how to manage future situations and could avoid the child's tantrum. This focus on replacement behaviours was discussed during weekly target setting.

Bedtime problem record

In this case, the dad is reporting being consistent in sticking with his clear instruction to get pyjamas on, and it works.

C's bedtime record

Date: Feb 12th
Who was at home? Mum/Dad/Other   *Dad*
What time did you start the bedtime routine?   *7.00*
What did it involve?   *I asked C to go and put his pyjamas on*
Any problems?*C said: No it's not bedtime, I'm busy*
What did you do?   *I repeated the instruction several times and he eventually went to do it*
What time does C go to bed?   *7.15*
Who went up with C to bed?   *Dad*
Who reads C a story?   *Dad*
What time do you leave him?   *7.45*
Any problems tucking him in/saying goodnight?   *Said he wanted to be alone*
What happens after that, how many times does C come down? *He did not come down*
What do you do, how does it work out? *Was asleep when I checked him at 8.15*

In discussing this record, it would be helpful to check whether C's eventual compliance was praised and how C gets his bedtime story despite his previous reluctance to get pyjamas on, which is good parenting, as this would not be something to use as a reward, as it is part of the consistent bedtime routine that the parents are establishing and is probably calming for the child.

It is not clear why C wants to be alone. He is learning that his father is being consistent and may by now have learned that there was no point in prolonging the farewell. It was good that Dad records going to check on him and finding him asleep.

Morning routines

Morning time, in households where children have to be ready and out for school, is identified as the most stressful time in the day for most families. Routines in general, but particularly morning routines, are often part of interventions.

The record sheet for mornings for B and S shows an example of a morning routine being established that was linked to a reward. In fact, the problem only applied to one child, B, but the parents liked the idea of making a rule that applied to both children. This was seen by the parents as fair. S was likely to complete the morning task every morning, because for her it was already a well-established behaviour, but for B it was more challenging. The parents reasoned that it might cause resentment from S if B was being rewarded for a behaviour that she already did well. In addition, rewarding the same behaviour for both children clearly demonstrates that the focus is on the behaviour, and not the child, and is a rule for both of the children.

This plan was set up several weeks into the intervention phase. Nevertheless it was ambitious in terms of targeting several behaviours.

Record of mornings for B and S

Rules: To earn their money for a snack to buy after school, the children must get up, wash and dress before having breakfast in the kitchen. After breakfast, if there is time, they can watch TV. If they do that without any problems, they get their 40p for the snack. Be prepared for a tantrum if B loses her 40p, but do not get into a row with her. Just say, "You knew the rules", and walk away. When she is calm, you can remind her of her previous successes and suggest that she can try again tomorrow. Do not debate whether the 40p has been earned or lost – just tell them. Remind them once of the rules when they get up in the morning.

If the children are getting up nicely, remember to praise them.

Put a star in the box for each day they earn the money.

Week beginning ....

Day	B	S
Monday		
Tuesday		
Wednesday		
Thursday		
Friday		

Parental monitoring of the required behaviour is important and this programme also involved one of the parents getting up earlier because, at baseline, B was always up first and watching the TV in his pyjamas before his parents were up. In order to stop this pattern and prompt the behaviour they wanted, one of the parents had to get up before B.

This programme worked well, particularly because the parents also sat down with the children and explained that mornings were not very pleasant times for any of them and that they had decided on a new plan to help everyone.

In some cases, it might be better to have two separate star charts, to avoid possible competition. In another situation it might be better to recognise developmental differences and identify a different behavioural target for S, who was a little older than B.

Separations

The record sheet that follows involved a preschool child who, at the start of the intervention, was unable to be separated from her mother. She had been hospitalised and had become very clingy towards her mother. Although this was a baseline record, it is clear that the process of record keeping was already prompting the mother to start to take steps to deal with the problem. The record covers two situations: the playgroup, and one where J was being encouraged to do something with her father.

J record sheet of separations from Mum

Day: *Monday*
Time: *9.30*   Place: *Playgroup at XXXX*

What did you want to do?
Wanted to leave her in playgroup for 5 minutes just to get her used to idea

What you said to J?
Told her I was going to toilet and would be back very soon and Aunty R (whom she knows well) would look after her

How did J behave about it and for how long?
Ok for 3 minutes then cried for mummy

How did it work out, did you go and for how long?
Went for 4/5 minutes out of room where J was.

If you did spend some time without her, what happened while you were apart and when you met up again?
See above – was crying when I came back but also saying bravely that she was alright now. Aunty R (in charge of playgroup) pointed out to her that mummy had come back as promised very quickly.

Any other information that may be relevant.
J has visited this playgroup many times with mummy. This was first time I have tried to leave her for even a short while and I am hoping to gradually increase the time left once she accepts me leaving.

The next record relates to the goal of J learning to spend time with her father

Dad's record of time with J

What you wanted to do with J?
Take her to the park for walk and swings.

Was J agreeable?
Initially yes.

How long did you go out for and how did it work out?
Started crying for mummy after couple of minutes. So distressed had to return home.

What happened when J met up with Mum again?
Needed a lot of reassurance and comforting before calmed down. Afterwards played quite happily with daddy whilst mum was upstairs.

In this case it became clear in discussion of these records with the parents that more time needed to be spent by Dad doing things at home with J, and that possibly Mum going out and briefly leaving them together might be an easier initial goal for J, who would be at home in a familiar environment, not only with Dad but also with her familiar toys, etc.

Daily log

The record sheet below shows extracts from B's daily intervention log. B is a single parent who lives at his workplace. He had acknowledged getting angry with his two children and is working on handling situations differently.

1 TIME	2 ACTIVITY	3 WHERE	4 WHO WAS THERE	5 WHAT YOU WANTED	6 WHAT YOU GOT	7 REFLECTIONS
8.15	Breakfast	Kitchen	Daughter	Time to collect thoughts	Recorder playing	Do not wish to stop her
1.15	Lunch	In garden	Alone	Relaxation	Disturbed by workmates	Needed the time to get myself sorted out and do domestic things
10.15	Fell asleep putting children to bed					

Dad's example of the recorder playing shows that he is doing well to stay calm and not shout at his daughter, but his own needs are not being met and that would make it hard for him to maintain this behaviour.

He needs to establish rules about time and place for recorder playing in discussion with his daughter. Similarly, he needs to learn to set limits around his entitlement to lunchtime, during which he wanted to do domestic tasks. The reference to bedtime suggests the need to explore it in more detail.

A blank daily log sheet can be found at the end of this chapter.

Continence problems and targets

Problems involving bedwetting or daytime wetting or soiling should be approached with caution. There are a number of issues to consider and you may need to rule out any physical problems, although these can be less common that parents might think. If the child has never been dry, you may be dealing with a bladder-training task that includes increasing the child's awareness of their bladder. This can be helped by increasing fluid consumption in the day to give the child more practise at identifying bladder cues and increase their bladder capacity. If the child is dry on some occasions, you may be able to use a reward system to increase the number of dry nights, as well as looking at all of the circumstances surrounding the wet nights. Is it related to the drinking pattern, time of going to bed or other factors?

Health visitors may have access to enuresis alarms to use in bedwetting training, but they usually only work as part of a structured plan to train the child in bladder control. The record sheet for 8-year-old W is an example of a programme using an alarm. Before the programme, there had been considerable conflict over the wet beds, and, although an alarm had been used previously, it had not worked, as the child had frequently switched it off. The new programme had initially included increasing daytime fluid consumption, and rewards for doing this had worked well. At this stage, well into the programme – which by now involved a process whereby after every wet night the child had the alarm back in the bed, until achieving three consecutive dry nights – the programme was working well. W took the responsibility for ensuring that the alarm was switched on and was rewarded for five dry nights with a choice of something from his reward menu that had been agreed with his mother.

W's record sheet for a dry bed

Mum – at bedtime remind W that he will get a star for a dry night. In the morning you must check the bed when W gets up and, if it is dry, praise him and give him a star to put on the chart (this approach would only be used for a child who was already having some dry nights, so would be earning some stars). W can stick his own stars on. Decide where to put the chart, stick it up with Blu Tack somewhere that the rest of the children will not be able to pull it down.

If W has a wet bed in the morning, remind him of his previous successes and predict success. Remind him that he needs to have the alarm in his bed again to help him until he has had three dry nights in a row.

Every time W has earned five stars, he gets to choose something from his reward menu.

	Fill in this side every day	*Fill in this side if the alarm is needed*		
Date	*Star for a dry night (Mum)*	*W tick that alarm is on*	*Mum tick that you checked it*	*W tick if alarm rings*
22	*			
23	*			
24	*			
25				
26	*	✓	✓	
27	*	✓	✓	
28	*	✓	✓	

This worked well. The reward motivated W to work with the programme, and within a month he was having consistent dry beds.

An adult who, at the start of intervention, wet the bed every night was depressed, felt unable to contemplate staying anywhere but at home, and was reluctant to develop a partner relationship. He worked first on a day-time bladder-training programme and then with an enuresis alarm to stay dry at night. He learned that he could stay dry on every night except when he drank more than six pints of beer, when he would still wet the bed. He was happy with this outcome, because he had the knowledge and control that he needed to avoid the problem when he wanted to.

If a child has been dry but has started to wet the bed, you should proceed with caution. The child may have an infection, but if this is not the case, you can try to establish the trigger, which could indicate some other problem. Even then, look for the simple explanations first. In one case, a child's bedwetting coincided with starting school. However, the problem was not related to anxiety about school, the parents' initial thoughts, but simply that the child was no longer drinking in the day and their bladder was unable to cope overnight, with the majority of fluid input occurring in the evening.

The book *Toilet Training in Less Than a Day* (Azrin and Foxx, 1989) is a good example of how to arrange contingencies to train a child to become daytime continent. It uses the idea of encouraging the child to drink a lot in the day, to maximise the opportunities to learn bladder cues, plus lots of prompting and reinforcing, asking the child whether they need the toilet or potty, etc. – and it works!

Soiling, or faeces incontinence, is another problem where it is important to have very detailed records of the current situation in order to set realistic targets and goals. This may be a physical problem which needs medical intervention, or where you need to work with colleagues (including a GP, who might prescribe a laxative to get the bowel into a regular pattern). Either way, records that include where, when and how problem incidents occur can be very useful.

Some children with faeces incontinence are fussy eaters, and the resulting incontinence can be caused by constipation and overflow of uncontrollable faeces around the solid mass of impacted faeces in the bowel. Constipation can be painful, causing children to hold back. Often these children have little fibre in their diet and are likely to have a between-meals diet of problem foods. Therefore, along with a programme of medication, the initial targets are likely to be around increasing healthy eating habits and reducing between-meal snacking on high-calorie, low fibre foods.

An important goal with all children, but especially for older children, is to involve them in taking responsibility for trying to solve the problem. This is the case in the record of bedtime wetting for M (a teenager) that follows. The programme involved M taking responsibility for setting the bedwetting alarm and, if it went off, he was to get up and go to the toilet and see if he could pass any more urine. The agreement with his parents was that they would wake him to go to the toilet with a gentle prompt each night following a night when he had had an accident with a large patch of urine and had been unable to pass more urine in the toilet. This was to give him practise in getting up in response to a light prompt. He was by this stage having five dry nights in the week and, on occasions, was able to finish passing urine in the toilet after he had been woken by the alarm. This meant that on those occasions he was waking quickly to the alarm, which was rightly seen by him and his mother as a sign of progress.

M's dry bed programme records

Week beginning 16 March

This chart is to be filled in by M.

Please fill all information in on the chart at the time that it is happening.

Day Please put the date and a tick if you think that it was a high drinks day	Tick that you have put the alarm on and note time that you go to bed	Time Mum wakes you for a wee	Time alarm rings and size of patch: small (S), medium (M), large (L)	Tick if you manage to wee in the toilet after the alarm has gone off	Tick if the bed is dry all night	Tick when Mum gives you your reward
Monday 16✓	✓10.30	/			✓	✓
Tuesday 17	✓10.30	/	3.30 a.m. L			
Wednesday 18✓	✓10.30	2 am			✓	✓
Thursday 19✓	✓10.30	/			✓	✓
Friday 20	✓1.00	/	4.30 a.m. S	✓		
Saturday 21✓	✓1.30	2 am			✓	✓
Sunday 22	✓10.30	/			✓	✓

Rather than restricting fluid in the evening, it is often helpful to increase fluid consumption in the day, as this generally results in training the bladder to increase its capacity. This then also helps to establish the normal diurnal rhythm whereby the kidneys tend to produce more urine during the daytime and less at night.

Time-out and consequences

Time-out or other consequences should only be included in your intervention when you are sure that the child has the skills and motivation to avoid the problem behaviour, so generally not in the first few weeks of intervention. It is also important to ensure that the parent has decided on a consequence if the child refuses to accept time out – this is far more effective than any physical attempt to put a child in time-out, which can result in a battle between parents and child.

Two time-out record sheets are included below.

J, A and N: record of use of time-out

Please record every time that you use it, which child it is, date and time, the reason and how it works out. Put your initials at the side to show if it is Mum or Dad who gave the time-out.

Remember that if a child refuses a time-out, you must have a plan as to the choice you will give them – that is, what they will lose if they do not take the time-out. For J, it is losing his skateboard for one hour. For A and N, it is losing half an hour of PlayStation time. Remember to present this as a choice: "You can take a time-out or you will lose your skateboard for one hour." Time-out only works if you give lots of praise for good behaviour. We call this "time-in". This is time in the sunshine of positive attention. If the time-out is for refusing to follow an instruction, the child must comply with the instruction at the end of time-out, or you repeat the time-out. Check the rules for time-out *The Little Parent Handbook* (Hutchings, 2013, Chapter 5).

Remember to praise the children when they complete the task, even if they do it with bad grace. Do not comment on that – just praise the fact that they are doing what you have asked. At the end, just praise them for the task done, not the way they did it.

If the time-out is for an aggressive or other unacceptable behaviour, remember to re-engage the child with praise after the time-out finishes.

Date, time, name of child	Reason for time-out	How it worked out and who gave it

Time-out record for L

What instruction did you give or what rule was broken?	Who gave the time-out?	How long did L stay on the chair? How many time-outs?	Did he get it right in the end? Please tick in the box if he did
To get changed from school uniform	Mum	Kicked me, said, or rather shouted, that he hated that bloody clock and I'm a stupid woman	✓

(continued)

(continued)

What instruction did you give or what rule was broken?	Who gave the time-out?	How long did L stay on the chair? How many time-outs?	Did he get it right in the end? Please tick in the box if he did
		He had to go twice on chair as first time didn't stay on the chair. 6 minutes	
Shouting and stomping around because my granddaughters were visiting	Mum	6 minutes but shouted to begin with then calmed down. 1 time-out	✓

In reviewing the record above, the parent was acknowledged as doing a good job in following through. The discussion also explored whether it might have been possible to ignore the shouting and stomping and focus attention on the grandchildren. The record also prompted recognition that more planning was needed for visits by the grandchildren, in terms of giving L a role and engaging him in helping to entertain them, etc. This would result in him getting attention for appropriate behaviour. We also discussed the need to agree what toys, etc. the grandchildren could use and whether L had particular toys that needed to be put away or kept out of the grandchildren's reach.

The above examples demonstrate the small and specific steps that each stage of the intervention process requires, and the value of parental record keeping in ensuring that what you and the parents share is a clear understanding of what is happening and whether the strategies are effectively addressing the agreed goals. At the end of the chapter, there is a session checklist for reviewing all of the steps for each intervention session.

References

Azrin, N. & Foxx, R. M. (1989). *Toilet training in less than a day*. New York: Simon and Schuster.

Hutchings, J. (2013). *The Little Parent Handbook*. Bangor, UK: Children's Early Intervention Trust.

Intervention worksheet

Name of child:

Task	Reason for task	Existing skills/assets that will enable this task to be completed

ABC chart for special time

Antecedents	Behaviour	Consequences
How you set up the play session, what you did to follow the child's lead, choices given, etc.	What the child did, what they played, how they played	How you behaved and what response you got from the child

Basic sticker chart

MY STICKER CHART						
(Name)						
Target behaviour						
Mon	Tues	Wed	Thurs	Fri	Sat	Sun

Bonus stickers for:

When I get _____ stickers, I will receive _____.

Daily log

1 TIME	2 ACTIVITY	3 WHERE	4 WHO WAS THERE	5 WHAT YOU WANTED	6 WHAT YOU GOT	7 REFLECTIONS

EPaS checklist for reviewing weekly intervention sessions

	Activity	Completed (yes/no)
1	Greet parents and thank them for their commitment to their child.	
2	Explore each of the weekly targets and whether they had achieved it.	
3	Take responsibility for any targets not met and plan a more achievable target.	
4	Agree and record a new set of targets and reasons that make them achievable.	
5	Design and leave a parent record sheet.	
6	Agree record keeping with parents.	
7	Decide whether to leave a reading assignment.	
8	Thank the parents for their commitment to their child and the EPaS process.	
9	Arrange next appointment.	

11 Teaching new behaviour

This chapter presents a summary of teaching tools and strategies to consider in the intervention phase when agreeing tasks with parents.

Parents sometimes complain that children do not tell them about things that they have been doing outside the home, but this can be an antecedent or timing problem, as reported by Suzy's mum. Asking how Suzy's day in school went is a very appropriate parenting behaviour. Taking an interest in children's education is associated with good educational outcomes (Hindman and Morrison, 2011; Kingston, Huang, Calzada, Dawson-McClure and Brotman, 2013), but it is important to choose the right time or to approach it in the right way. Five-year-old Suzy had been in school all day. She came running out of school and was met by a parent, who asked what she had done in school. But that was not what was on Suzy's mind; she was probably thinking about what she would do next – getting home, her favourite TV programme, etc. So she said "Colouring", and Mum then asked what she had for dinner and she said, "Chips." These may be truthful answers, but they are not very reinforcing for Mum, who wants to show an interest in and learn about Suzy's day at school. Seeing the world through Suzy's eyes helped Mum to solve this problem. Here is the plan that we worked out together:

1   When greeting Suzy tell her that you have missed her and been thinking about her.
2   Talk with Suzy about what she wants to do when she gets home.
3   Talk to Suzy about what you have been doing during the day (modelling!).
4   Choose a quiet time to ask Suzy about school – for example, at bedtime (a time when most children will talk, to delay saying goodnight).

Once we defined clearly what behaviour we wanted, this produced a surprising and very quick solution: once greeted, and Mum having chatted a bit with Suzy, as they walked home together Suzy began to tell her mother all about her schoolday without being prompted.

This example uses several key skills to achieve the behaviour that a parent wants. What follows is a summary of the key components of effective teaching.

Rewarding behaviour we want to see more of

Reinforcement of desired behaviour is a key teaching tool, so it is useful to help parents to understand how they become reinforcers, generally very early in a child's life. Usually one person, or a small number of people, provide the touch, gentle stimulation, attention and care needs of a new baby, plus the removal of any pain or discomfort that the baby experiences. Through these activities, carers establish themselves as reinforcers, and the attachment that develops between parents and children becomes a pattern that children ultimately copy in their own relationships with others. It is also the basis through which children can learn to enjoy a wide range of other experiences to which adults introduce them, from music to physical activities. This gradual process of learning to enjoy things – by their association with other things that are reinforcing for us – probably accounts for many of our behaviours that we think of as choices about how we spend our time and with whom.

Knowing that new experiences become rewarding through association with things that are already enjoyed, such as the company of friends, can be help-ful. Parents sometimes say that a child does not like an activity, for example, swimming. However, many activities that a child feared or did not initially like can become enjoyable through gradual encouragement from an important adult, especially with the addition of other rewards, praise and encouragement, maybe a special treat. Eventually, swimming (in this case) may be rewarding because it is enjoyed with school friends or because the child earns badges or competes and wins, so what maintains behaviour in the longer term can be different from what helped to establish it. Getting praised for doing homework initially helps to establish a pattern that builds the child's self-esteem in the short term, but it can also lead to longer-term rewards of success in school.

Young children with challenging behaviour can generate negative atten-tion, although if this is the only attention the child gets it can still be reinforcing. However, this does not provide a basis for the parent being effective in teaching new behaviour to the child and eventually the parent's criticism will become aversive to the child and other reinforcers, such as antisocial peer group reinforcement, will take over. At this point parental influence over the child and their behaviour is lost. This is why many par-enting programmes that aim to address challenging child behaviour start by helping to re-establish the parent as a reinforcer, through spending special time with the child.

To support effective learning of new behaviour, consequences/rewards should initially be *immediate*, but gradually we learn to do things for longer-term gains. A parent who teaches a child to save some of his sweets for later in the day probably achieves this by praising him for doing it, and a parent who teaches a child to save her pocket money probably praised her decision to do it and also talks to her about the benefits of saving. These parents are giving immediate attention to the child for learning to wait for longer-term rewards.

Many things that we do as we grow up are for longer-term rewards – things like working for pay, studying for exams, child-rearing or taking on a mortgage. Achieving these goals is successful when people have been reinforced for planning such goals with key people in their lives and these behaviours have been modelled. However, even in adult life, much of our behaviour is still influenced by immediate or short-term consequences. An adult may give in to a child's tantrums because the immediate consequence or reward for the parent is relief from the problem and the longer-term goal of being consistent towards the child is harder to achieve. Recognising how new behaviours become rewarding by association with other behaviours or rewards, such as parental attention, helps us to understand more about how to support children's learning. This is an example of the Premack Principle that says that if one behaviour is more reinforcing than another, by pairing it can be used to reinforce the less frequent behaviour (Mikulas, 1972).

If we help children to learn through praise and rewards, we build their self-confidence and self-esteem, which will help them to make good, and longer-term, choices when adults are no longer around. For young children, attention can be sufficient reward, but when dealing with a problem behaviour that has become stuck or has generated conflict, small incentives or rewards can help to bring about change.

Effective rewarding has several important characteristics.

i) Rewards must be *immediate* if we want the child to learn the relationship between their behaviour and our response as quickly as possible.

ii) Rewards should occur *every time* in order to establish new behaviour. Once the behaviour occurs regularly, such as cleaning teeth, and becomes part of a routine, our praise no longer needs to occur every time. But it is important that, initially, rewards occur every time, since they are an important component of motivation to learn.

iii) Praise must be *specific* and *positive* and tell the child exactly what it was that we liked about their behaviour. "Thank you for playing quietly while I was on the phone" is more effective than "Thank you for not shouting", as it tells the child what to do in the future to receive praise.

iv) When tangible rewards are used, they should always be *paired* with praise, as in the longer term, when rewards are faded out, it is the strength of the relationship that enables parents to have a continuing influence over their children as they grow up. If praise alone is not sufficiently reinforcing, pairing it with small incentives will, over time, help to establish praise as effective by association and strengthens the relationship between parent and child.

v) Rewards must be *effective*. They must be important to the child. Every child is different – most like praise, but not all do. A teenage son told his mum, "I'll tell you what I did in school, Mum, as long as you don't 'reinforce' me." His mum worked with profoundly learning-disabled adults and was in the habit of giving effusive praise to any adaptive behaviour. For a teenager, particularly in front of his friends, this was quite inappropriate.

Developing children's positive language and self-talk

What the world tells us affects our views about ourselves. Children get messages about how they are perceived, often that they are good, clever, kind, friendly, but for some that they are bad, naughty, careless, unkind, etc. Unfortunately, children with behavioural problems get less attention for their appropriate behaviour than children without such problems, and more attention for problem behaviour than other children get for the same behaviour (Webster-Stratton, 1999). As children's understanding of language develops, they internalise the messages that the world gives them and this is the process by which their self-esteem is developed. Self-esteem, or how we feel about ourselves, is not present in babies but comes from the gradual internalisation of the messages that the world gives us, and children acquire a positive or negative view of themselves that gradually becomes relatively fixed and independent of the world around us. Changing the self-image of children with low self-esteem takes time and encouragement to gradually eradicate or replace the negative messages that have been internalised. If a child has low self-esteem, they may not know how to behave differently or may not be reinforced for behaving well. Conversely, if a child has positive self-esteem and views themselves as kind or helpful, they may give up their seat on the bus to an old person. This may initially be because they have been taught to do so by their parents, but gradually they will only feel comfortable with themselves by continuing to do this, because this is consistent with their own view of the sort of person that they are. Their parents no longer have to be present for the behaviour to occur.

Once children become proficient in language, they start to use it to think and instruct themselves about the things that they are going to do. We talk about this in terms of feelings, thoughts and behaviour, the core components explored in cognitive therapy (Wills and Sanders, 2013). Learning to control their own behaviour by thinking, developing choices and evaluating them is another important developmental milestone for children. This process is often missing in children with behavioural problems, who often do not process situations but respond directly to their feelings. So an uncomfortable feeling – when another child does not want to play with you, for example – can produce an aggressive response.

Basic teaching strategies for learning

a. Learning to pay attention

This is a very important skill for a learner and, often parents and others try to give instructions or teach children without having established basic attending skills. For parents of children on the autistic spectrum, this can be particularly challenging and getting consistent eye contact may be a long-term goal in itself. Parents must teach a child to look at them, and this may mean removing the child from other distractions, such as TV, in order to encourage this. There are other good reasons for doing this, as there is growing evidence from teacher report and longitudinal data of an association between the amount of time spent watching TV and problems of attention and concentration, including ADHD (Landhuis, Poulton, Welch and Hancox, 2007; Levine and Waite, 2000). Getting a child's attention can reduce the necessity to say things several times to a child. Parents *often* repeat instructions to children, particularly to challenging children, and this may inadvertently teach them that paying attention is unnecessary because the message will be repeated. Getting a child to repeat what has been said is one way of encouraging attention. Using a child's name to get their attention is also helpful.

b. Imitation

Imitation supports learning, and parents usually start to teach children to imitate when they are very young. They do this in several ways, initially by imitating what the child does. For example, adults often repeat back the babbling noises that young children make. They also encourage children to imitate by physically helping them to wave bye-bye or blow kisses or by opening their own mouth as they take a spoonful of food towards a baby. As adults we are perhaps less dependent upon imitation, except when we are in novel situations and need to see what other people do. For example, when presented with food that we have not eaten before, we might look to see what others do. Do they eat it with a fork or a spoon? Do they eat the skin? Some children have learned to imitate only the most inappropriate things that they hear or see, such as swearing, perhaps because this leads to attention. However, more adaptive imitation can be encouraged by the parent repeating what the child says or copying what the child does – for example, in child-led play. This was particularly helpful for a mother of a deaf child who was initially encouraging her child's play by describing what he was doing in sign language (describing the child's activities is an important way of knowing that they have your full attention), but this was distracting him from his play. Therefore, we agreed that she would sit opposite him and copy what she saw him doing – for example, in his Lego play. Her son really appreciated this, as it was showing him that she valued what he was doing in an unobtrusive way.

c. Modelling

We can help children to learn by *modelling* the behaviour we want, particularly if they have already learned to imitate us. The mother of a learning-disabled child was anxious because he always sat down on the toilet whenever he was going to pass urine. Because he was disabled and needed help to undress, when outside the house his mother always took him into the ladies' toilets with her and, despite her verbal prompts, he had not learned to stand up to pass urine. Once his father took responsibility for teaching him, and demonstrated what to do, he quickly learned.

The way that new behaviour is learned is often unrelated to what might subsequently maintain the activity, as with the earlier example of praising a child for doing homework, and modelling can initially prompt behaviour. Learning to smoke is an example. The first cigarette is not usually a very pleasant experience, but it generally occurs in the presence of other people who are also smoking and maybe admired. It gradually becomes rewarding in its own right and also begins to happen when we are not in the company of friends.

Prompting the behaviour we want

Prompting can be done verbally or physically, and once the behaviour is established prompts can be faded out. In teaching toileting, for example, we can start by verbally prompting children to use the toilet by telling them when to go. We might do this because we are going to take them out and want to avoid an accident or because we notice cues that suggest that they have a full bladder, such as crossing their legs or increased fidgeting. With little children, we can prompt physically by actually sitting them on the potty or taking them to the toilet. Physical prompting is used when we put our hand over the child's hand to guide them through an action, such as holding a spoon or pencil. Another way of prompting is by gesture – pointing to the potty when suggesting that the child needs to use it and thereby focusing the child's attention on it.

Once going to the toilet is becoming established, often prompting might shift to asking questions of the child, such as "Do you need to go to the toilet?" This helps to give the responsibility for deciding what to do to the child. Verbal prompting can help in teaching social behaviour to children – for example, prompting asking politely or saying "Please" and "Thank you".

Once the child has started to learn, we can gradually fade our prompts. The child who initially went to the toilet because he was prompted by his parents soon started to go when he identified the signal that his bladder was full.

Making sure that the goal is achievable: identifying realistic targets

Many of the things that we want to teach children are quite complex and it is not surprising that they sometimes have difficulty in learning. This is apparent with independent toileting, which is successfully acquired by the average 2-year old. To be "independent" in toileting, the child must recognise bladder and bowel cues, know where the toilet is, be able to open doors, undress and dress, climb on to the seat, wipe themselves, flush the toilet, wash their hands, etc.

Often the child's failure to learn arises from failure on the part of the parent to analyse the task and teach all of the necessary skills. When a more detailed analysis is made, a more realistic teaching target can be established, probably with independent toileting becoming a longer-term goal. Analysis of task components can be helpful for many skills, such as toileting, dressing and eating. In the EPaS programme you have learned a lot in the assessment phase about the child's level of skills and, through the case analysis, can guide the parent towards developmentally realistic goals.

Teaching the last bit of the task first

Starting with the last bit of the task can be helpful. For example, putting on socks is a complex series of tasks and it is not surprising that some young children get frustrated and tell their parents that they can't do it. Rather than reinforce failure by doing the task for them, parents can start by putting the child's sock on for them and asking the child just to pull it up for the last 5 cm or so. The child can easily learn to do this and can be encouraged by this success to attempt more of the task, such as pulling the sock over their heel and then gradually adding more steps. This method of teaching is sometimes known as *backward chaining*. The advantage is that, as you teach the new part of the task, the child always arrives at a part that they have already mastered. This can be successful in teaching children to do jigsaw puzzles, or other tasks that will develop concentration: initially getting them to put just the last piece in, then the last two pieces, etc. always ending with the success of seeing the completed task/jigsaw puzzle.

Shaping

Shaping involves gradually getting closer to the performance that is required. This is particularly the case when we are teaching language. At first the child's approximation to a new word is acceptable to the parents. "Bish" was initially sufficient to send a parent of an 18-month-old searching for a book with a fish on the cover. When the mother subsequently prompted the child to say it again, it was improved to "pish", which again was initially accepted because the "p" sound was a more complex one, which the child had not been using at that stage. Next, the child was prompted to say "fish". This was soon mastered and over time the prompt was to say "fish, please" and eventually to put the word into a full sentence: "Please can I have the fish book." This shaping process is how we teach many skills. For example, it helped in teaching a child to play the recorder. Initially, the parent praised the child because the correct fingers were in place, although because they were not always properly covering the holes the notes did not always sound correct. Next, the child was encouraged to listen to the sound and wiggle her fingers to make sure that the holes were properly covered and also to ensure that the notes sounded right.

Conclusion

Successful teaching depends on a number of specific strategies. These include:

1   identifying achievable teaching targets for children
2   identifying the necessary skills required by the child in order to achieve the target
3   breaking teaching tasks into components or steps that the child can achieve
4   deciding on appropriate teaching strategies in the form of modelling, prompting and shaping
5   rewarding the child for small steps towards success with praise and small incentives.

Using these skills will support children in being successful learners and they are the tools that parents need to establish new replacement behaviours.

References

Hindman, A. H. & Morrison, F. J. (2011). Family involvement and educator outreach in Head Start: Nature, extent, and contributions to early literacy skills. *Elementary School Journal, 111*(3), 359–386.

Kingston, S., Huang, K. Y., Calzada, E., Dawson-McClure, S., & Brotman, L. (2013). Parent involvement in education as a moderator of family and neighborhood socioeconomic context on school readiness among young children. *Journal of Community Psychology, 41*(3), 265–276.

Landhuis, C. E. Poulton, R., Welch, D., & Hancox, R. J. (2007). Does childhood television viewing lead to attention problems in adolescence? Results from a prospective longitudinal study. *Pediatrics, 120*(3) 532–537. doi:10.1542/peds.2007-0978

Levine, L. E. & Waite, M. (2000). Television viewing and attentional abilities in fourth and fifth grade children, *Journal of Applied Developmental Psychology, 21*(6), 667–679. Retrieved from: https://doi.org/10.1016/S0193-3973(00)00060-5

Mikulas, W. L. (1972) *Behavior modification: An overview.* New York: Harper & Row.

Webster-Stratton, C. (1999). *How to promote children's social and emotional competence.* London, UK: Paul Chapman Publishing.

Wills, F. & Sanders, D. (2013). *Cognitive behaviour therapy: Foundations for practice.* London, UK: SAGE.

12 Concluding the EPaS intervention

This chapter reviews the rationale for the EPaS progamme, describes some of the problems associated with focusing primarily on problem behaviour and sets out the tasks for the final EPaS session.

Our ability to learn from our environment is a fundamental human characteristic. A lot of our character, relationship skills and habits are formed through our experiences, particularly those that occur early in our lives (Allen, 2011). Most parents are motivated to do the best for their children and many families do this well without help. Others can be helped without the level of intervention and support that is provided through the EPaS programme. However, using the EPaS process we can engage and help some of the families facing the biggest challenges, both with their children and personally, working as partners with them in supporting their children.

The good news is that, despite the fact that some parents have had bad early experiences themselves, are living in circumstances that are not ideal, are coping with their own mental health problems and finding themselves supporting children with challenging behaviour or developmental difficulties, they can be helped to develop new positive parenting skills (Patterson, Forgatch, Yoerger and Stoolmiller, 1998). This enables them to develop strong and positive relationships with their children and to promote positive child behaviour (Gardner, Hutchings, Bywater and Whitaker, 2010; Hartman, Stage and Webster-Stratton, 2003). This is also the case for parents whose children are temperamentally less easy to support and may have concentration and other difficulties (Jones, Daley, Hutchings, Bywater and Eames, 2008).

The EPaS approach was developed from evidence-based principles and strategies that have helped many parents of children with developmental and/or behavioural challenges to develop new skills and competencies and to replace some of their own and their children's (logical but costly) less adaptive behaviours with effective and pro-social behaviours.

Factors that contribute to the success of the EPaS programme are:

i) the focus on collaborating with parents (the experts on their own child)
ii) ensuring that we are addressing parental concerns
iii) identifying the functions of problematic (logical but costly) child behaviours
iv) identifying new ways for children to have their own needs met through socially appropriate behaviour
v) building on existing assets and skills within the family situation
vi) ensuring that goals (both long-term goals and weekly targets) are realistic and achievable
vii) providing an accessible and predictable service for families.

The EPaS goal is to teach children and parents alternative ways of meeting their needs. Focusing on problem behaviour – although sometimes necessary, particularly for dangerous behaviours – can be counter-productive and risks escalating the situation into a different and potentially more dangerous or challenging problem. Even if sanctions are sometimes necessary, they are not a substitute for teaching children how we want them to behave so that they can avoid sanctions in the future.

When we do have to use consequences for problem behaviours, how we do it matters. It needs to be done in a calm and planned manner or it may be achieved at a cost that parents would not wish to pay. We all learn by imitation and modelling, and when we are angry children learn more from how we handle the situation than they do about the specific problem. Bigger, stronger or more powerful people (or even countries) can influence the behaviour of the smaller and weaker people through aggression, nagging or verbal abuse. The modelling principle reminds us that children can learn to respond in the same way, both towards the person who is behaving in this way towards them and in their own interactions with other people. This is how the coercive cycle between parents and children gets established (Patterson, 1982). Most aggressive children have been treated in similar ways themselves.

Focusing on problems can also lead to avoidance. A husband who was always met by his wife waiting to nag him when he got home from the pub took to staying out later and later each night. By doing this, he was postponing the nagging for as long as possible and sometimes his wife had gone to bed before he got home, so he avoided it completely. In this case, helping his wife to change her response when he came home was one of the factors, in a programme to deal with child protection issues, that led to a change in both his pattern of drinking and support for his wife with the children.

A similar problem occurred for a child coming in from school and wanting to tell her mum about what she had been doing in school that day. She was told that she had torn her trousers, or got her clothes dirty, or that the teacher had said that she misbehaved, all of which reduced the likelihood of her telling her mum about her school day. This was not what the parent intended any more than what the wife intended by nagging her husband when he came home.

Another difficulty with focusing on problem behaviour is that it can teach children to lie in order to avoid consequences. While lying can have a number of functions – including attention, or avoiding tasks by saying that it has been done (cleaning teeth or doing homework, for example), or blaming others ("He started it") – once lying is reinforced by avoiding punishment, it is difficult to deal with because, invariably, it relates to a problem that occurred when the parent was not present.

The EPaS intervention is concluded when the initial contract goals or modified goals have been achieved. In the concluding session, you will review with the parents what has been learned, what successes they have had and, more importantly, why they have achieved success. The aim is not only to have achieved their goals, but to have given the parents a set of tools for tackling the inevitable future challenges that will arise. This is why the involvement of parents in collecting information and agreeing goals is so important. Goldiamond (1975) argues that the goal of therapy is to help people to become their own behaviour analysts, and the EPaS process facilitates this goal, enabling parents to learn about the function of both the child's behaviour and their own. In the final session, you review with parents how they have learned to recognise that – although costly for both the child and adults – the child's problem behaviour was functional and that the parents have either taught their child a different and more socially acceptable way of achieving their goals or a set of behaviours that provides them with alternative reinforcers.

We know that in families in which children present behavioural challenges the core parenting deficits are poor observation skills, global and negative recall focused in the problem, poor problem-solving skills and inconsistent responding. It is these skill deficits that get in the way of parents being able to analyse the circumstances that surrounded the problem behaviour and then plan a realistic strategy:

> "He never does what he is told."
> "She has a tantrum whenever she does not get her own way."
> "The minute I leave the room she hits her baby brother."
> "Whenever the phone rings he kicks off."

The evidence from our own studies, and those of others, highlights the association between poor problem-solving skills and inability to recall detail associated with events. The EPaS process has been training parents to be specific in their observation and recall of events and to assess the impact of small changes in their own behaviour on that of their child, by setting and achieving small developmentally achievable goals for their child. This has provided them with tools to address future challenges. Any changes or improvements achieved have been the result of the changes that the parents have made. You, the therapist, have facilitated these changes but not made them for the parent.

The final session is a celebration of the achievements of the parents and a reflection back on how these changes have been achieved. It is important to talk about the longer-term goal of maintaining changes and generalising the skills to new challenges. Parents may hit a bump in the road and things may deteriorate, so it is important to share with parents that, should this happen, they now have the tools to get themselves back on track. They have become their own problem-solvers. It might have been quicker or easier simply to tell the parents how to get their child to stay in bed, but that would not have given them the tools to address future and different challenges.

Goldiamond (1975) worked with adults with mental health problems, and he gives two detailed examples of the application of the constructional approach to adult mental health problems. Sadly, he died in the 1980s from injuries sustained in a road traffic accident, but not before he had written a fascinating article about how some of his fellow patients had adaptive behaviours punished rather than shaped. He gives the example of a man who, after brain surgery for a tumour, got out of bed and urinated in a tiled corner of the ward (which to him may have appeared much like a urinal and was described as such by some sarcastic visitors as a latrine). He was then confined to his bed and promptly soiled himself, having to be held down four times a day to be changed (Goldiamond, 1976). Goldiamond left us with a valuable approach to helping people to learn to resolve many problems that arise in human interactions. The EPaS programme has taken his work and successfully adapted it for work with children and families.

Our work, and that of others, has demonstrated that the co-occurrence of maternal depression and child behaviour problems arises due to the same set of skill deficits – poor observation skills, global and negative recall of events and poor problem-solving skills – resulting in the inability to set realistic and achievable goals (Hutchings, Nash, Williams and Nightingale, 1998; Hutchings, Bywater, Williams, Lane and Whitaker, 2012; Wahler and Sansbury, 1990). Therefore, it is no surprise that work with families that addresses these deficits produces improvements in maternal depression that are equivalent in effect size to the reductions in child behaviour problems. This finding is also confirmed in a Cochrane review of parenting programmes. Barlow, Coren, and Stewart-Brown (2003) found parenting programmes to be effective in improving both child behaviour and a range of parental factors, including maternal depression, anxiety and self-esteem.

The association between depression and child behaviour problems can arise in different ways, and there is no one explanation for this association. As we have argued:

> Some evidence suggests that maternal depression is causal in the development of CD (Patterson, 1982; Rutter, 1996). Depressed mothers exhibit low rates of praise and failure in monitoring their child's

behaviour, which are both associated with the development of CD (Webster-Stratton and Herbert, 1994). Even shortly after birth, coded videos of mother–infant interactions show differences in behaviour between depressed and non-depressed mothers (Field, 1995a, 1995b). Other research suggests that problematic child behaviour can precipitate maternal depression, particularly if the child displays characteristics that make parenting difficult, such as temperament problems and poor sleep patterns (Webster-Stratton and Spitzer, 1996). There can also be external predictors for both conditions such as socio-economic disadvantage that have been shown to be independently associated with both problems (Silberg and Rutter, 2002; Mensah and Kiernan, 2010).

(Hutchings et al., 2012, p. 795)

As our case analysis in Chapter 9 showed, in that situation the mother's depression was triggered by the break-up of her marriage following her husband's infidelity. Beck has defined the classic depressive triad as negative view of the world, the self and the future (Beck, Rush, Shaw and Emery, 1979). Peter's behaviour, in the situation of starting nursery and having to cope with the recent arrival of his baby brother, was logical (see Chapter 9). As Patterson et al. (1998) have demonstrated, challenging life circumstances can impact on parenting, not directly on the child, and it is the parenting that impacts on the child. Some parents do a great job, despite living in difficult circumstances. With support, other parents can change their interactions with their children, even if other aspects of their life are less easy to change.

Regardless of the initial triggers for problematic child behaviour, a premature and hard-to-parent child, a traumatic life event or external factors that appear to put solutions beyond the control of the parent, the EPaS programme has demonstrated the benefits of teaching the core skills of observation and problem-solving. These are focused around a set of parenting behaviours that include:

i)   strengthening the parent–child relationship
ii) increasing positive behaviour through praise and rewards
iii) having clear and realistic expectations and household rules
iv) giving positive and specific instructions
v)   removing attention from challenging behaviours that are annoying but not destructive or dangerous to either the child or others
vi) Having clear and consistent consequences for unacceptable behaviour.

The final EPaS session is an acknowledgement of the goals achieved by the parent and a review of what has been learned and why. This will equip the parent with the tools to maintain their present achievements and generalise their skills to new situations that inevitably will arise and may or may not be related to their child. There is a checklist for reviewing the final session at the end of this chapter.

References

Allen, G. (2011). *Early intervention: The next steps. An independent report to Her Majesty's Government.* London, UK: The Smith Institute and the Centre for Social Justice. Retrieved from: http://dera.ioe.ac.uk/14161/1/graham%20 allen%20review%20of%20early%20intervention.pdf

Barlow, J., Coren, E., & Stewart-Brown, S. (2003). Parent-training programmes for improving maternal psychosocial health. *Cochrane Database of Systematic Reviews, 4.* doi:10.1002/14651858.CD002020.pub2

Beck, A. T., Rush, A. J., Shaw, B. F., & Emery, G. (1979). *Cognitive Therapy of Depression.* New York: Guilford Press.

Field, T. (1995a). Infants of depressed mothers. *Infant Behaviour and Development, 18,* 1–13. doi:10.1016/0163-6383(95)90003-9

Field, T. (1995b). Psychologically depressed patients. In: M. H. Bornstein (Ed.), *Handbook of parenting,* Vol. 4, *Applied and practical parenting.* Mahwah, NJ: Lawrence Erlbaum.

Gardner, F., Hutchings, J., Bywater, T., & Whitaker, C. J. (2010). Who benefits and how does it work? Moderators and mediators of outcome in an effectiveness trial of a parenting intervention in multiple "Sure Start" services. *Journal of Clinical Child and Adolescent Psychology, 39,* 568–580.

Goldiamond, I. (1975). A constructional approach to self control. In: A. Schwartz & I. Goldiamond (Eds.), *Social casework: A behavioural approach.* New York: Columbia University Press.

Goldiamond, I. (1976). Coping and adaptive behaviours of the disabled. In: Gary L. Albrecht (Ed.), *The sociology of physical disability and rehabilitation.* Pittsburgh, PA: University of Pittsburgh.

Hartman, R. R., Stage, S. A., & Webster-Stratton, C. (2003). A growth curve analysis of parent training outcomes: Examining the influence of child risk factors (inattention, impulsivity, and hyperactivity problems), parental and family risk factors. *Journal of Child Psychology and Psychiatry, 44,* 388–398.

Hutchings, J., Nash, S., Williams, J. M. G., & Nightingale, D. (1998). Parental autobiographical memory: Is this a helpful clinical measure in behavioural child management? *British Journal of Clinical Psychology, 37,* 303–312. doi:10.1111/j.2044-8260.1998.tb01387.x

Hutchings, J., Bywater, T., Williams, M. E., Lane, E., & Whitaker, C. J. (2012). Improvements in maternal depression as a mediator of child behaviour change. *Psychology, 3*(9A), 795–801. doi:10.4236/psych.2012.329120

Jones, K., Daley, D., Hutchings, J., Bywater, T., & Eames, C. (2008). Efficacy of the Incredible Years Basic Parent Training Programme as an early intervention for children with conduct disorder and ADHD: long-term follow-up. *Child: Care, Health and Development, 34,* 380–390.

Mensah, F. K. & Kiernan, K. E. (2010). Parents' mental health and children's cognitive and social development. *Social Psychiatry and Psychiatric Epidemiology, 45,* 1023–1035.

Patterson, G. R. (1982). *Coercive family process.* Eugene, OR: Castalia.

Patterson, G. R., Forgatch, M. S., Yoerger, K. L., & Stoolmiller, M. (1998). Variables that initiate and maintain an early-onset trajectory for juvenile offending. *Development and Psychopathology, 10*(3), 531–547.

Rutter, M. (1996). Connections between child and adult psychopathology. *European Child and Adolescent Psychiatry, 5,* 4–7. doi:10.1007/BF00538535

Silberg, J. & Rutter, M. (2002). Nature–nurture interplay in the risks associated with parental depression. In: S. H. Goodman & I. H. Gotlib (Eds.), *Children of depressed parents: Mechanisms of risk and implications for treatment* (pp. 13–36). Washington, DC: American Psychological Association. doi:10.1037/10449-001

Wahler, R. G. & Sansbury, L. E. (1990). The monitoring skills of troubled mothers: Their problems in defining child deviance. *Journal of Abnormal Child Psychology, 18,* 577–589.

Webster-Stratton, C. & Herbert, M. (1994). *Troubled families: Problem children.* Chichester, UK: Wiley.

Webster-Stratton, C. & Spitzer, A. (1996). Parenting a young child with conduct problems: New insights using qualitative methods. *Advances in Clinical Child Psychology, 18,* 1–62.

EPaS checklist for reviewing final session

	Activity	Completed yes/no
1	Conclude the session by reviewing achievements.	
2	Review the parent skills and principles that contributed to the outcomes.	
3	Provide information on future access, etc.	
4	Thank the parents for working with you and their commitment to their child.	
5	Predict success with future problems using the skills that they have developed.	

Part III
Typical problems

13 A bedtime problem

Consequences significantly influence how we learn and whether things will happen again, so it is important to look first for the consequences or functions of problem behaviours to establish why they are happening. Night-time problems are common and, by considering what consequences there might be, we can find solutions for these problems for many children. The accumulating evidence of the importance of sleep and the extent to which both children and adults in our society are sleep-deprived highlights the importance of good sleep routines.

Andrew was 3 years old and his night-time behaviour was a major problem for his parents. His daytime behaviour was also challenging and he was described as hyperactive. However, his parents saw the night-time problem as imposing the most limitations on them as a family. If Andrew did not have a lot of attention at night he made his parents' life a misery. He would not go to bed when asked, and if they did get him into bed he would not remain there on his own. Despite living in a three-bedroom house, his bed was in his parents' bedroom, although generally he ended up sleeping in their bed.

At bedtime, usually at the fourth or fifth time of asking, he would go upstairs to his bedroom with one of his parents. Once in bed, he would demand a drink and snack and the parent would go downstairs to get this for him, and then, after stories, they would stay with him until he fell asleep. This could last for well over an hour. Once he was asleep, they would creep downstairs only to find that (at least five times a week) Andrew would wake up and either call for someone to come upstairs or come downstairs himself. Generally, he came downstairs and then remained there until they all went to bed. If he remained asleep until after his parents had gone to bed, he then got into their bed when he did wake, so invariably ended up in their bed in the morning. Whilst downstairs, he would sit or lie on the settee between his parents – he would not let them sit together – and finally all three went to bed together and Andrew slept between his parents, in their bed, for the rest of the night. Andrew's younger sister did not have these problems, but she was still in a cot, so (as yet) she did not have a choice about getting up.

When Andrew was 3 years, 6 months, his parents asked for help. Tranquillisers had already been tried without much effect, so their doctor referred them for help, with his management. By this point, the night-time problems had been occurring for over two and a half years and were affecting many other aspects of family life. His parents said that the hyperactive and challenging daytime behaviour had developed more recently. Andrew's parents could not get a babysitter, so could not go out together, and they had little privacy. They disagreed about the best way to solve the problem and blamed each other for the situation. They said that they had tried everything, including threats, bribes and punishment.

It was easy to see why Andrew continued to behave in this way. There were many rewards for him. He got attention from his parents, as well as drinks and food through the night. But how had he learned it?

When Andrew was born, his parents had lived in a one-bedroom flat, so he had always slept in the same room with them. When he was 10 months old, he had been quite ill and had had several disturbed nights. His parents had got up when he cried to see what was wrong and soothed him to sleep. This led to demands for attention at night that gradually increased in frequency. By the time Andrew's parents began to realise that he was not in pain, there was a well-established pattern that they had since not managed to change.

There were several reasons for Andrew's parents failing to get to grips with the problem. His Mum said, "Well, we have tried putting him back in his own bed, but he makes such a fuss and cries. That disturbs my husband and he has to get his sleep just now, because he's hoping for promotion and he's being watched at work to see whether they think he could do it." A further issue was their concern that he would wake his sister. In fact, Andrew's dad sometimes slept in a separate bedroom.

Andrew's problem was typical of those that many parents report, and there is usually a logical explanation for how the behaviour became established – in Andrew's case, during illness, or following a period in hospital. By the time the problem was established, Andrew had learned the rewarding consequences of his behaviour and his parents had learned that, in the short term, giving in was the least painful way to cope.

Andrew's parents agreed to a plan to teach him more acceptable ways of behaving at bedtime and during the night. First, before trying to change things, they kept simple records of what was happening. These included recording what time Andrew went to bed, how long they lay with him, whether he had drinks or food in bed, what time he got up, and also whether he spent the night in his parents' bed. Andrew's parents kept records over eight nights, which showed that they were lying with him for, on average, 47 minutes each night before he fell asleep. He spent every one of the eight nights in his parents' bed. Andrew's parents could see that there were many rewarding consequences for him, and these were maintaining his difficult behaviour. A new routine was devised:

1 Tell Andrew that you have a new plan for him to earn stickers for sleeping in his own bed each night.
2 Tell Andrew that he can have food or drinks before going to bed. Andrew was a fussy daytime eater. This is not surprising, when he had food during the night – including quite a lot of milk, which substitutes for food!
3 Going to bed: take Andrew to bed and read stories for 10 minutes. Tell him that he is a big boy now and that he is learning to stay in his own bed. Explain to him that if he shouts after you have gone downstairs, you will not reply. Remind him that if he comes downstairs, he will be taken back to bed.
4 Tell Andrew that he can tell his grandmother all about learning to sleep on his own. Andrew was very fond of his grandmother and also liked to speak on the phone.
5 In the evening, if Andrew comes downstairs, take him back to bed without speaking to him. The same applies if he comes to your bed during the night when you are in bed. You may, at first, have to do this a lot of times. He must end the night sleeping in his own bed.
6 In the morning, remind Andrew that he is a big boy and that he has stayed in his own bed all night and give him a sticker to put on his chart. Make it very clear how pleased you are that he is in his own bed, regardless of how many times you have had to put him back in his own bed.
7 During the day remind Andrew – at first, several times – that he stayed in his own bed during the night. Also tell any other visitors to the house, or anyone that you see with Andrew, about his good behaviour. Let Andrew speak to his grandmother on the phone to tell her he stayed in his own bed.

The plan was discussed in detail before commencement and Andrew's parents were prepared for the fact that Andrew's initial response would probably be challenging. However, they were reassured that if they were consistent, this plan was likely to produce observable changes within less than a week. It was also important to establish that they would support one another in carrying out the plan to put Andrew back to bed without getting angry with him. This involved coaching the parents in some positive self-talk about the benefits for Andrew, as well as for themselves. On the first night, Andrew came downstairs 47 times, but he learned to sleep in his own bed very quickly. On the second night, he came down once. He did not come downstairs again after being put to bed until night 10, when he again tried once.

This clearly demonstrated to the parents how children's behaviour will change, usually quite quickly (sometimes very dramatically) when the consequences change. Under the new system, the rewards for staying in his own bed, and the removal of the rewarding consequences previously associated with the problem, rapidly taught Andrew to do this.

Within less than a month Andrew was sleeping in a room on his own all night. His parents had felt that moving him out of their bedroom was too large a step for him, so they decided to move themselves into a slightly smaller bedroom (which they had previously intended for Andrew), leaving him in the room that he was familiar with. They also did a great job in rearranging the consequences for his behaviour, using a combination of giving positive attention for the behaviour they wanted, with reinforcement for target behaviour, and ignoring the behaviour that they wanted less of. They also said that having the plan meant that they handled the situation much more calmly than they had previously, thereby modelling positive behaviour towards Andrew. Having a very structured plan made it possible for Andrew's parents to approach the situation calmly and explain to him in advance what the new system involved and what his rewards would be.

Another benefit was a significant improvement in Andrew's daytime behaviour, something that can occur quite often. Recent studies suggest that children, adolescents and adults are getting insufficient sleep, and that this can have a major impact on daytime levels of concentration (Gregory and Sadeh, 2012; Wheaton, Liu, Perry and Croft, 2011; Wolfson and Carskadon, 1998).

It is important to establish what is reinforcing the night-time problem, which is usually clearly demonstrated by the record sheets and discussions with parents. It could be the child can obtain access to food and drinks or to TV or toys in the bedroom, or the problem may be anxiety-based and the parents remaining with the child might reduce the child's anxiety. Some children are afraid of the dark – usually ones that have not experienced it – and strategies such as installing dimmer lights or sitting with the child in the bedroom in the dark may be needed to help children learn to feel comfortable in the dark. Light of any sort in the bedroom reduces the production of melatonin during sleep and this can disrupt sleep rhythms and the body's care and repair mechanisms (Scheer and Czeisler, 2005; Pandi-Perumal et al., 2008). Other children may be ill-prepared for sleep due to being overstimulated as a result of too much time in front of screens, particularly if the content includes violent games. A review of many studies by Browne and Hamilton-Giachritsis (2005) confirmed the effects of exposure to violent media, significantly on younger children, particularly on boys. Current advice suggests the need for two screen-free hours prior to going to bed in order that the brain is prepared for sleep (Chatterjee, 2017).

Key points that led to success in the work with Andrew were:

1   The problem was described clearly, to enable the identification of probable reinforcers or rewards.
2   This information was used to negotiate a plan with the parents.
3   The plan was introduced to the child in a positive way.

4   The parents knew what challenges would be faced in implementing the plan, e.g. that on the first night the child is likely to get out of bed many times.
5   The parents talked through how they would support one another in ensuring that they stayed calm and stuck to the plan.

For this, and many other problems, it can be helpful to introduce the plan in stages – for example, first establishing the rule that food is only eaten in a certain place or getting a structured bedtime routine in place, then addressing the larger aspect of the problem or only returning the child to their own bed if they wake during the night. In Andrew's case, we decided that developmentally he was capable of learning the new behaviour if the parents implemented the whole plan at once. The fact that both parents were willing to support each other in doing this also contributed to their decision to address the problem in this way.

References

Browne, K. D. & Hamilton-Giachritsis, C. (2005). The influence of violent media on children and adolescents: A public-health approach. *Lancet*, *365*(9460), 702–710.

Chatterjee, R. (2017). *The 4 Pillar Plan: How to relax, eat, move and sleep your way to a longer, healthier life*. Harmondsworth, UK: Penguin.

Gregory, A. M. & Sadeh, A. (2012). Sleep, emotional and behavioral difficulties in children and adolescents. *Sleep Medicine Reviews*, *16*(2), 129–136.

Pandi-Perumal, S. R., Trakht, I., Srinivasan, V., Spence, D. W., Maestroni, G. J. M., Zisapel, N., & Cardinali, D. P. (2008). Physiological effects of melatonin: Role of melatonin receptors and signal transduction pathways. *Progress in Neurobiology*, *85*(3), 335–353. doi.org/10.1016/j.pneurobio.2008.04.001

Scheer, F. A. L. & Czeisler, C. A. (2005). Melatonin, sleep, and circadian rhythms. *Sleep Medicine Reviews*, *9*(1), 5–9.

Wheaton, A. G., Liu, Y., Perry, G. S., & Croft, J. B. (2011). Effect of short sleep duration on daily activities – United States, 2005–2008. *Morbidity and Mortality Weekly Report*, *60*(8), 239–242.

Wolfson, A. R. & Carskadon, M. A. (1998). Sleep schedules and daytime functioning in adolescents. *Child Development*, *69*(4), 875–887. doi:10.1111/j.1467-8624.1998.tb06149.x

14 A morning problem

In the previous example (Chapter 13), changing the consequences helped Andrew to learn to stay in bed at night. In this example, a similar approach was used to address a morning problem.

Steven was 11 and had difficulty getting up in the morning and it was getting worse. First his dad woke him. Then, on her way downstairs, his mum said good morning to him and asked him to get up. She started to prepare the breakfast and, if she could not hear Steven moving, she would go to the foot of the stairs and call him, often several times. The calls would escalate to shouts and, since this seldom worked, she often had to go upstairs and actually shake him out of bed. When he finally arrived in the kitchen Steven usually got a telling off for his disobedience and for making himself late for school.

For Steven, there were not many pleasant consequences associated with mornings. His mum nagged and shouted at him, not only when he remained upstairs, but also when he came down. But the consequence for Steven's mum was that the end result of all her nagging was that Steven finally got up – so she continued to do it day after day, not very happy about it, but trapped by a situation in which nagging and shouting seemed to be the only thing that worked. She had inadvertently taught Steven that she took the responsibility for getting him up and, in order to achieve this, she had to do a lot of nagging and shouting.

Steven's mum knew that something needed to change, and keeping records of what was happening helped her to identify the problem more clearly. With help, she rearranged the consequences to teach Steven to get up more readily. Given Steven's age, it was important to include him in the discussion of both the problem and the plan. First we defined what Steven needed to do in the morning. He must get out of bed, wash his hands and face, get dressed and come downstairs (his mum put out his morning clothes the previous evening). Steven agreed that it should be possible to do this in 25 minutes and he readily agreed with his parents that if he did achieve 25 minutes or less, he could have an extra half-hour of television time in the evening. Steven's mum agreed to ask Steven only once to get up and not to call or nag him. She also agreed to smile and say something pleasant when he came down, regardless of how long he had taken in getting up.

Sometimes when working on strategies to solve problems like this, it is necessary to inform schools or employers that the child might be late for school for a day or two or the parent late for work. However, most children do not like being late for school, and helping them to take responsibility for their own behaviour is usually a very powerful tool in helping them to change.

On *day one*, following the usual routine, first Steven's dad woke him, then his mum, on her way downstairs, said good morning to him and asked him to get up. Steven took 55 minutes to get downstairs. It was difficult for his mother to refrain from doing what she had previously done, but once Steven came downstairs she smiled, and said, "Nice to see you," and then later said, "I am sorry to say that you have not earned your half-hour of extra TV time tonight. I think that tomorrow you will manage to do it." By expressing her sympathy for Steven's failure to earn the reward, his mum was modelling her own concern for him and her wish for him to succeed. His behaviour had previously generated anger from her, and this was a very different response.

On *day two*, Steven took 26 minutes to get downstairs and his mum greeted him cheerfully and acknowledged that he had been quicker, but repeated what she had said the previous day. She almost relented, since it was so close, but she reasoned that 26 minutes today would be 27 minutes tomorrow, and so on. Thereafter Steven was down well inside the 25 minutes and earned his extra TV time. Within a couple of weeks, they had stopped timing him or mentioning the routine but continued to praise him on arrival downstairs. As well as gaining the extra TV time, both Steven and his mum were rewarded for their new behaviour by pleasant mornings.

In this situation, the behaviour that had achieved consequences for Mum (nagging and shouting) had continued – however unpleasant she found it – because it worked, and she did not know how else to get Steven to get up. For Steven, the consequence of getting up was a further telling off, so was delayed as long as possible. Mum had taken on responsibility for getting him up and Steven had learned to ignore what she said for as long as possible.

It is important to ensure that the behaviour you want has happened, and in Steven's case his mum was certain that he did wash his hands and face and that this did not need supervising.

However, for some children a much greater level of supervision is needed to ensure that the behaviour occurs and that each step can be praised and rewarded. It is not uncommon for parents and children to argue about whether the child has done something, such as their homework or cleaning their teeth.

Many parents find themselves in the same situation as Steven's mum – knowing very clearly what they want their child to do, but having got into a trap of providing consequences for the wrong behaviour and/or having failed to set up consequences for the right behaviour. Solutions generally require the following steps: (a) careful observation of what is currently happening, to identify what consequences are currently operating; (b) deciding what the desired behaviour is and that it is developmentally achievable; and (c) ensuring that a rewarding consequence is arranged for the appropriate behaviour rather than for anything else.

We can learn a lot about consequences from the examples of Steven and Andrew. Two sorts of consequences encourage behaviour to occur again. Behaviour is repeated when something pleasant follows. Steven soon learned to get up quickly on his own because he got more TV and his mum was nice to him. Andrew stayed in bed at night because he got praise and attention for it. Behaviour is also repeated when what we do removes something unpleasant. Andrew's parents gave in to his demands at bedtime and during the night because it was an end to the difficulties presented if they tried to manage the situation in any other way. Before Steven had learned to get up through his own efforts, he got up only when the nagging and shouting became so unpleasant that it was impossible to stay in bed any longer. Getting up put an end to this unpleasant nagging.

The key message from these examples is to give attention to behaviour we want more of and remove attention from behaviour we want less of. It is also important to remember that parents are models for their children and that children learn as much from the way that parents handle situations (in Steven's mum's case, calmly and pleasantly rather than by nagging) as they do about the situations themselves.

In learning to recognise and change the consequences of problem behaviour, it can be helpful to keep records of the problem and what follows it, as has been happening throughout the EPaS programme. Record keeping sometimes resolves problems because the mere fact of recording shows parents what is happening and what needs to change. In some cases, writing down what is happening when a problem occurs changes how parents respond to it (they become detectives looking for clues to explain behaviour, and so are responding differently to it) and this too can produce changes in children's behaviour.

During a visit to Monash University, Australia, in 1970, I learned of work involving parents recording typical things their child did that they found problematic. They developed lists of typical behaviours for children of different ages. For 3-year-olds, it included tantrums, hitting, spitting, swearing, running off and throwing objects. Parents were asked to keep the list on their fridge or cupboard door and go to the list whenever the problem behaviour occurred, then to mark it down and say to themselves, "This is what 3-year-olds do." They found that the act of walking away and recording the problem actually reduced it. This was because the behaviour no longer got the attention that it previously had. It also served to help the parents to recognise that these problems were typical of children of that age, so provided developmental knowledge that helped parents to have more realistic expectations.

Two things are important to consider in the case of Steven. He was expected to undertake getting up, washing, dressing, etc. before coming downstairs and without supervision. In his case he was already doing all of these things without supervision, so the task was developmentally achievable and he did not need teaching. The only teaching that was needed was for Steven to respond to the initial prompt. For many children, more supervision would be needed and the programme might need to focus on one step at a time and need teaching and/or supervision. In addressing a morning problem, it would also be important to consider whether the child had an adequate amount of sleep or whether tiredness was playing a part in the problem, as discussed in Andrew's bedtime example in Chapter 13.

15 A shopping trip

A common problem for parents can be seen at the till in the supermarket. Some parents with young children may try to leave them at home when they go shopping and other children cope well in the supermarket. However, for some, being confronted by tiers of sweets at the till can be a challenge and you might overhear the following:

> Child asks "Can I have . . .?"
> Mum says "No!"
> Child starts to repeat more loudly "Can I have?" or cry.
> Mum says "No" rather more loudly.
> The child tries to grab the sweets or to tantrum – Mum tries to maintain her position.
> Other people start to take notice.
> Mum picks up the sweets and puts them in the shopping trolley.
> Child beams and peace is restored.

Two things have been rewarded. First the child was rewarded, by the tantrum, for shouting and getting sweets, and therefore they will do it again. Second, the mother was rewarded for giving in to the child's difficult behaviour, because the child became quiet and other customers stopped taking notice of what was happening. She is also likely to cope in the same way next time. This is the same pattern as we saw with Andrew's night-time problem (Chapter 13). The child's behaviour is rewarded by the positive consequence – in this case, by the sweets – and the mother is rewarded because the child stops behaving badly and the problem goes away.

What has happened makes sense in terms of consequences for both the child and the parent. The problem that it produces is a longer-term one, reminding us that behaviour that is reinforced will be repeated.

Sometimes the consequence of, or reward for, problem behaviour is attention, but often it involves other things: sweets, extra computer time, staying up later to watch TV, etc. By identifying and removing the rewards for problem behaviour, and by ensuring that they only follow desired behaviour, problems can be resolved without having to resort to punishment, as was demonstrated in the solutions to the night-time and morning problems (Chapters 13 and 14).

The till in the supermarket illustrates something else. People, even children, are very good at learning what will pay off in different situations and with different people, so it is important to look for the triggers – to what prompts them to behave in a particular way at that time. These antecedents or triggers (the things that occur before the problem behaviour) can set off particular chains of events.

At the supermarket till, there are several very important antecedents/ triggers for problem behaviour. One is that people often have to wait in a queue, so children have nothing to do. Another is that the supermarket managers and owners (who also understand human psychology) put out an array of easily available goods, often within children's reach, intended to prompt people to spend more money while they wait. Another antecedent/trigger is that there are usually other people standing around who might take notice. All of these things combine to make some things much more likely to happen than others. So, looking at Antecedents (or triggers), Behaviour and Consequences – the ABC model – helps to sort out what is happening.

In the supermarket, the situation looks a bit like this:

Antecedent [for the child]	[Child's] Behaviour	Consequences
Nothing to do, sitting in trolley by the till	Asks for sweets	Mum says "No"
Sweets within reach	Asks again louder	Mum says "No"
Other people join the queue	Starts crying	Mum says "No"
People start to pay attention	Child tries to grab the sweets	Mum is embarrassed and says "OK"
Mum gives sweets to child	Child has the sweets	People stop paying attention
	Child is no longer crying	Mum feels more comfortable

Linda was 3 years, 6 months old and had a younger sister of 18 months. Linda would touch things in shops, pick them up and demand (successfully) that Mum bought her some sweets. Her mother had got so upset about taking her shopping that she tried to do all her shopping in the two mornings that Linda was in the playgroup. Mum also had difficulties in getting Linda to follow instructions at home.

Before Linda's mum started taking her shopping again, she first helped Linda to follow instructions at home. Once this was done, she tried the following:

1   Mum got Linda a small bag so that she could be like Mum and carry something home.
2   Mum told Linda that she would like her to hold the side of the trolley walking round the shop, but that when she wanted something Linda could fetch it and put it in the trolley.
3   Mum told Linda that if she helped in the shop, she would be able to choose something for herself to take home in her bag (since Linda was already being bought something when she went shopping, her Mum decided that it was important that Linda got something for acceptable – rather than unacceptable – behaviour).
4   If there were choices about things that Mum was buying – for instance, which sort of biscuits – Mum was asked to involve Linda in the choice.
5   Mum agreed to talk to Linda and help to retain her interest while shopping by telling her what they were going to buy, what meals they could make with it, and so on, and also by asking Linda to remind her to get things. For an older child, writing and carrying the shopping list and searching for things can be helpful.
6   While in the shop, Mum praised Linda and reminded her what a good girl she was for helping with the shopping and how nice it was to have such a good helper.

Initially, Mum took Linda on very short shopping expeditions and into smaller shops – in fact, first to the local village post office, where Linda was able to post a letter in the postbox. Gradually, as Mum learned how to keep Linda's interest and teach her to help, she was able to extend the length of time and the locations in which she could shop with Linda without having problems. On the first few occasions Linda's mum also took along a set of reins. She explained to Linda before leaving home that she would have to put them on if Linda wandered off, like she had previously.

If we look at Linda's behaviour in ABC terms, we can see what has happened.

Antecedent [for problem]	Behaviour	Consequences
Shops	Walks around, touches things, pick things up	Mum's attention – "Put that down", etc.
Seeing other people pick things up generally, including Mum, and seeing sweets at the till	Demands sweets	Sweets

Antecedent [for solution]	Behaviour	Consequences
Shops	Linda helps Mum	Mum praises her
Mum involves Linda in shopping	Linda helps with the shopping	Linda chooses something for herself

Other useful strategies for solving shopping problems include: getting the child to help to write the shopping list, cutting out parts of cereal boxes, etc. so the child could look for them, giving the child a sticker at the end of each shopping aisle for holding onto the trolley, helping to push it, etc. The stickers can earn a small reward, which the child will be able to choose – say, something costing less than a pound.

The antecedents or triggers that produce problem behaviour may be a particular person previously associated with that behaviour when it has been rewarded. Granny, for example, might say "Yes" to requests for sweets or ice creams more often than other people. Granny's arrival might become a trigger for asking for sweets. Children learn that there are times when parents will say "Yes" and times when they will say "No". They may say "Yes" in the supermarket and "No" at home, so the trigger for the problem is a particular place, such as school, a shop, or frustration because someone called you a name or took your toy. Being tired or hungry can also be a trigger for a particular behaviour, as is a parent being otherwise occupied (perhaps on the phone or talking with a friend).

All of these examples show the importance of observing and describing very carefully, not only the child's behaviour and the consequence, but also the situation in which the behaviour occurs. Describing the situation means looking at where it is occurring, who is present, what people were doing, and so on. Only by careful observation of this sort can we understand children's behaviour sufficiently to be able to help them to learn what we want them to do.

16 A toileting problem

The problems described in Chapters 13, 14 and 15 – going to bed, getting up and going shopping – were resolved by understanding how the situation was rewarding to both the child and parents. They also showed how teaching the desired behaviour and providing consequences for it was effective in replacing problem behaviour with pro-social behaviour. Sometimes what is rewarding the problem behaviour can be used as a reward for the new behaviour. For example, an older child who delays going to bed could earn half an hour of extra time out of bed (that could be spent at weekends) for going to bed on time on school nights. This would only work with an older child, however, as developmentally younger children are not yet likely to have learned to wait and they would need a more immediate reward. The shopping problem in Chapter 15 involved helping Linda to earn the reward for acceptable behaviour rather than problem behaviour. The shopping trip also highlighted the importance of looking for triggers or antecedents, the situations that set up or prompt behaviour.

It is often easier to understand the effect of triggers for (or antecedents of) behaviour by looking at learning failures, rather than successes. For example, a mother was giving 3-year-old son Peter lots of attention for sitting on the potty, so why wasn't he learning to use it? Her description of what was happening was "I notice that his pants are damp, so I sit him on the potty and give him lots of attention. I make sitting on the potty pleasant, I read books to him while he sits there, and so on, but he does not do anything in it." A more careful description of the problem revealed the following:

Antecedent	Behaviour	Consequences
Bladder's signal indicating that Peter must empty his bladder	Peter wets his pants	Mum sits Peter on potty and gives lots of attention, reads to him, etc.

Peter was sat on the potty and given attention after he was wet, and not when he was dry. He learned to use the potty within a week when his mum changed the consequences.

Peter's mum was asked to check his pants at frequent intervals, initially every 15 minutes. If Peter had wet pants, he was changed without comment and not sat on the potty. If he was dry, she praised him and also asked him, "Do you want a wee?" If he said "Yes", he was praised and encouraged to sit on the potty, where he was praised for a good decision but was not read to. If he said "No," that he did not want a wee, he was praised for being dry. If he used the potty, which she checked frequently, he was praised again. If, after five minutes on the potty, he had not performed, he was praised for remaining dry and told that he could try again when he was ready. This simple change was sufficient to teach Peter to use the potty very quickly.

For Peter, being dry led to a consequence of praise, and being wet led to being changed without anything being said. Obviously, since he became dry so quickly, the praise was a rewarding consequence. His mum also continued to read frequently to Peter – something that is important for all children, – but not when he was on the potty.

It is important that children are praised more for being dry than for performing, although it is sometimes helpful to prompt children – if we are going on a long journey, for example. In general, we want children to learn to respond to a signal from their bladder that tells them that they need to go to the toilet. Both the presence of Mum and the bladder signals can be antecedents, which lead to the behaviour we want, but it is only when the child learns to respond to bladder cues that they become independent in toileting. There is a maturational process underpinning bladder control and children are generally not ready to learn until they have developed control and have sufficient urine in their bladders to become aware of bladder cues. This can be judged by the frequency and content of urine when the child does pass urine, and that becomes more apparent with the dry-pants checks. Had Peter's mum found that his pants were wet very frequently, she would have needed to consider whether he was developmentally capable of learning at that stage or whether he needed some other form of assessment.

Another example of the power of antecedents comes from another toileting example. A colleague had worked with a mother on toilet training Tommy, a child with a developmental difficulty, and had taken an active part in helping with his toilet training. Unfortunately, the wrong message had been learned. Tommy had learned to associate my *colleague* with sitting on the potty rather than to respond to *bladder cues*. Every time she arrived at the house, Tommy rushed off and got his potty and sat on it. He usually managed to perform something and got her attention, but he was not responding to his bladder cues:

Antecedent	Behaviour	Consequences
Jane arrives	Tommy sits on potty – passes a small amount of urine	Praise from Jane

This was easily resolved by my colleague shifting her attention from Tommy sitting on the potty to looking at the stars he had earned by staying dry since her last visit. An analysis of the antecedents or triggers, as well as of the consequences, was necessary to explain what had been happening.

The programme described in *Toilet Training in Less Than a Day* (Azrin and Foxx, 1989) is a fun way to help to toilet train a child. It uses all of the behavioural principles used in the examples above and the teaching strategies in Chapter 11, on teaching new behaviour. Their programme starts with modelling by a doll that pees and then is based on prompting and reinforcing the behaviour that is wanted i.e. includes a lot of reinforcement for being dry and practising with frequent checks for dry pants. Whil Azrin and Foxx suggest using sweets as reinforcers (something that we would no longer encourage) along with praise, cuddles and involving other significant adults, the programme works well with other reinforcers, such as special stickers. It was interesting to see the review below, from a mum that had used it with her four children and who has recently bought it for one of them to use with one of their *own* children.

A review from Amazon

To be honest, I bought this book way back in the 70s and used it to potty train my four children. Of course it doesn't work in less than a day (neither do Father Christmas nor the Tooth fairy exist, you know), but I found it a brilliant way to get the children started and compared to other mums my kids were potty trained relatively quickly.

The reason why I am writing this review is that I was looking for something to help my own daughters potty train their kids – and was delighted to find the book is still in print – no mean feat after more than 40 years!

These examples show the importance of clearly defining the target behaviour and all of the steps to achieve it and also of identifying both possible reinforcers and achievable goals leading to effective interventions to support our children's learning.

Reference

Azrin, N. & Foxx, R. M. (1989). *Toilet training in less than a day*. New York: Simon and Schuster.

17 An eating problem

A behaviour that a child engages in often is, by definition, reinforcing, and one way of increasing a behaviour that does not occur very often is to link it to the reinforcing behaviour. This is often referred to as "When . . ., then . . ." For example, Johnny loved watching TV but would not do homework, and hated showing work to his parents. When he had to earn his TV viewing by doing half an hour's homework and showing it to his parents, he soon learned to do the homework willingly, and subsequently (although this can take time), as a result of parental praise, to enjoy it. Homework can be a cause of stress and arguments between parents and children, so it was also important that, initially, his parents praised Johnny's *effort* rather than commenting on the quality. In time this also led to other rewards, like better marks and positive teacher attention. Therefore, it can be helpful to arrange for activities that children like to do as a reward for doing those they find hard, which in the end leads to longer-term rewards that were initially established by immediate rewards.

Current rates of childhood obesity are concerning: 26 per cent of 5-year-old children in Wales and 22 per cent in England are classified as overweight, and over 11.5 per cent obese, with the majority of obese children (82.5 per cent) remaining obese four years later (Bailey, 2017). Not surprisingly, therefore, given the health problems related to obesity, making sure that children eat a healthy diet is a concern for many parents. Children whose diets have plenty of fruit and vegetables are less likely to become obese than children on poorer diets and eating plenty of fruit and vegetables in the longer term protects against many cancers, lowers the risk of coronary heart disease and helps prevent diabetes (Erjavec, Viktor, Horne and Lowe, 2012). However, teaching children to eat a healthy diet can be a challenge for parents and a child saying that they don't like something, particularly refusing certain foods, is a common problem. The key to changing children's food preferences is repeated tasting – children come to like fruit and vegetables because the taste buds learn to recognise and accept new tastes.

The school-based Food Dudes Healthy Eating Programme, developed at Bangor University, has demonstrated the effectiveness of using the behavioural principles of role modelling, rewards and repeated tastings in getting children to taste new foods and increasing their regular consumption of fruit and vegetables (Erjavec et al., 2012). The fun programme targets children and, indirectly, their families. Children watch the DVD adventures of the Food Dudes, a group of children who are fun, cool, slightly older than themselves and very successful. By eating fruit and vegetables, the Dudes equip themselves with the superpowers they need to vanquish General Junk and his Junk Punks, who are taking away the energy of the world by depriving it of healthy food. Through words and catchy songs, children are encouraged to taste fruit and vegetables and earn Food Dudes rewards, pencil cases, pencils, juggling balls and other small rewards.

In the Food Dudes programme, children develop pride in seeing themselves as fruit and vegetable eaters, with the greatest gains shown by the children who ate the least fruit and vegetables at the start and who needed them most. The programme effects extended beyond the school context into the home environment and were long-lasting.

Whilst not every child has access to the Food Dudes programme, the principles are relevant to helping parents to solve problems of children's fussy eating, particularly the idea of making eating healthy food fun. Lucy was 6 years old. Her parents were concerned that she ate very few foods. They had tried a variety of approaches suggested by friends and relatives, from what they called bribery to confrontation and punishment, but the problem remained. Lucy's parents kept records about what she ate and about mealtimes in general, and once we had a clear picture of the problem it was obvious that mealtimes had become an unpleasant and anxiety-provoking time for both Lucy and her parents. It was also clear that there was not a lot of role modelling of mealtime behaviour for Lucy, as the family did not often eat together.

The first step in the plan was to arrange for her parents to eat with Lucy and to let Lucy have the foods she liked. The initial goal was to make mealtimes fun in other ways. Her parents talked with her about things unrelated to food – what they had been doing during the day or what they might do after the meal was over, for example – and they gave Lucy attention for appropriate behaviour, such as coming to the table when asked or using a knife and fork. After a couple of weeks, when the initial goal of making mealtimes a pleasant joint family activity was reached, they moved on.

Lucy was offered food that her parents were eating, and whenever she refused a particular food her parents were encouraged to say, "You haven't learned to like this yet, but you probably will when you are a bit older." Introducing the idea that we learn to like foods and that getting used to new foods is a learning process is really helpful to children. Next, the parents started to put very small quantities of foods Lucy did not like on to her plate – maybe two or three peas. They explained to Lucy that she did not have to eat it, but that if she did she would be rewarded by having a choice of pudding or ice cream. At first, she ignored the peas and her parents said nothing, but after a couple of days she pushed them into the mashed potato and ate them. They immediately gave her lots of praise and attention for eating the peas and the choice of a pudding. They repeated giving her peas for several days, before introducing another food that she had previously rejected. This time it was very small florets of broccoli. Throughout this process she was praised for trying new and healthy foods that she had previously rejected. Her parents reminded her that learning to eat new foods was not easy but was part of growing up, and explained why certain foods were important for her health.

Another way that her parents helped Lucy was to let her prepare and help cook the food. This gave her another reason for wanting to try it: to taste the results of her own efforts. With these gradual changes in the way that Lucy's parents approached her eating problems, which took place over several months, they helped her to eat and enjoy many foods that she had previously rejected. They had also learned six basic rules about teaching new behaviour and coping with problem behaviour. These are:

1 Make learning fun.
2 Model the behaviour that you want.
3 Set small, achievable goals for children in order to make it easy for them to succeed.
4 Offer the same food once the child has tried it, to ensure repeat tastings before moving on to new foods.
5 Arrange small rewards, and ensure that they are accompanied by parental praise and attention.
6 Predict success by reminding the child that it is a learning process and is part of growing up: "You haven't learned to like broccoli yet, but you will do."

These ideas enabled Lucy's parents to help Lucy to learn to eat a range of different foods and to become better at teaching other new behaviours to her. They now knew how to focus on ways of helping her to learn rather than on provoking confrontation about activities they had failed to teach her.

Another family used a different strategy. Simon was a fussy eater and observations showed that his parents put a lot of food on Simon's plate in the hope that he would eat some of it. Instead, he played with it, ate a little of the things he liked and never had the experience of a clean plate. We agreed that the parents would give Simon mini-meals, initially only with foods that he was already eating. This meant a very small amount of each item – for example, a third of a fish finger, a dessertspoon of mashed potato and a small spoonful of baked beans. When he had a clean plate, Simon was praised for having a clean plate and was given the choice of more of the same food or that he could have a pudding, generally an ice cream. Like Lucy, the praise that Simon received made mealtimes a lot more pleasant. Simon responded immediately and his plate was clean from the start. Initially he immediately opted for the pudding, but over time he started to ask for more of his first course before asking for pudding. We left this plan in place for two weeks before moving on and starting to add very small amounts of other foods to Simon's plate. In the meantime, Simon's parents told Simon that they could remember times when they had not liked food but had now learned to do so, suggesting that some things – olives, for example – were tastes that they had only learned to enjoy as adults. They also told him that learning to like foods takes time. This plan worked well, and within a couple of months Simon had significantly extended the range of foods that he would eat.

A key feature in the success of these programmes was that the parents recognised that what they wanted to achieve was a long-term goal, and that enabled them to stay calm and make mealtimes a pleasant time. Using key strategies from the Food Dudes programme, role modelling, rewarding and repeated tasting enabled these parents to support their children in learning to make, and enjoy, healthy food choices.

References

Bailey, L. (2017). *Child Measurement Programme for Wales 2015/16*. Cardiff, Wales: Public Health Wales NHS Trust. Retrieved from: www.wales.nhs.uk/sitesplus/doc uments/888/12518%20PHW%20CMP%20Report%20%28Eng%29.pdf

Erjavec, M., Viktor, S., Horne, P., & Lowe, F. (2012). Implementing a healthy eating programme: Changing children's habits for life. *Community Practitioner, 85*(4), 39–42.

18 Avoidance and anxiety-based problems

As we have seen in earlier chapters, some behaviours are reinforced by the removal of negative consequences – as, for example, when parents give the child what they are demanding, to stop the child from crying, having a tantrum or demanding. But the same applies also to children who might eventually do something to stop the nagging.

Antecedent	Behaviour	Consequences
Mum finds coat lying on the floor. Mum tells Joanne off. "How many times have I told you . . .."	No response from Joanne, who is texting her friend	Mum becomes angry
Mum begins to shout and threatens to stop Joanne from going out	Joanne hangs up the coat reluctantly	Mum stops shouting, but says, "Why didn't you do it the first time?" Joanne returns to texting

In this example, like the morning example with Steven in Chapter 14, Joanne's behaviour was eventually reinforced by the removal of an aversive situation – Mum's nagging and threat of punishment. Unfortunately, even when children respond in these situations, they are unlikely to get praise, because the parent is still feeling angry. However, this is a poor way of teaching children to do something, as it only teaches them to hang the coat up when Mum's reminders become irritating (they hang it up in order to stop the nagging). So the reinforcer for the child is the removal of an unpleasant event, nagging. It does not teach the child to hang up their coat when they come through the door. This requires a different strategy. This distinction is important, since it explains why we should always teach and reward appropriate behaviour, because when behaviour is rewarded with praise the reward can eventually be faded out and the behaviour – cleaning teeth, for example – will be maintained because it feels more comfortable to do it.

A different sort of problem occurs when what are being experienced are negative sensations in our own bodies. This is the case with anxiety-based problems in which, our uncomfortable feelings are cues to avoid the stressful situation altogether (rather than doing something to avoid or remove nagging). If we respond to the anxiety produced by anticipation of a problem by avoidance, this can become a pattern which, in cases of extreme avoidance, we call a phobia.

As humans we have two responses to perceived danger or distress. One is to fight or challenge the danger, and the other is to run away. When we find ourselves in a situation of danger, we experience a series of physical bodily changes, our blood pressure rises, we become tense, we may start to shake or feel hot and to breathe more rapidly, and our body releases adrenalin. This prepares us for the "fight or flight" response. Depending on the nature of the perceived threat and how we interpret it, we then respond. Avoidance is triggered by the flight response and removes us from the anxiety-provoking event. It is reinforced because we become calm in a different place, where the perceived threat is no longer present.

Many people dislike things like spiders and mice, but this only occasionally leads to extreme avoidance. The avoidance behaviour is reinforced because we see a rapid movement (say, a mouse) that triggers arousal and our flight response, so we run away. Our behaviour is reinforced by a change in how we feel, because we become calm and feel OK again in a situation away from the perceived threat. This makes it likely that we will do it again and also likely that we will avoid the situation where we had this negative experience.

Post-traumatic stress is an anxiety-based condition where people, as a result of a bad experience, become overwhelmed by fear and can have repeated flashbacks to the situation that make it impossible for them to continue to live normally. Examples of situations that can produce post-traumatic stress include: seeing someone get injured or killed, being injured personally or being the subject of domestic abuse or rape. It is particularly common following experience of wartime or following natural disasters. News coverage of anxiety-provoking situations – wars, road traffic accidents, abuse and stories of murders or burglaries – can act as triggers and add to people's anxieties.

Sometimes an avoidance response arises from a one-trial learning experience and sometimes it is repeated exposure to a lower-level threat. An example of a one-off experience happened to a child who as a toddler, was stung by a wasp that he tried to pick up, and this generalised to a fear of *any* flying insects. At other times avoidance can develop as a result of lower-level, but repeated, exposure to a stress-producing situation. So a child who is teased at school might, over time, develop a dislike of school that becomes a phobia, with even the thought of being at school triggering an anxiety response that is only calmed by refusing to go to school.

Some avoidance behaviours are conditioned by seeing other people behave in particular ways. One mother reported having seen her own mother scream and jump on to a chair at the sight of a mouse, for example. This example of the modelling principle left her with a manageable, but uncomfortable, feeling in their presence.

It is important to consider whether the anxiety arises from a lack of skills to deal with the situation. Some children are easily aroused and seem programmed to have an anxiety response more quickly than others. In the case of children on the autistic spectrum, many situations can provoke anxiety, such as transitions from one activity to another, or having to manage social situations. It is important to consider ways of making the world very predictable for these children, and the strategies that have been developed to treat phobias or anxiety are also helpful in supporting them.

Many social phobias arise because the individual did not have the skills to deal with the situation. This may be being bullied, called names or teased at school, or not being able to do the expected schoolwork. These problems require a strategy to manage the situation, as well as teaching the child to manage their emotional responses. If the problem arises because the child cannot do what is expected or required in school, they need an individualised learning plan. If they are being bullied, they need to be taught strategies for getting help. In addition to teaching the child to manage their anxiety, work needs to be done to arrange for the demands of the situation to be achievable for the child.

In the case of bullying, it is important to work with other children to ensure that they learn to support the child who is being bullied. Most children say that bullying is wrong, but many do not know what to do to stop it, and research shows that the long-term effects of being bullied are significant, with ongoing mental health problems into adulthood (Ttofi, 2011) Furthermore, adults who were victimised say that it was not so much the behaviour of the bully that they remember, but the fact that no one did anything about it. A very effective school-based programme called KiVa was developed in Finland to help to reduce bullying (Salmivalli, Kärnä and Poskiparta, 2011). KiVa is a whole-school approach which, while directly supporting the victimised child, focuses on the behaviour of bystanders by giving them skills and strategies to support the victims of bullying (Salmivalli, 2010). KiVa is now being introduced into schools in the UK and is demonstrating similarly beneficial results (Hutchings and Clarkson, 2015).

A child on the autistic spectrum who needs extra transition time to cope with a change of activity may need extra scaffolding, both at home and at school. At school, letting them be the child that rings the bell in the classroom to let others know that a transition to another activity is coming up can help, as it gives them this extra bit of transition-time warning. Other strategies include: giving them personal picture timetables; ensuring that they do not spend too long in a situation that is stressful for them, such as circle time or other social activities; and arranging that a brief stay will be rewarded with an activity that they like (often a solitary play activity).

Once we understand the triggers for anxiety-based responses, we can start to help children to deal with them. In fact, the release of adrenalin is quite short term, allowing for bodily preparation to run away or to stand and fight. If a person with a flight response can be persuaded to remain in the presence of an anxiety-promoting object, such as a mouse or spider, their anxiety will reduce fairly quickly and they will learn that the feared object is not a threat. However, persuading people to stay in the presence of feared objects is not easy, but a number of well-tried and -tested strategies have been developed to address phobias.

Training in relaxation skills helps the body to counteract the negative physiological effects of anxiety. There are a number of programmes and resources for children, but one of the best researched is the Coping Cat programme developed by Kendall, which includes workbooks and a CD-ROM (Khanna and Kendall, 2008; Podell, Mychailyszyn, Edmunds, Puleo and Kendall, 2010). When this approach is paired with gradual exposure to the feared situation, this is called desensitisation. Relaxation means learning to monitor bodily sensations and do things to counteract them, such as controlling breathing by practising taking deep breaths, doing activities to relax the body through self-talk and through focusing on tensing and relaxing muscles. It is particularly useful, initially, to train these skills at a time when the person is not feeling anxious.

Teaching stress-reducing self-talk that challenges the negative thoughts associated with the anxiety has been shown to be helpful. Teaching children to say "I can stay calm, I can calm myself", "This situation is difficult but it is possible to manage" or "I can take some deep breaths" gives them self-instructions about how to handle the situation, and also serves as a distraction.

Desensitisation of a fear of mice

A grandmother whose fear of mice had resulted in her becoming almost housebound was referred for help with this problem. The successful programme involved:

1　Teaching relaxation, including monitoring to identify how her body was feeling, tensing and relaxing muscles and practising breathing skills. (There are lots of audio aids to teaching relaxing including the Coping Cat resources mentioned earlier – Khanna and Kendall, 2008).
2　Learning positive self-talk about the fact that she was seeking help, that her problem was not unusual (*normalising*) and that she was doing something about it. It also included reminding herself about the things she would be able to do once she overcame this fear – this included visiting her children and grandchildren.
3　Encouragement to visualise a mouse and then to use her relaxation skills to self-calm, whilst holding on to the image of the mouse.
4　Exposure to pictures and video footage of mice, again pairing this with relaxation and positive self-talk until she was able to look at the pictures and stay calm.

5   Exposure to actual mice in cages, again practising all of the earlier steps in managing her anxiety and remaining calm.
6   Watching another person handling a live mouse.

Of course, it is difficult to arrange real-life exposure to mice, but following this programme she felt sufficiently confident that she had the skills to remain calm if she did see one – probably a fairly unlikely event, as she certainly did not have any in her home – and was able to resume normal life.

Relaxation skills and positive self-talk form part of the desensitisation and gradual exposure strategy, regardless of whether the problem seems logical or not. Fear of mice might seem less logical than fear of being bullied or ridiculed in public, but the bodily sensations and effects in terms of avoidance are the same. In the bullying situation, learning alternative (more assertive) responses can be very effective, but these skills need to be rehearsed after having first practised managing anxiety through relaxation and self-talk.

Many parents report that children are afraid of the dark, but if their parents allow them to sleep with the light on they are not exposed to the feared situation and therefore can never learn that it is safe. This is a problem that is important to address, since there are now plenty of studies that demonstrate that quality sleep is compromised by sleeping with a light on, as this has a significant effect in depressing the production of melatonin, which regulates sleep cycles (Pandi-Perumal et al., 2008; Scheer and Czeisler, 2005). Other studies demonstrate the importance of at least nine hours of good sleep for children, even more when they are younger (Gregory and Sadeh, 2012; Wheaton, Liu, Perry and Croft, 2011; Wolfson and Carskadon, 1998). These are good reasons for a desensitisation programme, which could involve a dimmer switch (allowing for the level of light to be gradually lowered), a timer that puts the light off after a while, sitting in the dark with a parent present and being rewarded for learning to stay in the dark.

Help for children's anxiety-based problems involves talking initially with confidence with the child about the fact that anxiety is a normal bodily response and that solutions are possible, and then to use the following steps:

1   Identify very clearly exactly what the situation is where the anxiety response occurs.
2   Help the child to identify the cues in their body that they are becoming anxious.
3   Teach relaxation skills, body monitoring and breathing.
4   Identify clearly the goal that the child is working on.
5   Prompt positive self-talk about the problem.
6   Introduce the problem situation in imagination, and again practise relaxation and self-talk.
7   Identify and talk with the child about other ways to behave in the situation. Pinpoint what alternative skills or strategies need to be taught in order to handle the situation.

8 Role-play/rehearse alternative coping strategies.
9 Set up a reward programme to encourage the child to work towards a solution, and reward small steps.
10 Where appropriate, work with others in the situation to support the child – for example, by offering support to the victims of bullying.

Careful attention to the anxiety-provoking situation and the pattern of avoidance that arises from it will enable us to ensure that the demands placed on children are realistic, that the environment is encouraged to support them and that they are given help to develop the skills to handle difficult situations and overcome anxieties.

References

Gregory, A. M. & Sadeh, A. (2012). Sleep, emotional and behavioral difficulties in children and adolescents. *Sleep Medicine Reviews*, 16(2), 129–136.

Hutchings, J. & Clarkson, S. (2015). Introducing and piloting the KiVa bullying prevention programme in the UK. *Educational and Child Psychology*, 32(1), 49–61.

Khanna, M. S. & Kendall, P. C. (2008). Computer-assisted CBT for child anxiety: The Coping Cat CD-ROM. *Cognitive and Behavioral Practice*, 15(2), 159–165. Retrieved from https://doi.org/10.1016/j.cbpra.2008.02.002

Pandi-Perumal, S. R., Trakht, I., Srinivasan, V., Spence, D. W., Maestroni, G. J. M., Zisapel, N., & Cardinali, D. P. (2008). Physiological effects of melatonin: Role of melatonin receptors and signal transduction pathways. *Progress in Neurobiology*, 85(3), 335–353. doi.org/10.1016/j.pneurobio.2008.04.001

Podell, J. L., Mychailyszyn, M., Edmunds, J., Puleo, C. M., & Kendall, P. C. (2010). The Coping Cat program for anxious youth: The FEAR plan comes to life. *Cognitive and Behavioral Practice*, 17(2), 132–141. doi.org/10.1016/j.cbpra.2009.11.001

Salmivalli, C. (2010). Bullying and the peer group: A review. *Aggression and Violent Behavior*, 15(2), 112–120.

Salmivalli, C., Kärnä, A., & Poskiparta, E. (2011). Counteracting bullying in Finland: The KiVa program and its effects on different forms of being bullied. *International Journal of Behavioral Development*, 35, 405–411.

Scheer, F. A. L. & Czeisler, C. A. (2005). Melatonin, sleep, and circadian rhythms. *Sleep Medicine Reviews*, 9(1), 5–9.

Ttofi, M. M. (2011). Do the victims of school bullies tend to become depressed in later life? A systematic review and meta-analysis of longitudinal studies. *Journal of Aggression, Conflict and Peace Research*, 3(2), 63–73.

Wheaton, A. G., Liu, Y., Perry, G. S., & Croft, J. B. (2011). Effect of short sleep duration on daily activities – United States, 2005–2008. *Morbidity and Mortality Weekly Report*, 60(8), 239–242.

Wolfson, A. R. & Carskadon, M. A. (1998). Sleep schedules and daytime functioning in adolescents. *Child Development*, 69(4), 875–887. doi:10.1111/j.1467-8624.1998.tb06149.x

Appendix 1

The Strengths and Difficulties Questionnaire (SDQ) (Goodman, 1997)
Additional information

Sample items from each of the subscales

Emotional Symptoms scale: "Often unhappy, downhearted or tearful"
Conduct Problems scale: "Often has temper tantrums or hot tempers"
Hyperactivity scale: "Constantly fidgeting or squirming"
Peer Problems scale: "Picked on or bullied by other children"
Pro-social scale: "Often volunteers to help others"

Administration

Respondents are asked to provide answers based on the child's behaviour over the last six months. For young children, the inventory is a self-administered parent (or teacher) report measure and takes approximately five minutes to complete.

Scoring information

The respondent is asked to rate how true of the index child a particular behaviour is, using a three-point scale ranging from 0 (*not true*) to 2 (*certainly true*). A sample item would be:

	Not True	Somewhat True	Certainly True
Considerate of other people's feelings	☐	☐	☐

In addition to the 25 items on psychological attributes, the scale has an impact supplement. The respondent is asked whether they think that the index child has a problem and, if so, are asked to respond to seven further questions about chronicity, distress, social impairment and burden to others.

Scoring may be done by hand by summing the items within each of the five subscales (5 items per subscale, minimum score = 0, maximum score = 10). A Total Difficulties score is calculated by summing the scores from all scales except the Pro-social scale (minimum score = 0, maximum score = 40). For more detail on scoring, see the SDQ website (www.sdqinfo.com), where a syntax file for SPSS is also available.

SDQ score ranges

Parent completed	Close to average	Slightly raised/ slightly lowered	High (/Low)	Very high/ very low
Total Difficulties score	0–13	14–16	17–19	20–40
Emotional Symptoms score	0–3	4	5–6	7–10
Conduct Problems score	0–2	3	4–5	6–10
Hyperactivity score	0–5	6–7	8	9–10
Peer Problems score	0–2	3	4	5–10
Pro-social score	8–10	7	6	0–5

Source: Goodman, R. (1997). The Strengths and Difficulties Questionnaire: A research note. *Journal of Child Psychology and Psychiatry, 38,* 581–586.

When using a version of the SDQ that includes an "impact supplement", the items on overall distress and social impairment can be summed to generate an impact score that ranges from 0 to 10 for the parent-completed version and 0 to 6 for the teacher-completed version. Responses to the questions on chronicity and burden to others are not included in the impact score. If the answer is "No" to the first question on the impact supplement, i.e. when the parent does not perceive the child as having any emotional or behavioural difficulties, they do not proceed to the subsequent questions and automatically receive a score of zero. Scores can be classified as "very high/very low" (a score of 3 or more), "high" (a score of 2), "slightly raised/ slightly lowered" (a score of 1) and "close to average" (a score of 0).

Although the SDQ is free to download, and can be manually scored, due to the level of scoring errors, use of the online scoring version is recommended for a fee of $0.25. For more information, see https://admin.sdqscore.org.

Appendix 2

Additional information on the Arnold-O'Leary Parenting Scale (Arnold, O'Leary, Wolff and Acker, 1993)

Scoring

The following items have 7 on the left-hand side: 2, 3, 6, 9, 10, 13, 14, 17, 19, 20, 23, 26, 27, 30. The following items have 7 on the right-hand side: 1, 4, 5, 7, 8, 11, 12, 15, 16, 18, 21, 22, 24, 25, 28, 29. To calculate the total score, add the responses on all items and take the mean score. To calculate a factor score, take the mean for the sum of responses on that factor.

Laxness contains 11 items: 7, 8, 12, 15, 16, 19, 20, 21, 24, 26, 30
Over-reactivity contains 10 items: 3, 6, 9, 10, 14, 17, 18, 22, 25, 28.
Verbosity contains 7 items: 2, 4, 7, 9, 11, 23, 29.

Two items (7 and 9) occur on more than one scale, and four items (1, 5, 13, 27) load only on to the total score and are not on a factor subscale.

To date, there are no published population norms for this scale and its subscales; however, data from parents of clinic-referred children whose parents were reporting extreme difficulties in handling their children's behaviour are reported and have shown higher levels of problematic parenting behaviour scores than those of parents of non-referred children, and this can guide interpretation (see table).

Parenting Scale scores for clinic and non-clinic groups

	Clinic group (n = 26)		Non-clinic group (n = 51)	
	Mean	SD	Mean	SD
Child's age (months)	29.9	4.5	28.6	3.3
Mother's age (years)	29.6	6.7	31.7	3.9
Parenting Scale				
Laxness	2.8	1.0	2.4	0.8*

(continued)

(continued)

	Clinic group (n = 26)		Non-clinic group (n = 51)	
	Mean	SD	Mean	SD
Over-reactivity	3.0	1.0	2.4	0.7**
Verbosity	3.4	1.0	3.1	1.0
Total score	3.1	0.7	2.6	0.6**
* p < .05				
** p < .01				

Source: Arnold, D. S., O'Leary, S. G., Wolff, L. S., & Acker, M. M. (1993). The parenting scale: A measure of dysfunctional parenting in discipline situations. *Psychological Assessment, 5,* 137–144.

Appendix 3

The Warwick-Edinburgh Mental Well-Being Scale

The scale is available to download from www.healthscotland.com/scotlands-health/population/Measuring-positive-mental-health.aspx.

Please note the copyright statement that must be included on the downloaded scale.

If you wish to use the scale in your routine practise, you should register as an individual with the University of Warwick (see www.healthscotland.com/documents/4742.aspx).

Copyright for the scales rests with the University of Warwick and NHS Health Scotland. Once the registration form has been submitted, a member of the WEMWBS team will be in contact to confirm your use.

Parents can complete WEMWBS online on the NHS choices website where they can see how their score compares with national survey data (see www.nhs.uk/Tools/Pages/Wellbeing-self-assessment.aspx).

Please note the information taken from the following website: www.healthscotland.com/documents/4742.aspx.

Should you decide to use WEMWBS (or SWEMWBS), we ask that when you seek permission for use and that you indicate how you are planning to use WEMWBS. Please complete the request for use questionnaire available from: http://www2.warwick.ac.uk/fac/med/research/platform/wemwbs/researchers/register/ and return to Frances. Taggart@warwick.ac.uk. We also ask that after use you feed back to Frances how WEMWBS has performed. Frances is also the person to contact should you have more technical questions regarding the scale and its use.

If the scale is reproduced, it must include the copyright statement that appears with it, and no changes to its wording, response categories or layout must be made. Any report regarding use of WEMWBS also needs to include the following text:

The Warwick-Edinburgh Mental Well-Being Scale was funded by the Scottish Government National Programme for improving Mental Health and Well-being commissioned by NHS Scotland, developed by the University of Warwick and the University of Edinburgh, and is jointly owned by NHS Health Scotland, the University of Warwick and the University of Edinburgh

A user manual is accessible via the following link: www.cppconsortium.nhs.uk/admin/files/1343987601WEMWBS%20User%20Guide%20Version%201%20June%202008.pdf

Index

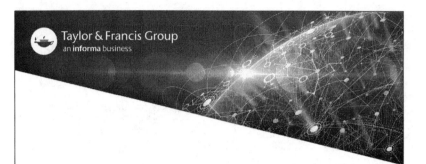